DRIVING TOURS
BRITAIN

Macmillan • USA

Written by Roy Woodcock, John McIlwain

Revised second edition 1995
First published January 1991

Edited, designed and produced by AA Publishing.

ISBN 0-02-860452-0

Published in the United States by
Macmillan Travel
A Prentice Hall Macmillan Company
15 Columbus Circle
New York, NY 10023

Macmillan is a registered trademark of Macmillan, Inc.

Color separation: L C Repro Ltd, Aldermaston

Printed and bound in Italy by Printers SRL, Trento

Title Page: *A windmill on the River Ant at How Hill*

Above: *Sunset at Godrevy Lighthouse*

Right: *A summer view of Canterbury Cathedral*

CONTENTS

INTRODUCTION

This book is not only a practical touring guide for the independent traveller, but is also invaluable for those who would like to know more about the country.

It is divided into 6 regions, each containing between 4 and 6 tours. The tours start and finish in major towns and cities which we consider to be the best centres for exploration. Each tour has details of the most interesting places to visit en route . Side panels cater for special interests and requirements and cover a range of categories – for those whose interest is in history, wildlife or walking, and those who have children. There are also panels which highlight scenic stretches of road and which give details of events, crafts and customs. The numbers link them to the appropriate main text.

The simple route directions are accompanied by an easy-to-use map of the tour and there are addresses of local tourist information centres in some of the towns en route as well as in the start town.

Simple charts show how far it is from one town to the next in miles and kilometres. These can help you to decide where to take a break and stop overnight, for example. (All distances quoted are approximate.)

Before setting off it is advisable to check with the information centre at the start of the tour for recommendations on where to break your journey and for additional information on what to see and do, and when best to visit.

ENTRY REGULATIONS

Passports are required by all visitors except citizens of EU countries, but they must be able to prove their identity and nationality. Visas are not required for entry into Britain by American citizens, nationals of the British Commonwealth and most European countries.

CUSTOMS

For goods bought outside the EU, you can import, duty free, 200 cigarettes or 100 cigarillos or 50 cigars or 250g of tobacco; two litres of still table wine; one litre of spirits, strong liqueurs over 22 per cent volume or two litres of fortified or sparkling wine or other liqueurs or an additional two litres of still table wine; 60cc/ml of perfume and 250cc/ml of toilet water. For goods bought within the EU there are no further taxes to be paid as long as the goods are for personal use. Please check current guidelines before making purchases.

EMERGENCY TELEPHONE NUMBERS

Police, fire and ambulance tel: 999.

A sunny day's outing on the nature reserve trail at Cwm Idwal and Tryfan in Gwynedd

Garden flowers enhance the unique warmth of Cotswold stone at Bibury, Gloucestershire

HEALTH

Inoculations are not required for entry to Britain. Health insurance is recommended for non-EC citizens.

CURRENCY

The unit of currency is the pound (£), divided into 100 pence. Coins are in denominations of 1, 2, 5, 10, 20 and 50 pence and one pound (£1); notes are in denominations of £5, 10, 20 and 50.

CREDIT CARDS

All major credit cards are widely accepted throughout Britain.

BANKS

Banks are generally open between 9am and 3.30pm weekdays, though times do vary from bank to bank, and some are open on Saturday mornings until noon. In Scotland, times vary – some banks have different opening times and some close for lunch.

POST OFFICES

Post offices open from 9am to 5pm or 6pm Monday to Friday and 9am to noon on Saturdays.

TELEPHONES

Insert coins after lifting the receiver; the dialling tone is a continuous tone.

Useful numbers:
Operator – 100
Directory Enquiries – 192
International Directory
  Enquiries – 153
International Operator – 155

To make an international call, dial 010 (the international code), then the country code, followed by the area code and the local number.

TIME

The official time is Greenwich Mean Time (GMT).
British Summer Time (BST) begins in late March when the clocks are put forward an hour. In late October, the clocks go back an hour to GMT. The official date is announced in the daily newspapers and is always at 2am on a Sunday.

PUBLIC HOLIDAYS

1 January – New Year's Day
2 January – holiday in
  Scotland only
Good Friday
Easter Monday (not Scotland)
1st Monday in May – May
  Day (8 May in 1995)
Last Monday in May – Spring
  Bank Holiday
1st Monday in August – Bank
  Holiday in Scotland only
Last Monday in August –
  August Bank Holiday (not
  Scotland)
25 December – Christmas
  Day
26 December – Boxing Day

ELECTRICITY

The standard electricity supply is 240 volts, 50 cycles AC. Plugs are three-pin. Shavers operate on 240 or 110 volts. Since most American appliances are designed to operate on 120 volts, 60 cycles, a transformer will be required. Visitors from Europe will need an adaptor. Most hotels have special razor sockets which will take both voltages.

MOTORING

Documents
You must have a valid driver's licence or an International Driving Permit. Non-EC nationals must have Green Card insurance.

Route directions
Throughout the book the following abbreviations are used for British roads:
A – main roads
B – local roads
unclassified roads – minor roads (unnumbered)

Breakdowns
Visitors who bring their cars to Britain and are members of a recognised automobile club may benefit from the services provided free of charge by the AA.

Accidents
In the event of an accident, the vehicle should be moved off the carriageway wherever possible. If the vehicle is fitted with hazard warning lights, they should be used. If available, a red triangle should be placed on the road at least 165 feet (50m) before the obstruction and on the same side of the road.

Speed limits
In built-up areas 30mph (48kph). Outside built-up areas 70mph

The tumbling white and ice-blue of the River Dochart on Tayside, beneath Ben Lawers

(112kph) on motorways and dual carriageways; other roads 60mph (96kph).

Driving conditions
Driving is on the left.
Seat belts are compulsory for drivers and front seat passengers. Passengers travelling in the rear of the vehicle must wear a seat belt if fitted.
Tolls are levied on certain bridges and tunnels.
Roads in the northwest of Scotland are sometimes narrow. On single track roads, pull into passing places only if they are on your left. Stop level with those on your right – the oncoming traffic will make the detour.

Car hire and fly/drive
Drivers must hold a valid national licence or an International Driving Permit. The minimum age for hiring a car ranges from 18 to 25, depending on the model of car. With some companies, there is a maximum age limit of 70 years.
You can arrange to pick up your car in one town and return it in another. If you are going to hire a car, you can often get a good deal if you arrange a fly/drive package tour.

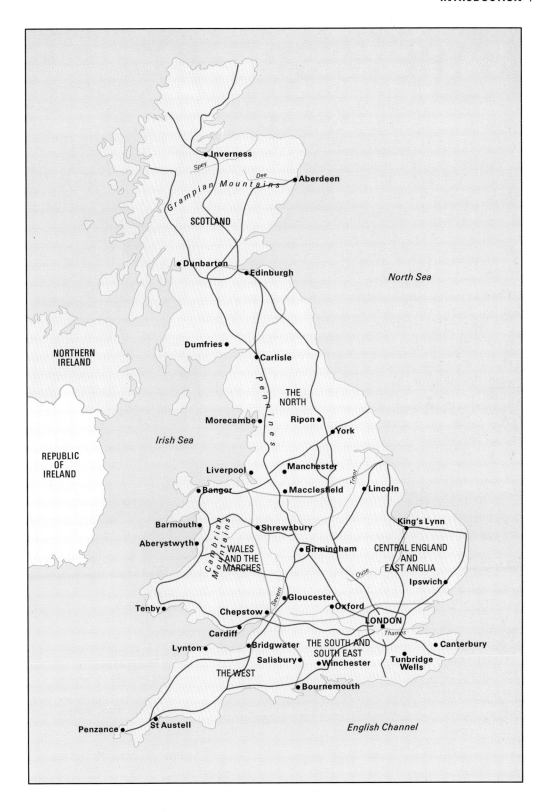

THE WEST

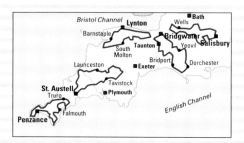

The rich, rural lands of the counties from Dorset and Wiltshire westwards contain some spectacular scenery. Soft chalklands around Salisbury give way to harder and older rocks, which create the steep and dramatic hills of the Quantocks, Exmoor and Dartmoor.

An alternating sequence of cliffs and beaches forms the western coastline: there are the precipitous granite cliffs near Land's End, and stupendous sandstone cliffs on the northern fringe of Exmoor. Steep roads are an indication of the resistance of the rocks. As a contrast to hills and cliffs, the flat fen lands of the Somerset Levels stretch away from the coast.

The Levels are dotted with dairy cattle grazing on lush green meadows, many of which, thanks to conservation techniques, still contain buttercups and other wild flowers. West Country towns are situated round the edges of the high ground and in the river valleys. Many coastal towns which grew up as fishing ports have become holiday resorts, and traffic tends to be congested during the summer. Even the M5 motorway can become crowded at peak holiday weekends.

Early settlements left their mark on this area, too: Dartmoor probably has the greatest number of relics, but more famous and popular are the sites at Glastonbury, Avebury and Stonehenge. More recent evidence of human activity can be seen in many areas of mining, which is still practised near St Austell, where china clay is obtained for the paper industry. Copper and tin were important minerals in Cornwall from the time of the Romans until earlier this century, when richer and larger deposits in other countries made the British mines uneconomic. The history of mining can be traced in the mining museums which are among the increasing number of the southwest's indoor centres, adding to the many attractions of this most scenic part of Britain.

Penzance
The end of the railway line and the most westerly major town of England enjoys a mild climate which enables palm trees to grow along the coastline. Penzance was immortalised by Gilbert and Sullivan in *The Pirates of Penzance*. The National Trust's Trengwainton Gardens, 2 miles (3km) inland, contains magnolias and many delicate shrubs. A maritime museum and a natural history museum are among the other attractions, and there is still plenty of activity in the harbour. The *Scillonian* makes regular sailings to the Isles of Scilly.

St Austell
Originally noted for tin mining, St Austell has recently become associated with the china clay industry, which is why the landscape to the north is scarred with hollows overlooked by lunar mounds of white debris. The Wheal Martyn Museum will give a fascinating

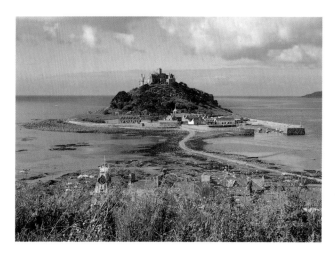

A granite island, cut off at high tide; a castle, a priory, but above all a place of mystery and magic – the romance of St Michael's Mount

depiction of mining history. This regional market centre grew up around the Market Hall, one of many local buildings built from granite, and other buildings of architectural interest include the parish church, the White Hart Hotel and the Quaker Meeting House.

Lynton

Steep tree-covered cliffs make up the northern edge of Exmoor, with Lynton at the top of the slope and Lynmouth down by the sea below. The Catholic church is an out-standing building with decorative marble work, and the Lyn and Exmoor Museum has interesting displays about the local area. Joining Lynton with Lynmouth is the dramatic cliff railway, built by the Victorian lawyer Sir George Newnes out of the fortune he made by publishing the famous Sherlock Holmes stories.

Salisbury

This ancient town was originally at Old Sarum, 2 miles (3km) to the north, where there was an Iron Age settlement and the Romans kept a strong military force. In 1220 the foundations of the new cathedral

Fishing boats at rest in Mevagissey Harbour on Cornwall's sun-washed south coast, Britain's best-loved holiday resort

were laid at New Sarum, now called Salisbury, and gradually the new town developed. The cathedral is beautiful, built in the shape of a double cross, with a graceful spire rising to a height of 404 feet (123m). Among many features of interest are the Poultry Cross, St Thomas's Church, the Playhouse and the delightful River Avon.

Bridgwater

Situated on the edge of Sedge-moor, where James II defeated the Duke of Monmouth's rebellion in 1685 in the last battle fought on English soil, Bridgwater grew up as a port and still has a tidal river linking it to the sea. The church is a fine and imposing building, well worth a visit; Monmouth used the tower as a look-out while trying to locate the King's infantry. Another famous figure in the Bridgwater area was Admiral Blake, and his birthplace is now a museum which contains exhibits of his life, as well as a history of the town.

3 days – 158 miles (255km)

BAYS, CLIFFS & GRANITE

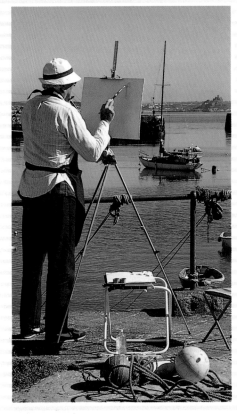

Penzance • Newlyn • Lamorna • Porthcurno • Land's End
St Just • Zennor • St Ives • Lelant • Hayle • Portreath
Porthtowan • Truro • St Mawes • Penryn • Gweek
Cadgwith • Mullion • Helston • Marazion • Penzance

Small bays, sandy beaches and steep rugged cliffs alternate around the Cornish coast on this tour, which then heads inland across green, undulating countryside, dotted with relics of the mining industry. Granite is everywhere, in the walls and villages and in tors on the hilltops.

Few sights evoke Cornwall more than an artist at work – here overlooking Newlyn Harbour with St Michael's Mount beyond

ⓘ Station Road, Penzance

From Penzance, drive south along the coast for a mile (1.6km) to Newlyn, and a little further to Mousehole.

Newlyn, Cornwall

1 Really a suburb of Penzance, this is a lively and colourful fishing port, once famous for its artist colony. The **Passmore Orion Picture Gallery** shows some of their work. Further along the coast is Mousehole. Pronounced 'mowzel', this delightful old fishing village consists of a semi-circle of colour-washed and granite houses round its harbour. Some of the roofs are specially weighted down to combat strong sea winds. Dolly Pentreath, supposedly the last person to speak Cornish as her native language, died here in 1777.

Continue on unclassified road for 5 miles (8km) to Lamorna.

Lamorna, Cornwall

2 Lamorna is a holiday centre. The tempting golden sand of its spectacular cove is surrounded by steep blocks of granite cliffs and rocky outcrops.

Join the B3315, then at Trethewey turn left on to an unclassified road to Porthcurno.

Porthcurno, Cornwall

3 Porthcurno's beach of almost-white sand is overlooked by a remarkable theatre in the cliffs. The **Minack** is Britain's equivalent to an ancient Greek theatre, set 200 feet (60m) above the waves. It was created by Miss Rowena Cade, who cut it out of the cliffs in 1931.The theatre has a 16-week season, and can seat 750 on its granite terraces.

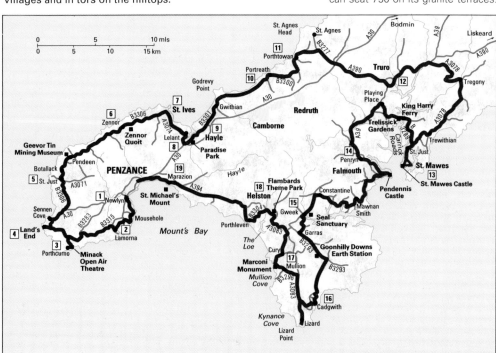

The end of England: the haunting majesty of Land's End

Return to the B3315 and continue for another 4 miles (6km), then join the A30 to Land's End.

Land's End, Cornwall

4 England's most westerly point, Land's End is 873 miles (1,405km) from John O'Groats, Scotland's most northerly town. On a fine day the Isles of Scilly, 28 miles (45km) away, can be seen, along with **Wolf Rock Lighthouse** and the **Longships Lighthouse**, only a mile and a half (2km) offshore. Land's End is the setting for wild coastal walks and amazing rock formations. Further along is the small village of Sennen, the battleground of the last Cornish fight against invading Danes. **Sennen Cove** has a good sandy beach and excellent bathing.

Continue with the A30, then left on to the B3306 for 5 miles (8km) to St Just.

St Just, Cornwall

5 This enchanting village and its neighbourhood are rich in antiquities. St Just is noted for the contents of its large medieval church: a stone of the 5th or 6th century inscribed with **XP**, the first two letters of the Greek word for Christ, and the shaft of a 9th-century Hiberno-Saxon cross. Abandoned and ruined mines litter the countryside north of the town. At Botallack, along the B3306, is a very deep mine which extended out beneath the sea, and at the **Geevor Tin**

Mining Museum at Pendeen, a little further on, you can take an underground tour of this working mine.

Keep going along the B3306 to Zennor.

Zennor, Cornwall

6 Zennor, named after St Senara, is a grey stone village huddled round its restored 12th-century church in a wild, bleak landscape. The **Wayside Museum**, the oldest private museum in Cornwall, recaptures the flavour of this area from 3000BC onwards, with displays on archaeology, tin mining and many other aspects of Cornish life. The writers D H Lawrence and Virginia Woolf both lived here in the 1920s. **Zennor Quoit**, to the southeast, is a chambered tomb from about 2000BC.

A further 5 miles (8km) along the B3306 is St Ives.

St Ives, Cornwall

7 St Ives was a prosperous pilchard port in the 19th century, but now is more noted for tourism, with its two fine sandy beaches and many excellent museums and galleries. Sculptress The town has managed to preserve its old-world charm: quaint houses and narrow streets cluster round the 15th-century church. Be sure to visit the **Barbara Hepworth Museum and Sculpture Garden**, and the **Model Railway Museum**.

i The Guildhall, Street-an-Pol

Take the main A3074 for 3 miles (5km) to Lelant.

FOR CHILDREN

4 The legendary **Last Labyrinth** at Land's End is a major attraction using electronic equipment and including a life-size galleon with scrambling nets and cabins. You can also watch the glass-blower or wood-carver at work, and there is a fascinating collection of shells.

SCENIC ROUTES

The drive along the B3306 reveals new views at every bend in the road, with the coastal scenes and the inland moors competing for attention.

Approaching St Mawes along the A3078, there are suddenly views of **Carrick Roads** to the right, with closer views of **Pencuil River** on the left.

The writer Virginia Woolf lived in Zennor in the 1920s

Street has many fine Georgian structures, and **Walsingham Place** is a beautiful early 19th-century crescent off Victoria Place. The whole town is dominated by the **cathedral**, which has three spires and was built on the site of the 16th-century church of St Mary. The **County Museum** in Silver Street is considered to be the finest in Cornwall and now there is also a fine new art gallery.

[i] Municipal Buildings, Boscawen Street

Follow the A39 eastwards, then turn right along the A3078 for St Mawes.

St Mawes, Cornwall

13 Smart shops and houses and many narrow old streets make this an interesting place to wander round. You should try to visit **St Mawes Castle**, built by Henry VIII in the 1540s to guard the mouth of the Fal estuary, and still in excellent repair. The views across Carrick Roads, a stretch of sea, to Falmouth are particularly impressive. **Trelissick Gardens**, north of St Mawes, boasts a fine collection of exotic plants from all over the world.

Turn north on the A3078 then the B3289, using King Harry ferry, which closes before dusk, then join the A39 to Penryn.

Penryn, Cornwall

14 Almost everything in Penryn is built of granite – granite buildings, a granite port and granite blocks lying around everywhere waiting to be shipped out. The narrow streets of this old town stretch up the sides of the valley in an untidy but appealing way.

Further on is Falmouth, on one of the finest natural habours in the world. There are beaches to the south of the town, and on the northern side of the peninsula are the docks and 18th- and 19th-century buildings. **Pendennis Castle** was built at the same time as its twin, St Mawes Castle, to guard the harbour entrance.

[i] 28 Killigrew Street, Falmouth

Leave Falmouth on unclassified roads passing through Mawnan Smith, Porth Navas, Constantine and Brill to Gweek.

Gweek, Cornwall

15 This lovely little stone village with two stone bridges across the channels of the Helford River is now better known as a **Seal Sanctuary**. Along the picturesque and tranquil banks of the Helford, sick and wounded seals and birds are treated. There are displays which show the work of the centre, and a safari bus will take you round the park to see the convalescent pool and nursery and exercise areas.

Travel to Garras on unclassified roads. Then take the B3293 and unclassified roads across Goonhilly Downs, south to Cadgwith and on to Lizard Point on an unclassified road and the A3083.

RECOMMENDED WALKS

16 Walks along the cliffs are numerous and some are quite exposed and steep. Among the most dramatic is the path from Cadgwith towards Landewednack. On the west coast of the Lizard, the coast near **Kynance Cove** can look most romantic and appealing.

9 From the B3301 it is possible to walk to **Godrevy Point** and **Navax Point** on a circular walk of 3 miles (5km).

Lelant, Cornwall

8 Lelant has a fine Norman and Perpendicular style **church** with a 17th-century sundial, but is now noted for **Merlin's Magic Land**, which claims to provide a 'Funtastic' day out for the whole family, with bumper boats, motor bikes and many other attractions.

Follow the A3074, then the B3301 to Hayle.

Hayle, Cornwall

9 During the 18th century Hayle developed as a port for the copper trade, but now it is a small industrial town with a good sandy beach, though there are still a few boats to be seen in the harbour. **Paradise Park**, just off the road before entering Hayle, is a conservation theme park with otters and endangered species of birds. There is also a first-class falconry display.

The B3301 runs along the coast for 8 miles (13km) to Portreath.

Portreath, Cornwall

10 Portreath's tiny harbour cottages cluster around the port and the 18th-century pier, at the foot of windswept cliffs. It is a marvellous place to go walking along the coast path and there are spectacular views from **Reskajeage Downs**, above.

Turn inland along the B3300, then left on unclassified roads for Porthtowan.

Porthtowan, Cornwall

11 Porthtowan is a pleasant little place with a sandy beach and magnificent cliffs to north and south. If you have time, walk up on to the cliffs for fantastic views inland and over the Atlantic.

Follow unclassified roads, then the B3277 and A390 to Truro.

Truro, Cornwall

12 The cathedral city and administrative centre for Cornwall, Truro is a fascinating town with a mixture of old and new buildings. Lemon

---

FOR HISTORY BUFFS

19 St Michael's Mount is accessible by foot at low tide, and you should make time to get across to see the **castle** and **priory**, both founded by Edward the Confessor in the 11th century. This was the legendary home of the giant Cormoran, who was slain by Jack the Giant Killer.

Cadgwith, Cornwall

16 Attractive thatched cottages clustered round the small beach and harbour create a beautiful setting for local fishermen and tourists. Sandy caves alternate with rugged cliffs along this stretch of coast, but the most dramatic feature is the noisy water of the **Devil's Frying Pan**, created when a vast sea cave collapsed.

Further on, **Lizard Point** is the southernmost point in England with dramatic 180-foot (55m) cliffs and a lighthouse, open to the public.

*Head north from Lizard Point for 4 miles (6km) along the **A3083**, then the **B3296** to Mullion.*

Cadgwith is still a busy harbour with working fishermen

Arthur's sword Excalibur. Nearby **Flambards Theme Park** provides entertainment for the whole family, open in the evenings in July and August. It features a Victorian village, a simulation of the World War II blitz and many other themes.

*Take the **B3304** through Porthleven, then along the **A394** for 7 miles (11km) to Marazion. Take an unclassified road before the bypass in to the village.*

Marazion, Cornwall

19 This ancient port is famous for **St Michael's Mount**, the granite island located offshore, but is a remarkable place in its own right. Cornwall's oldest chartered town, it has the safest beach in Cornwall and some of the best wind-surfing

Mullion, Cornwall

17 The village of Mullion boasts a fine 14th- and 15th-century **church**, whose carved oak bench-ends are worth inspecting. The church tower is partially built of the local multi-coloured serpentine. Nearby **Mullion Cove** is surrounded by steep cave-pocked cliffs and has splendid views.

*Drive on for 8 miles (13km) on unclassified roads via Poldhu and Cury to the **A3083** and on to Helston.*

Helston, Cornwall

18 Radio buffs should visit **Poldhu Point** before entering Helston, to see the **Marconi Monument**, which commemorates the first transatlantic transmitting station. The ancient **Furry Dance** takes place in Helston on 8 May, when there is dancing in the streets all day. In the past this town was a port, before the Loe Bar, a 600-foot (183m) ridge of shingle, blocked it off from the sea. Behind Loe Bar is **The Loe**, a pretty lake, in to which, according to legend, Sir Bedivere threw King

in Europe. Henry III granted the town a charter in 1257 and for hundreds of years tin and copper ores were exported from here. The small town still attracts visitors, in spite of the bypass, which has reduced the amount of through-traffic.

*Return the 3 miles (5km) to Penzance via an unclassified road to the **A394**.*

Penzance – Newlyn 1 (2)
Newlyn – Lamorna 5 (8)
Lamorna – Porthcurno 7 (11)
Porthcurno – Land's End 5 (8)
Land's End – St Just 6 (10)
St Just – Zennor 9 (14)
Zennor – St Ives 5 (8)
St Ives – Lelant 3 (5)
Lelant – Hayle 2 (3)
Hayle – Portreath 9 (14)
Portreath – Porthtowan 4 (7)
Porthtowan –Truro 10 (16)
Truro – St Mawes 19 (31)
St Mawes –Penryn 13 (21)
Penryn –Gweek 14 (23)
Gweek – Cadgwith 10 (16)
Cadgwith – Mullion 10 (16)
Mullion – Helston 11 (18)
Helston – Marazion 12 (19)
Marazion –Penzance 3 (5)

3 days – 150 miles (240km)

MINING, MOORLAND & LEGENDS

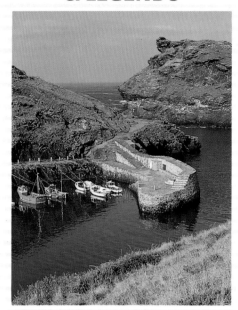

St Austell • Bodmin • Camelford • Tintagel
Boscastle • Launceston • Lydford • Okehampton
Moretonhampstead • Princetown • Tavistock
Morwellham Quay • Liskeard • Dobwalls
Lostwithiel • St Austell

This tour leads through granite scenery, market towns and green river valleys, before crossing the moorland expanse of Dartmoor, with its famous ponies and notorious prison, and finally descending to the farmlands around Tavistock.

BACK TO NATURE

The wilds of Dartmoor have a surprising variety of wildlife. Cottongrass, sundew, bog asphodel and bog bean grace many of the wetter areas, and birdlife includes curlews, dunlin, lapwings, kestrels and buzzards. In winter, look for short-eared owls, merlins and hen harriers.

ⓘ Bypass Service Station, St Austell

Leave St Austell and drive 12 miles (19km) north on the A391, then cross the A389 to Bodmin.

Bodmin, Cornwall

1 The only Cornish town recorded in the Domesday Book, Bodmin lies on the steep southwest edge of

At the full moon, the Rivers Valency and Jordan meet the sea at Boscastle with dramatic effect

Bodmin Moor, which overlooks the town. The Celts, Romans and King Arthur have all had links with the town, and the **parish church**, the largest in Cornwall, is dedicated to St Petroc, the greatest of all Celtic saints. Further north, just off the **A389**, is **Pencarrow House,**begun in the 1700s by Sir John Molesworth. In the grounds is an ancient **Iron Age encampment**, and there are walks through the flower gardens, a play area and a pets' corner.

ⓘ 80 Bradford Street, Shire House, Mount Folly Square

From Pencarrow return to the A389. Turn left, then after half a mile (0.8km), left again on to the B3266 to Camelford.

Camelford, Cornwall

2 Camelford is thought by some to have been Camelot, the fabulous city of King Arthur, and Slaughter Bridge, one mile (1.6km) to the north, is said to have been Arthur's last battleground. **The North Cornwall Museum** contains many items of rural life in Cornwall, with sections on agriculture and slate and granite quarrying.

ⓘ 80 Bradford Street, North Cornwall Museum, The Cleave

From Camelford continue on the B3266, turning left on to the B3314 and almost immediately right to join the B3263 to Tintagel.

Tintagel, Cornwall

3 Romance and legends connect this area strongly with King Arthur. The dramatic cliffs of slate on 'the Island', which is a peninsula and not really an island, have caverns and a waterfall. The 12th-century ruins of **Tintagel Castle** are in a spectacular setting on a wild, wind-lashed promontory. In the small town the highlight for most visitors is the **Old Post Office**, a small 14th-century manor house built of local slate.

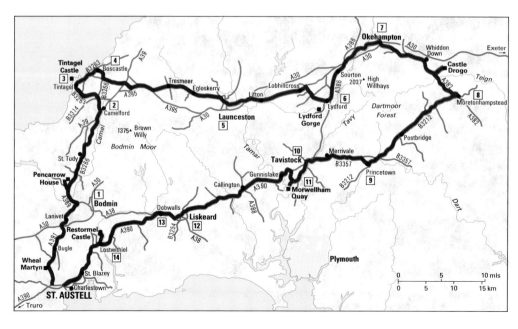

Excellent and beautiful walks can be found along the coast paths near by and in the **Rocky Valley**, a few miles further north.

Follow the B3263 along the coast for 4 miles (6km) to Boscastle.

Boscastle, Cornwall

4 Boscastle is a picturesque harbour at the head of a deep S-shaped inlet between high cliffs. A few houses are actually built in to the side of the road and oak woods, river valleys and the sea combine to make this a classic beauty spot. The river and the tide occasionally meet with explosive collisions just beyond the outer breakwater.

From Boscastle take the B3266 and unclassified roads east across the A39 to join the A395. Turn left on to the A395 and follow it for 3 miles (5km) before branching left on to unclassified roads again through Tresmeer and Egloskerry to Launceston.

Launceston, Cornwall

5 Launceston is an ancient town standing on the hill top around the ruins of a **castle**. This was the only walled town in Cornwall and the South Gate, a narrow arch, remains. **St Thomas's Church** has the largest font in Cornwall, and the **Church of St Mary** is famed for the carvings completely covering its external walls. A nostalgic **steam railway** runs into the Kensey Valley through 3 miles (5km) of glorious countryside. At the station there is a model railway and a small **museum**. The **Tamar Otter Park and Wild Wood** has peacocks and golden pheasants strutting about, and deer roam the woods.

i Market House Arcade, Market Street

Continue eastwards on the old A30, now unclassified, then just past Lobhillcross turn right on to unclassified roads to Lydford.

Lydford, Devon

6 Formerly a major centre for tin, this secluded village on the edge of Dartmoor is dominated by the remains of its 12th-century **castle**. Its old prison, a reminder of the harsh conditions of the past, was described as 'one of the most heinous, contagious and detestable places in the realm'. **Lydford Gorge**, scooped out by the River Lyd is a mile (1.6km) to the southwest, where the 90-foot (27m) high White Lady Falls and Devil's Cauldron are to be found.

Follow the A386 north from Lydford, then after a short stretch east on the A30 take the B3260 to Okehampton.

Okehampton, Devon

7 Okehampton, the 'capital of the northern moor', is at the foot of the highest part of Dartmoor, accessible to walkers when the army is not using the firing range. An old ruined castle, one of Devon's largest, sits on a hill to the west. The **Museum of Dartmoor Life** is an innovative museum portraying life in the area for hundreds of years. Southeast of town is Okehampton Camp, the remains of an Iron Age hill-fort on a steep ridge.

i 3 West Street

Return to the old A30 (now an unclassified road) past Sticklepath and South Zeal. Just before Whiddon Down turn right on to the A382 for Moretonhampstead, at which take the B3212 to Postbridge.

Moretonhampstead, Devon

8 Before reaching this town you will pass the remarkable **Castle Drogo**, a massive granite castle designed by Edward Lutyens, to the left of the road near Drewsteignton. Drive on across the heart of Dartmoor to Moretonhampstead, a small market town with some fine old buildings. At Postbridge you can see the finest of the **clapper bridges**. One of England's oldest man-made bridges, it was used by pack horses to carry ore from the mines.

Drive across Dartmoor for 14 miles (23km) along the B3212 to Princetown.

Princetown, Devon

9 Princetown, the highest town in England, is noted for its **prison**, which was built for French prisoners-of-war brought to Dartmoor to work for Sir Thomas Tyrwhitt, who built a magnificent house near by.

Head west along the B3357 to Tavistock.

Objects from Cornwall's agricultural past on display at the North Cornwall Museum, Camelford

SCENIC ROUTES

Near Camelford, on the B3266, there are views of moorland and rough stone tors; **Brown Willy**, the highest point on Bodmin Moor, is in this area.

There are many fine views along the coastline, but outstanding is that from Tintagel Castle, looking north and south along the full length of the coast from Hartland Point to Padstow.

From the B3212 you can see Dartmoor's wild moorland stretching away in to the distance, with small groups of ponies dotted here and there.

RECOMMENDED WALKS

3 Trethevy car park, north of Tintagel, is a good starting point for walks in the Rocky Valley, especially to St Nectan, for beautiful woodland scenery.

6 Follow the River Lyd in to the famous Lydford Gorge, and you will see the whirlpools and tumbling water of the Devil's Cauldron.

8 From Castle Drogo a circular tour leads through the delightful village of Drewsteignton, down to Fingle Bridge and then back along the wooded valley of the River Teign.

Once a manor house, the Old Post Office at Tintagel is built of distinctive Cornish slate

Tavistock, Devon

10 Famous for its October Goose Fair, Tavistock is also of considerable interest for its association with tin and copper mining. The town is largely Victorian, but there are many older buildings – the remains of a Benedictine **abbey** founded in the 10th century, and 15th-century **St Eustace's Church**. The statue of **Francis Drake** is a reminder that the Elizabethan sailor was born at nearby Crowndale Farm.

i Town Hall Buildings, Bedford Square

Leave Tavistock on the A386 and just before crossing the river bridge, turn right along an unclassified road for 4 miles (6km) to Morwellham Quay.

Morwellham Quay, Devon

11 Formerly a port, Morwellham, at 350 feet (107m) above water level, is linked to the river by a remarkable inclined plane. It was the greatest copper port in Victorian times, and the old harbour and quays have been repaired by the Morwellham Trust. Crafts and costumes of 100 years ago are on show and there are underground reconstructions of working conditions and early mining techniques.

Return to the A390 and head westwards for 17 miles (27km) to Liskeard.

Liskeard, Cornwall

12 Liskeard is a small, lively town with attractive buildings including **Webb's Hotel** and **Stuart House**, where Charles I slept for a week during 1644. Relics of the past can be found at **St Keyne Station** on the B3254 just outside town. Fair organs, street organs and a mighty Würlitzer

are on show here in **Paul Corin's Musical Collection**.

A short drive of 3 miles (5km) along the A390 brings you to Dobwalls.

Dobwalls, Cornwall

13 The remarkable family theme park has eight adventure areas, with ropewalks, towers to climb and two railroads on a gauge of 7¼ inches (18cm). You can roar through tunnels and canyons on the *Queen of Wyoming*, or one of the other engines pulling the mini trains.

Continue with the A390 for Lostwithiel.

Lostwithiel, Cornwall

14 Lostwithiel sits at the highest point reached by the tide on the River Fowey. The **old bridge** dates from the 14th century, and **Restormel Castle**, overlooking the River Fowey, is even older, having first been built as a wooden fort in the 11th century. At Charlestown, a few miles along the road, is the **Shipwreck and Heritage Centre**, with an assortment of treasures from the sea bed. Outside the museum is the unspoilt harbour, which still looks much as it did in the 1790s.

i Lostwithiel Community Centre, Liddicoat Road

Return to St Austell on the A390.

3 days – 133 miles (215km)

WHERE EXMOOR MEETS THE SEA

Close to natural beauty: the rolling hills of legendary Exmoor in a gentle mood

ⓘ Town Hall, Lee Road, Lynton

*Take the **B3234** for a mile (1.6km), dropping very steeply down in to Lynmouth.*

Lynmouth, Devon

1 Lynmouth is on a junction where the East and West Lyn meet. The 1890 **cliff railway** still provides a link with Lynton by means of two railcars; the top car uses water ballast to haul the other one up from the bottom. The poet Shelley lived in Lynmouth for a time with his young bride. The River Lyn is very strongly embanked now and on leaving the town you will see the gorge down which the flood water came with such devastation in 1952.

*Leave on the **A39** towards Barnstaple, turn left on to the **B3223** signed Simonsbath and then immediately left again up a narrow steep road which leads through Rockford and Brendon to Malmsmead.*

Malmsmead, Somerset

2 This isolated village is set in idyllic scenery, and is reached along narrow roads with gradients of 1 in 4. The East Lyn is a rocky stream, and if you walk up the valley of the tributary Badgeworthy Water, you will see some of the best of Exmoor. This is popularly assumed to be Doone country, though Blackmore, who wrote *Lorna Doone*, always refused to say where his tale of bandits was actually set. R D Blackmore, grandson of a 19th-century rector of Oare, further on from Malmsmead, named his characters after local people. The 500-year-old church here was the setting for Lorna Doone's violent wedding. At the Robber's Bridge further along the road there is a picturesque spot by the East Lyn, now only a tiny stream called Oare Water.

*Take the unclassified road then join the **A39** to Porlock and eventually on to Selworthy.*

Lynton • Lynmouth • Malmsmead • Porlock • Luccombe
Minehead • Watchet • Brendon Hills • Winsford
Simonsbath • South Molton • Great Torrington • Bideford
Barnstaple • Arlington • Blackmoor Gate • Lynton

Bright bays, steep coasts, low coastlines, lonely moorland and delightful stone villages combine to make this a memorable and varied tour.

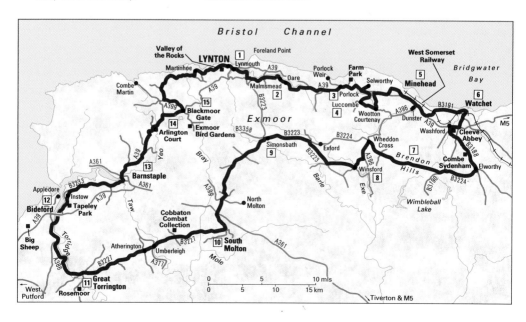

RECOMMENDED WALKS

1 Many footpaths lead from Lynton, notably a coastal walk in to the **Valley of the Rocks**. Take the narrow road between the parish church and the Valley of the Rocks Hotel, and follow a path carved out of solid rock on Hollerday Hill.

2 Starting from Malmsmead, walk upstream along Badgworthy Water, where you might see a dipper or a kingfisher. From the memorial in Blackmore, walk on to the waterslide and Lank Combe, the probable location of Doone Valley.

BACK TO NATURE

1 The wooded valley of **Watersmeet**, near Lynmouth, is safeguarded by the National Trust. Along the paths, look for the bright yellow flowers of Welsh poppy, sometimes growing alongside clumps of the rare Irish spurge. Woodland birds are common and dippers and grey wagtails have become accustomed to human visitors.

SPECIAL TO...

5 The **Minehead Hobby Horse** (or 'Obby 'Oss) procession takes place on the eve of May Day, and is said to have originated as an attempt to frighten off Danish invaders, using a strange, multi-coloured beast accompanied by musicians to create a fearsome sight and sound. There is also an 'Obby 'Oss procession in Padstow, and some dispute about which town used the idea first.

Porlock, Somerset

3 Once down the notorious steep hill, and a descent of 1,350 feet (411m), pause to admire **Porlock Weir**, a small village of thatched cottages fringing a tiny harbour. **Culbone Church** is possibly the smallest surviving medieval church in England, and can only be reached on foot.

Farm Park at Bossington is a must for family outings, with donkey rides, a hay bounce and quiz sheet. Just off the **A39** is **Selworthy**. Much of this pretty village is owned by the National Trust.

Return to the A39 and turn left towards Minehead. Shortly, turn right on an unclassified road to Luccombe.

Luccombe, Somerset

4 Pause in this secluded village to visit the fine **church** and churchyard, entered through a charming lychgate, and have a gentle stroll past the thatched cottages. Church lovers will enjoy seeing Wootton Courtenay, on the road to Minehead, where the magnificent **church** has a saddleback roof.

From Wootton Courtenay, turn north to rejoin the A39 and continue to Minehead and 2 miles (3km) further to Dunster, just south of the A39, up the A396.

Minehead, Somerset

5 A large expanse of sand and an attractive harbour area have encouraged the growth of the tourist industry in this bright and breezy town. Take a ride on the **West Somerset Railway**, which runs through 20 miles (32km) of superb scenery from the coast to the Quantocks. Just outside Minehead is **Somerwest World**, a large holiday camp with a cable car, monorail, and funfair. A little further on, Dunster's **Norman castle** looks out over the village and at the opposite end of the main street is the **Conygar Tower**,

A thatcher practising his traditional craft at Porlock Weir

built in 1775 as a landmark for shipping. There is a 16th-century yarn market, and you can see the working water mill, on the River Avill, which dates from 1680 and is still producing flour for local bakeries. **Blenheim Gardens** are fine to sit and relax in.

ℹ️ 17 Friday Street

Follow the A39 for about 2 miles (3km), then the B3191 towards Blue Anchor and Watchet.

Watchet, Somerset

6 Much of Watchet's early growth was due to iron mining in the Brendon Hills; paper-making is now the main industry. The poet Coleridge found the main character for his epic poem *The Rime of the Ancient Mariner* in this historic seaport.

Just outside **Washford**, 3 miles (5km) south of Watchet, is **Tropiquaria**, where you might find the owner wearing a snake round his neck! South of Washford is **Cleeve Abbey**, founded by Cistercian monks in 1198, with a well-preserved refectory, gate house and chapter house. Further along the road is **Combe Sydenham Country Park**, in a hidden valley on the edge of the Brendons, where there is a restored 11th-century corn mill and a deer park.

From Washford, follow the unclassified road southwards to join the B3188 via Monksilver to Elworthy, then take the B3224 west through the Brendon Hills.

Brendon Hills, Somerset

7 These undulating slopes, where Exmoor merges in to the distinctive patchwork of Brendon Hills, are not high enough for moorland, but have lush fields and trees and long views across the countryside. In earlier times small mining towns grew up to work the local deposits of iron ore, but the last one closed down in 1883. You can still see Bronze Age round **barrows** along the Ridgeway.

Continue along the B3224, turn left on the A396 and then follow an unclassified road to Winsford.

Winsford, Somerset

8 Winsford is one of the best centres for tourism on Exmoor, with its church standing over the village. The mysteriously inscribed **Caractacus Stone**, a mile (1.6km) to the south, probably dates from between the 5th and 7th centuries.

From Winsford take the unclassified road to join the B3223 and continue for about 10 miles (16km) to Simonsbath.

Simonsbath, Somerset

9 Situated 1,100 feet (335m) above sea level, Simonsbath is the highest village in Exmoor, in the centre of what used to be the Royal Exmoor Forest. Climb steeply out of the hamlet and on to the moors. In places the traditional old Exmoor hedges block the fabulous views.

Use unclassified roads to cross the moor southwards, and join the A399, then the B3226 for South Molton.

South Molton, Devon

10Formerly important for the wool trade, but now a cattle market and tourist centre, South Molton is known to have existed as a Saxon colony. The square is given grandeur by the **Guildhall** and **Assembly Rooms** which overlook it, and the splendid church has a magnificent tower and a remarkable stone pulpit. On the road west, the **Cobbaton Combat Collection** recalls World War II with tanks, artillery and radio equipment.

i 1 East Street

Follow the B3227 for 15 miles (24km) to Great Torrington.

Great Torrington, Devon

11Great Torrington was a market town in Saxon times and the scene of fierce fighting in the Civil War. The original church was used as a gunpowder stores but an explosion blew it to pieces. At **Dartington Glassworks** you can watch fine crystal glass being blown, and just outside the town the Royal Horticultural Society has a garden at **Rosemoor**. The **Gnome Reserve** at **West Putford** boasts the world's largest population of gnomes.

i Town Hall, High Street

Take the A386 to Bideford.

Bideford, Devon

12This interesting little town was a major port in the 16th and 17th centuries with a busy trade in tobacco. There is a new high bridge for the main road, but ships still move upstream to the old stone bridge across the estuary. The **Royal Hotel**, which dates from 1688, was where Charles Kingsley wrote part of his novel *Westward Ho!* Follow the old road to Barnstaple and you will pass Instow, a resort by the dunes with colourful views across to the port of Appledore. **Tapeley Park**, on the way to Instow, has medieval banquets and is the home of the Jousting Association.

i The Quay

Follow the coast road along the B3233 for 10 miles (16km) to Barnstaple.

Barnstaple, Devon

13Barnstaple is one of North Devon's major market towns. It was once a busy ship-building town and a port trading with America, but the River Taw became too silted in the 19th century. There are many fine examples of Georgian architecture. **Queen Anne's Walk** is a pleasant colonnade, and you can still see the **Tome Stone**, where merchants used to set their money to make their contracts binding. **St Anne's Chapel**, dating from the 14th century, houses the local **museum**. The fine long bridge over the River Taw has 16 arches and dates from the 13th century.

i North Devon Library, Tuly Street

Continue northwards on the A39 for Arlington.

The church at Oare where Lorna Doone was shot in Blackmore's tale

Arlington, Devon

14Arlington Court is one of the few great houses of North Devon. Formerly the home of the Chichester family, it has been owned by the National Trust since 1949. Sir Francis Chichester, the yachtsman, is the most famous descendant of this old family. The house contains a rich collection of model ships and there are walks in the park and woods. During the summer there are horse-and-carriage rides between the house and the collection of old carriages kept in the stables.

Another 3 miles (5km) along the A39 brings you to Blackmoor Gate.

Blackmoor Gate, Devon

15Blackmoor Gate is really a road junction, but the **Exmoor Bird Gardens** are near by along the B3226, and **Tarzan Land** provides entertainment for the children. For the next few miles the road is narrow, winding and very steep in places, with dramatic views of coastal cliffs. There is a short stretch of toll road, before entering the **Valley of the Rocks**, a gorge littered with enormous slabs of granite. Walk up to the top of **Castle Rock**, where the vertical drop is 800 feet (244m).

Take the A399 and then an unclassified road via Trentishoe and Martinhoe back to Lynton.

Lynton – Lynmouth 1 (2)
Lynmouth – Malmsmead 7 (11)
Malmsmead – Porlock 7 (11)
Porlock – Luccombe 5 (8)
Luccombe – Minehead 6 (10)
Minehead – Watchet 9 (14)
Watchet – Brendon Hills 14 (23)
Brendon Hills – Winsford 8 (13)
Winsford – Simonsbath 10 (16)
Simonsbath – South Molton 11 (18)
South Molton – Great Torrington 15 (24)
Great Torrington – Bideford 7 (11)
Bideford – Barnstaple 10 (16)
Barnstaple – Arlington 8 (13)
Arlington – Blackmoor Gate 3 (5)
Blackmoor Gate – Lynton 12 (20)

FOR CHILDREN

12At Abbotsham, 2 miles (3km) west of Bideford, is the **Big Sheep**, where you can watch the free demonstration of sheep milking and sheep shearing, and have a go at spinning. Other attractions include sheep racing, a nature trail and an adventure playground.

FOR HISTORY BUFFS

12Like most towns of the north coast of Devon, Bideford has strong maritime traditions. It was a busy port in England in the 16th century, with many links to the East Indies and the Americas. Smuggling as well as legal trading were part of the life in this area, and some of this history can be seen in the **North Devon Maritime Museum** in Appledore, north of Bideford.

SCENIC ROUTES

From the **A39** approaching Porlock there are excellent views down in to Porlock Bay. Towards Watchet on the **B3191** the view of harbour and cliffs beyond is an interesting mixture of town and coast. Moorland views can be enjoyed on Exmoor between Winsford and Simonsbath, though most of Exmoor is green farmland, and there are outstanding views near Trentishoe and Martinhoe.

3 days – 130 miles (209km)

SOMERSET'S CHARMING HAMSTONE TOWNS

Bridgwater • Taunton • Ilminster • Chard • Crewkerne
Beaminster • Bridport • Abbotsbury • Dorchester
Cerne Abbas • Sherborne • Yeovil • Montacute
Westonzoyland • Bridgwater

Wooded hills and rich valleys combine with the mellow dignity of country towns in golden stone to make South Somerset and Dorset one of the least spoiled parts of England. Add to this a splendid sea view and you have a tour to linger long in the memory.

The young Thomas Hardy worked on the restoration of St Peter's Church, Dorchester, in the 1850s

ⓘ High Street, Bridgwater

Leave Bridgwater on an unclassified road to Enmore. Continue to Bishops Lydeard then turn left on to the A358 to Taunton.

Taunton, Somerset

1 As you drop steeply down from the Quantock Hills, a stunning view of the Vale of Taunton Deane opens up, with the undulating ridge of the Blackdown Hills in the distance. Somerset's county town, Taunton, lies in the heart of this rich vale. The largest town between Bristol and Exeter, it has one of the biggest livestock markets in the southwest. In the Great Hall of **Taunton Castle**, the infamous Judge Jeffreys sent over 500 rebels to their deaths at his 'Bloody Assize'. A walk down Hammet Street gives the best view of the elegant Perpendicular tower of 15th-century **St Mary's Church**. The town is a mecca for cricket lovers, and next to the **County Ground** is Somerset's **Cricket Museum**, in the 13th-century **Priory Barn**.

ⓘ The Library, Corporation Street

Leave Taunton on the B3170 heading south. Shortly after crossing the M5, turn left for Staple Fitzpaine. Continue on unclassified roads towards Buckland St Mary and the A303. Turn left on to the A303, then right on to the B3168 to Ilminster.

Ilminster, Somerset

2 Dabinetts, Brownsnouts, Kingston Blacks and Red Streaks are all local varieties of apples. Somerset is cider country, and near Ilminster, at

SCENIC ROUTES

The whole drive through the Quantock Hills from Enmore, near Bridgwater to Bishops Lydeard, is a delight. There are few views to rival those from the B3157 between Burton Bradstock and Abbotsbury. On the right is one of the finest sea views in Britain, on the left steep chalky downs and deep valleys.

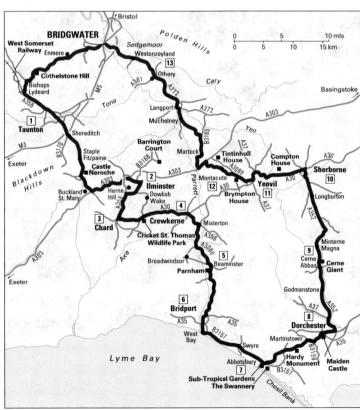

Dowlish Wake, are **Perry's Cider Mills**, where this powerful apple brew has been made for centuries. Visitors can wander through the farm to see how it is done and afterwards sample some 'scrumpy' for themselves. Ilminster has a lovely little shopping centre, built in the local Hamstone (a golden limestone). Of particular note are the pillared **market house** and the 15th-century minster **Church of St Mary**. Herne Hill is a local beauty spot and vantage point to the southwest of the town. One of the earliest National Trust properties, **Barrington Court**, lies to the north – an intriguing model estate with Tudor manor house and gardens transformed in the 1920s by the Lyle family.

ⓘ Shudrick Lane

From Ilminster go south on an unclassified road, turning left on to the A358 for Chard.

Chard, Somerset

3 This market town astride the busy A30 claims to be the birthplace of flight. To find out why, visit the **Chard Museum** in High Street. Besides flight, you can find out more about blacksmiths, early funerals, historic costumes and even artificial limbs – they were invented here too!

ⓘ The Guildhall, Fore Street

Leave Chard on the A30 for Crewkerne (8miles/13km).

Crewkerne, Somerset

4 Crewkerne is an ancient market town whose wealth was founded on minting coins, and in later centuries on flax-weaving and sail-making. It was here that HMS Victory's sails were made, and more recently the sails for several contenders for the Americas Cup. Captain Hardy, Nelson's flag captain on the *Victory*, was a pupil at the ancient grammar school.

From Crewkerne on the A356, signposted Dorchester/Bridport, turn right on to the A3066 for Beaminster (4½miles/7km).

Beaminster, Dorset

5 'The forgotten county' and 'the hidden valley' are two of the epithets ascribed to the scenery around Beaminster. This town, in the Brit Valley, is virtually unspoilt. Three fires in 200 years once rendered the town ' the pityfullest spectacle that Man can behold' but the mellow honey-coloured Hamstone houses testify to the healing power of time. Most streets offer a view of the fine pinnacled tower of the golden **church**, built in 1503. The Tudor manor house at **Parnham**, near Beaminster, enjoys world renown as a centre for craftsmanship in wood, and is open to the public on certain days of the week.

Continue south on the A3066 for 6 miles (10km) to Bridport.

Bridport, Dorset

6 In olden times, the term 'Bridport dagger' used to strike fear in to the heart of many a criminal, for that was the nickname for the hangman's noose. Ropes and nets have been made here for a thousand years now, and this is still Europe's biggest net-making centre. The unusual width of the streets allowed for rope-walks, where the flax strands were laid out to be twisted in to shape. In South Street, look out for **St Mary's Church** with its Hamstone tower and 13th-century knight's tomb.

ⓘ 32 South Street

Leave Bridport heading for West Bay, then turn on to the B3157 for 8 miles (13km) to Abbotsbury.

Abbotsbury, Dorset

7 Abbotsbury shelters in a valley between high chalk downs and the shingle coast of Chesil Bank, that sweeps round to the 'Isle' of Portland. A long main street of thatched limestone cottages heralds your approach to the village centre, clustered round the 15th-century **church** and the **Ilchester Arms** public house. From opposite here a narrow, unsignposted road leads high up over Black Down Hill to the **Hardy Monument**, an obelisk commemorating Vice-Admiral Hardy. **St Catherine's Chapel**, built for seamen in the 15th century, looks down from its grassy knoll near by, and near the church are the remains of an 11th-century Benedictine **abbey**. The one surviving feature is a fine thatched **tithe barn**, the largest in England.

Leave Abbotsbury uphill on an unclassified road to Martinstown; then turn left and on to the B3159, then left again for Dorchester.

Dorchester, Dorset

8 The county town of Dorset is in the heart of Thomas Hardy country and is still the busy market town portrayed in *The Mayor of Casterbridge*. **Hardy's statue** stands near the top of High West Street. Founded as Durnovaria by the Romans in AD70, Dorchester has many fine Georgian buildings. Judge Jeffreys was sent here by King James to punish rebels after the Battle of Sedgemoor in

The distinctive Giant dominates the village of Cerne Abbas

SPECIAL TO...

1 The **West Somerset Railway** is the longest preserved line in Britain, running through some of the finest scenery in the West Country. Starting off at Bishops Lydeard, at the foot of the Quantocks near Taunton, it runs 20 miles (32km) down to the coastal plain and beaches of the Bristol Channel.

FOR CHILDREN

3 The **Wildlife Park** at Cricket St Thomas is set in a deep, wooded valley just off the A30 between Chard and Crewkerne. The park is home to a great variety of animals and birds – from wild deer to penguins, elephants and parrots. There are plenty of leisure park features, including a scenic railway and an adventure playground.

BACK TO NATURE

7 The **Fleet** is a large brackish lagoon which lies behind the shelter of Chesil Beach. Towards the western end, the **swannery** at Abbotsbury is worth visiting, while at the eastern end, the mudflats revealed at low tide support thousands of birds such as waders, gulls and other wildfowl. The shingle flora of Chesil Beach is worth studying, and in the heart of nearby Weymouth lies **Radipole Lake**, an RSPB reserve.

FOR HISTORY BUFFS

8 Maiden Castle, 2 miles (3km) southwest of Dorchester, is the finest prehistoric hill-fort in Britain. The massive oval earthworks can be seen for miles around. Three huge ditches were dug by Iron Age men to protect some 5,000 inhabitants. Archaeological excavations have revealed a history stretching back to the Stone Age, and among the finds have been the skeletons of 34 people. Maiden Castle is best approached from the Weymouth road out of Dorchester.

RECOMMENDED WALKS

12 There are several enjoyable walks from Montacute, notably the woodland **Ladies' Walk**, or the paths that lead to the folly of **St Michael's Hill** near by. An extra burst of energy will take you to the top of the recently restored tower for glorious views across south Somerset.

1685. At **Old Crown Court**, six local farmworkers were sentenced in 1834 to be transported to Australia for forming a trades union: they became known as the Tolpuddle Martyrs. There are numerous sites of interest, including the floor of a **Roman town house** and **Maumbury Rings**, a Roman amphitheatre. The town boasts three museums: the **Dinosaur Museum**; the **Military Museum**, which is the unlikely location for Hitler's desk; and the **Dorset County Museum**.

ⓘ 7 Acland Road

From Dorchester head north on the A352 for Cerne Abbas.

Cerne Abbas, Dorset

9 Before entering Cerne Abbas, as you pass through Godmanstone, look out for the smallest pub in England, the Smith's Arms, just 20 by 10 feet (6 by 3m). Cerne Abbas itself is a charming village and its main source of interest is not difficult to spot. Cut in to the steep chalk hillside behind the village, the Cerne Giant, a well-endowed figure 180 foot (55m) high, is a fertility figure dating from Roman times.

Continue north on the A352 for Sherborne.

Sherborne, Dorset

10 Sherborne claims, with some justification, to be one of the most beautiful towns in England. Set in a gentle valley among wooded hills, it has a charming stone-built centre. Two kings of Wessex were buried in Sherborne's Saxon **abbey**, the mother cathedral of the Southwest

Sir Walter Raleigh crowned his success by building Sherborne Castle

until 1075. Sherborne Old Castle dates from the 12th century, and **Sherborne New Castle** was built by Sir Walter Raleigh in the 1590s. It was here that Sir Walter was 'extinguished' by a servant who first saw him smoking the tobacco he brought back from the New World. At **Compton House** near by is **Worldwide Butterflies** where exotic species can be seen in 'tropical' surroundings. You can also see Britain's only silk farm, where many royal wedding dresses were made.

ⓘ 3 Digby Road

Leave Sherborne on the A30 heading west for 6 miles (10km) to Yeovil.

Yeovil, Somerset

11 Yeovil is a thriving industrial and administrative centre, nationally known for its gloves and helicopters. It suffered disastrous fires in 1499, 1623, and 1640 and during World War II air raids destroyed many of its oldest buildings. One to survive was the 14th-century stone **church**, impressive for its simplicity and size.

ⓘ Petter's House, Petter's Way

Leave Yeovil on the A30 and turn right on to the A3088, turning left in 3 miles (5km) for Montacute.

Montacute, Somerset

12 This is yet another delightful Hamstone village. In a corner of the square is the entrance to its showpiece, **Montacute House**, a splendid Tudor mansion in formal, landscaped gardens. It was built by Sir Edward Phelips, chief prosecutor of Guy Fawkes in 1605. Although on a smaller scale than Montacute, nearby **Brympton House** and **Tintinhull House** attract many visitors each year.

From Montacute take the A3088 to Stoke-sub-Hamdon, then the A303 and right on to the B3165. Join the A372 heading for Westonzoyland.

Westonzoyland, Somerset

13 Westonzoyland's 100-foot (30m) church tower looks boldly over Sedgemoor, once covered by sea and now a vast expanse of fenland – the largest wetland of its type anywhere in Britain. A map in the church porch will show you how to explore the historical connection, for near here the last battle on English soil was fought. A granite **monument** on this quiet open land is all that marks the spot for posterity.

From Westonzoyland continue on the A372 to Bridgwater.

Bridgwater - Taunton 16 (26)
Taunton - Ilminster 15 (24)
Ilminster - Chard 5 (8)
Chard - Crewkerne 8 (13)
Crewkerne - Beaminster 7 (11)
Beaminster - Bridport 6 (10)
Bridport - Abbotsbury 10 (16)
Abbotsbury - Dorchester 9 (14)
Dorchester - Cerne Abbas 8 (13)
Cerne Abbas - Sherborne 11 (18)
Sherborne - Yeovil 6 (10)
Yeovil - Montacute 5 (8)
Montacute - Westonzoyland 20 (32)
Westonzoyland - Bridgwater 4 (6)

3 days- 137 miles (220km)

Avalon perhaps? Glastonbury Tor preserves its secrets still

ⓘ Fish Row, Salisbury

Leave Salisbury on the A345 signed Amesbury and in 1 mile (1.6km) reach Old Sarum.

Old Sarum, Wiltshire

1 Iron Age men, Romans, Saxons, Danes and Normans in turn chose this windy hilltop for their settlements. Within a huge circular mound are the foundations of the Norman cathedral and castle that once stood here. Bishops Osmund and Roger built the cathedral, but cathedral life wasn't easy, and castle and clergy did not get on. In 1220 the bishop chose a new site in the valley, known today as Salisbury, and materials from the demolished cathedral were then used for Salisbury's new glory.

Continue on the A345, then take the first left on to unclassified roads for the Woodfords. In 5 miles (8km) reach Amesbury and 1 mile (2km) further north on the A345 is Woodhenge. Return to the A303 and head west signed Honiton, then right on to the A360 to Stonehenge (2 miles/3km).

Stonehenge and Woodhenge, Wiltshire

2 A henge is a prehistoric monument, usually of religious significance. Woodhenge, the Neolithic precursor of Stonehenge, had six concentric rings of timber posts, surrounded by a ditch. The holes marking the site are now marked by concrete posts.

At Stonehenge huge stones 15 to 20 feet (4.5 to 6m) high have been the subject of enormous speculation. Is it a temple for Romans or Druids? How were 26-ton stones brought here with no modern lifting gear? One thing is certain – the axis is aligned with the midwinter and midsummer sun; perhaps this revered monument is a giant calendar.

From Stonehenge continue on the A360, turning left on to the B390 just past Shrewton. On reaching the A36 turn right, then right again after 1 mile (1.6km) on to the B3414 to Warminster.

THE HILLS & VALES OF WEST WESSEX

Salisbury • Old Sarum • Stonehenge and Woodhenge
Warminster • Frome • Wells • Cheddar
Glastonbury • Bruton • Stourhead • Shaftesbury
Wilton • Salisbury

From Wiltshire's gentle valleys and downlands to the rugged hills and expansive wetlands of Somerset, the Wessex scenery constantly changes. This tour takes in one of Britain's finest cathedrals, one of Europe's loveliest gardens and the world's most famous prehistoric temple.

Warminster, Wiltshire

3 Warminster was formerly a wool town and corn market; today it is the home of the **Army School of**

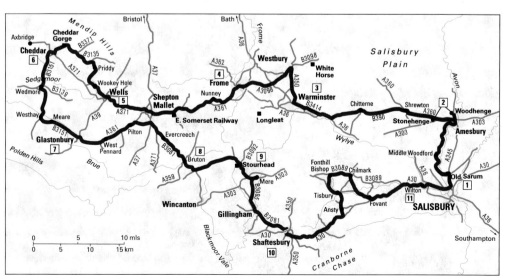

Built for ceremonies long forgotten, Stonehenge remains a mystery

SPECIAL TO...

4 The **Royal Bath and Wells Show**, held on the first weekend in June, attracts huge crowds from far and wide to the show ground near **Shepton Mallet**, 11 miles (16km) from Frome. As well as the agricultural activities, attractions include aerobatics, show-jumping and motorcycle displays.

FOR CHILDREN

5 Stalactites and stalagmites, soaring caverns and bottomless pits are all to be found at **Wookey Hole Caves** near Wells, first inhabited 50,000 years ago. On the surface, visitors can walk around a mill which still produces watermarked paper from rags, distort themselves in the mirrors of the old fairground and change new pence for old to play original one-arm bandits at the **Penny Pier Arcade**.

RECOMMENDED WALKS

Westbury's **White Horse**, cut in to the chalk escarpment of Salisbury Plain in the 18th century, is said to replace one carved in AD879 to commemorate King Alfred's victory over the Danes at Ethandun. The view from the downland here is tremendous. Climb from the church at Bratton on the **B3098**, 2 miles (3km) east of Westbury, or drive up to Westbury Hill, turning right from the **B3098**, just before the cemetery.

Infantry and the **REME** (Royal Electrical and Mechanical Engineers) workshops. Four miles (6km) to the west is **Longleat**, Elizabethan seat of the Marquesses of Bath and nationally famous as a wildlife park.

[i] Central Car Park, Three Horseshoes Mall, Warminster; Library Car Park, Edward Street, Westbury

*Take the **A350** for Westbury 4 miles (6km). Leave by the **A3098** for 7 miles (11km) to Frome.*

Frome, Somerset

4 'Friendly Frome' (say Froom), on the River Frome, is an attractive market town which grew rich on trade in woollen cloth. Its steep narrow streets are scattered with medieval and Tudor buildings. **Cheap Street**, with its ancient shops and leat gutter is a must, as are the 1726 **Blue House**, the bridge with its integral shops, and **St John's Church**. Three miles (4.8km) from Frome, on the **A361**, is Nunney, with its romantic moated 14th-century **castle**.

[i] Cattle Market Car Park

*Leave Frome to join the **A361** for Shepton Mallet, 11 miles (16km), then by the **A371** to Wells (6 miles/10km).*

Wells, Somerset

5 Wells is England's smallest city, lying in the shadow of the Mendip Hills, and gets its name from the springs that bubble in to a pool in the **bishop's garden**. The splendid **cathedral** was begun in the 12th century and finished in the 15th, and its astronomical clock in the north transept is one of the oldest working clocks in the world. South of the cathedral is the moated **Bishop's Palace**, where the swans used to ring the bell by the bridge for food. **St Cuthbert's Parish Church** in High Street is the largest in Somerset, with a 122-foot (37m) tower.

[i] Town Hall, Market Place

*Leave Wells on an unclassified road to Wookey Hole (1½ miles/2km), and shortly after the Wookey Hole Caves fork right for Priddy, (2 miles/5km), then left on the **B3135** for Cheddar (5 miles/8km).*

Cheddar, Somerset

6 The rugged grandeur of Cheddar Gorge unfolds slowly and magically as you descend a meandering road. Cliffs tower to a height of 450 feet (137m) here, and the 'Beware of falling rocks' sign is no idle warning. Climb the 274 steps of **Jacob's Ladder** at the south end for the best views, or rest in the **Garden of Fragrance**, especially created for the blind. At the bottom of the gorge, **Gough's and Cox's Caves** offer a chance to go subterranean in search of the lost Yeo. Cheddar would not be Cheddar without its cheese, but the product outgrew the place and has largely gone elsewhere. A 1990 replica of a 1920s factory shows how it used to be made.

[i] The Gorge

*Leave Cheddar on the **B3151** for Glastonbury (12 miles/9km).*

Glastonbury, Somerset

7 Said to be the 'cradle of English Christianity', Glastonbury is a town steeped in Christian and Arthurian legends. The focal point is the ruined **abbey**, which may have originated in the 1st century, but was sacked at the Dissolution in 1539. Joseph of Arimathea is reputed to have come here as a missionary in AD63, and a thorn in the **Abbot's kitchen** is said to derive from his wooden staff, which turned in to a thorn bush. The **chapel** on the Tor dates from AD179. Through the ages, writers have speculated that this is the site of Avalon, King Arthur's final resting place. The chalice which Christ used at the Last Supper is said to be beneath the **Chalice Spring** on the Tor. Of particular note in the town are the **Abbey Barn**, now housing the **Somerset Rural Life Museum**, the fine 14th-century **George and Pilgrims Hotel**, and **The Tribunal**, once a courthouse and now a museum.

ⓘ The Tribunal

Leave Glastonbury on the A361 and in 7 miles (12km) turn left on to the A37, then right on to the A371 signposted Castle Cary. Shortly, fork left on to the B3081 for Bruton, (4 miles/6km).

Bruton, Somerset

8 Little Bruton, on the River Brue, has a charm of its own. Be sure to explore **The Bartons**, narrow alleys leading down to the river, which is crossed by an unusual **packhorse bridge**. St Mary's Church, with its twin towers, is particularly fine, and prominent in the town is **King's School**, established in the 16th century. The tall building on the hill as you leave is the **Bruton Dovecote**, formerly belonging to the abbey which once existed here.

Leave Bruton by the B3081, signposted Wincanton. In Redlynch turn left at crossroads and in 3 miles (5km) right, and shortly right again to join the B3092 to Stourhead (½ mile/1km).

Stourhead, Wiltshire

9 Henry Hoare, an eminent banker, decided to landscape his Palladian Wiltshire home, Stourhead, in the grand manner. He began in 1740 by damming springs of the Stour to create a sweeping lake with wooded islands. This is one of the finest gardens in the world, now in the care of the National Trust. An unmistakable landmark on the border of the Stourhead estate is **Alfred's Tower**, a triangular brick structure 160 feet (49m) high, built in 1772. It marks the spot where King Alfred rallied his troops to fight the Danes in AD879.

Leave Stourhead on the B3092 for Mere (2 miles/3km). Take the B3095, then turn left on to the B3092 to Gillingham (2½ miles/4km), then Shaftesbury (3 miles/5km) via the B3081.

Shaftesbury, Dorset

10 Perched on a hill 700 feet (213m) above sea level, the pretty town of Shaftesbury commands marvellous views across Dorset's Blackmoor Vale. The **Local History Museum** near St Peter's Church contains the **Byzant**, a strange ornamental relic, formerly carried by townsfolk in a ceremony confirming their rights to draw water from wells at the foot of the hill.

ⓘ 8 Bell Street

Leave Shaftesbury on the A30 signposted Salisbury. In 6 miles (10km) turn left for Ansty and Tisbury. Continue north, then turn right on the B3089 at Fonthill Bishop. In 2 miles (3km) turn at Chilmark to Fovant (3 miles/5km). Go left on the A30 to Wilton (6 miles/10km).

Wilton, Wiltshire

11 In Saxon times, Wilton was capital of Wessex. Thousands now flock here each year to visit **Wilton House**, built in the 1540s and remodelled by Inigo Jones in the 17th century. The Double Cube Room, recently restored, is especially ornate. There is a world-famous collection of paintings by Rubens, Van Dyck and Tintoretto, among others. Near by is the **Royal Wilton Carpet Factory**, here since 1655.

Leave Wilton by the A36 for Salisbury (4 miles/6km).

Salisbury – Old Sarum 1 (2)
Old Sarum – Stonehenge 11 (18)
Stonehenge – Warminster 16 (26)
Warminster – Frome 11 (17)
Frome – Wells 17 (27)
Wells – Cheddar 11 (18)
Cheddar – Glastonbury 13 (21)
Glastonbury – Bruton 15 (24)
Bruton – Stourhead 7 (11)
Stourhead – Shaftesbury 10 (16)
Shaftesbury – Wilton 21 (34)
Wilton – Salisbury 4 (6)

Nature tamed: the classical order and opulence of Stourhead

FOR HISTORY BUFFS

6 Axbridge, near Cheddar, is a fine example of a close-knit winding medieval town. The jewel is **King John's Hunting Lodge**, at the corner of High Street and The Square. This handsome three-storeyed building has nothing to do with either King John or with hunting, but has been exquisitely restored by the National Trust, and now houses the **Axbridge Museum**, open on summer afternoons.

BACK TO NATURE

Ebbor Gorge on the route between Wookey Hole and Priddy, is thought by many to be the loveliest and most unspoilt Mendip gorge.

SCENIC ROUTES

On the B3151 south of Cheddar, it is worth stopping as you approach Wedmore to look back over **Sedgemoor**, one of England's few wetlands, stretching away to the marvellous backdrop of the Mendip limestone ridge. As you ascend the steep hill to enter Shaftesbury, look back over the rich farmland of Dorset's lovely **Blackmoor Vale**, with the wooded ridge of Stourhead and Alfred's Tower beyond.

THE SOUTH & SOUTHEAST

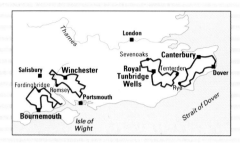

Despite being well populated, the five counties of Surrey, Sussex, Kent, Hampshire and Dorset have retained large areas of rich farmland, commons and heaths and forested areas. Perhaps the most famous area is the New Forest in Hampshire, much of which is heathland; 'forest' was originally a term for hunting ground.

Architectural styles are especially distinctive in the Weald of Sussex and Kent, where tile-hung houses can be seen in many villages, as well as thatched houses and oasthouses – though most of these are now residences, having ceased production of beer from locally grown hops. Further west is Hardy Country: many of Dorset's attractive towns and villages can be related to the writings of Thomas Hardy and his views of life in the 18th century.

The scenery varies from gentle, undulating landscapes to steep escarpments on the edges of the North and South Downs and dramatic coastal cliffs, notably at Beachy Head, where the South Downs reach the sea. At the foot of the white cliffs of Dover, where the North Downs reach the coast, the Channel Tunnel dives beneath the sea on its way of France.

Seaside resorts such as Bournemouth and Folkestone attract large numbers of visitors, especially in the summer months and at weekends, although many of the beaches are not very sandy in the south-eastern part of England.

Religion plays an important part in the life of this region, where Winchester and Canterbury are at opposite ends of the Pilgrims Way. Fine cathedrals can be seen in both these towns, and many impressive churches are hidden away in small villages. These were often financed from agricultrual profits and competition was fierce, with villages trying to outdo their neighbours with bigger or better churches. Near the chalk hills, many of these churches are built of this soft rock, but are faced with a layer of resistant flint.

Winchester
There is so much to see in this City of Kings that it might be worth taking a guided walking or driving tour. Winchester is a place of history and legend. The Round Table in the castle's Great Hall is actually a medieval creation which celebrates the romanticised King Arthur legend. From here you can walk past the old Butter Cross in the centre of town and make a diversion to the fine cathedral – before taking a look at the statue of King Alfred, which recalls Winchester's past status as his kingdom's capital.

Bournemouth
This town developed along with the Victorian enthusiasm for the seaside, when a few rich families built villas on what used to be a fairly desolate

The elegant Regency charm of the Pantiles in Royal Tunbridge Wells

heath. An attractive golden beach stretches for miles along the coast, and windsurfing, swimming and boating are popular activities. There are beautiful gardens to visit with sub-tropical vegetation which thrives in the mild climate. Quiet, wooded walks can be taken in the steep valleys called chines, which slope down from the cliff tops to the shore.

Royal Tunbridge Wells

This spa town has been a fashionable market and trading centre for many years; even in the 17th century, the Pantiles was an established shopping centre. The town first developed as a spa when its chalybeate spring was discovered in 1606; it can still be seen, in Bath Square. The surrounding countryside consists of miles of common, on which stand the spectacular High Rocks.

The distinctive white coastline of southern England, here seen in the Seven Sisters Country Park, has inspired nostalgia and national pride for centuries

Canterbury

Canterbury's cathedral dominates the landscape for miles around, but there is much more to see in this ancient city, often thought of as the birthplace of English Christianity. A walk round the streets is a walk through history, and a visit to the Canterbury Heritage Exhibition is a good way to start a tour. The city walls, St Martin's church, the ruins of St Augustine's Abbey, the Royal Museum and the Old Weavers' House are among the buildings you must not miss. There are also modern entertainments, including two theatres and an excellent pedestrianised area for shopping.

3 days – 122 miles (197km)

A JOURNEY ACROSS THE WEALD

Royal Tunbridge Wells • Penshurst • Hever • Limpsfield
Sevenoaks • Ightham • Mereworth • Lamberhurst
Cranbrook • Tenterden • Northiam • Bodiam • Burwash
Rotherfield • Royal Tunbridge Wells

Over undulating sandstone hills, through the orchards of the 'Garden of England', and the once vast Forest of Anderida, this is an area of delightful villages, superb castles and immaculate gardens. Church spires and towers and tile-hung Wealden houses all add to its beauty, as the buildings and countryside compete with each other to provide the most delightful views.

A stretch of line on the Kent and East Sussex Railway at Tenterden

ℹ️ Monson House, Monson Way, Royal Tunbridge Wells

Leave Tunbridge Wells on the A264, then take the B2188 north to Penshurst.

Penshurst, Kent

1 Penshurst is a small village with stone houses and a magnificent church, but the main attraction is 14th-century **Penshurst Place**, one of the outstanding stately homes of Britain, set in superb Tudor gardens. The famous chestnut-beamed Great Hall dominates the manor with its medieval splendour, and its scale and grandeur are almost beyond belief. It also houses a fascinating toy museum. The Elizabethan poet, Sir Philip Sidney, was born here in 1554, and the Sidney family still lives in the manor. The family became Earls of Leicester, and the village has the original **Leicester Square** – named after a favourite of Elizabeth 1. The **Church of St Michael the Archangel** dates from the 13th century and contains impressive memorials to the Sidney family.

Take the road past the church and follow the B2176, B2027 and unclassified roads for 6 miles (10km) to Hever.

Hever, Kent

2 Hever is known for its associations with Anne Boeyn, Henry VIII's second wife. The village inn is called **King Henry VIII**, and the fine **church** has a memorial to Sir Thomas Bullen, Anne's father, who is buried here. **Hever Castle** was the family home, Anne spent her childhood here, and it was here that Henry VIII courted her.

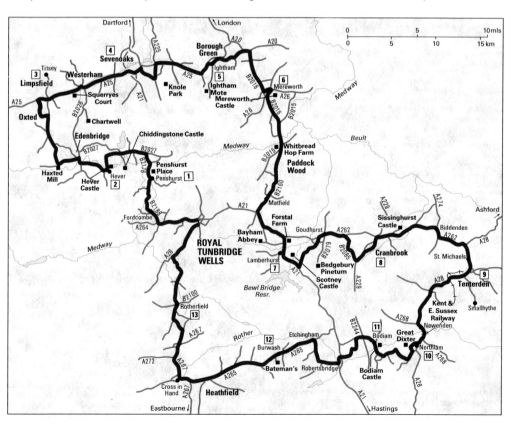

This fine, moated manor house was acquired by William Waldorf Astor in 1903, who did much work restoring it. He created the modern lake and superb Tudor-style gardens, including a spectacular Italian Garden, and built a mock-Tudor village behind the house. The house itself contains a superb collection of furniture and paintings, and the Tudor Long Gallery features a fascinating exhibition of scenes from the life and times of Anne Boleyn. Just east of Hever is Chiddingstone. The entire village is owned by the National Trust,

tains a collection of furniture, porcelain and military items. A littlefurther is the village of **Westerham**. General Wolfe, who beat the French in Quebec in 1759, was born here. His boyhood home, 17th-century **Quebec House** is near the green. Near by is **Squerryes Court**, a William and Mary manor house built in 1681 and owned by the Warde family for over 250 years. Wolfe received his commission here, and a room is set aside for Wolfe memorabilia. The house also contains fine paintings, tapestries and furniture, and the magnificent

RECOMMENDED WALKS

Many excellent walks can be found near **Titsey**, to the north of Limpsfield, southwards towards Edenbridge along the Vanguard Way, and east and west along the North Downs Way, which follows much of the old **Pilgrim's Way** from Winchester to Canterbury, giving fine views of southern England. On a clear day you can see as far as the South

The ill-fated Anne Boleyn was courted by a king at Hever Castle

including **Chiddingstone Castle**, a late 18th-century Gothic manor house.

The main street is lined with beautifully preserved half-timbered 16th- and 17th-century houses. The **Chiding Stone**, after which the village is named, is a piece of local sandstone where nagging wives were publicly chided by the assembled village population. Three miles (5km) west of Hever is **Edenbridge**. The 16th-century **Crown Hotel** is noteworthy. The 13th-century **church** here has a massive tower crowned with a spire of a later date. Near by, at **Haxted**, is a late 16th-century watermill, now a **museum** which contains mill machinery, two working waterwheels and a picture gallery.

From Haxted Mill take unclassified roads north to Limpsfield.

Limpsfield, Surrey

3 This small town nestles at the foot of the North Downs in wooded countryside. The composer Frederick Delius is buried among the yews in the churchyard here. **De Tillens** is a fine 15th-century Wealden Hall House with a splendid king-post roof. Built by the yeomen of the weald, it con-

garden has lakes, spring flowers and shrubs. There is a statue of Wolfe in the High Street, and on the tiny green one of Sir Winston Churchill, who lived at **Chartwell**, 2 miles (3km) south of town, from 1924 until his death. The interior of the house is preserved as a museum, with many souvenirs of the great man's life, including some of his paintings.

*Follow the **A25** to Sevenoaks.*

Sevenoaks, Kent

4 The traditional seven fine oaks which gave the town its name were reduced to only one in the great storm of October 1987, but new trees have been planted. Sevenoaks is notable for **Knole Park**, which dates from 1456 and is the largest private house in England. Thomas Sackville, the 1st Earl of Dorset, was granted the house by Elizabeth I. Set in a wide-rolling deer park, it contains an important collection of 17th-century furniture, fine staircases and fireplaces, two state beds of James II and galleries hung with original tapestries. Beer has been brewed in the area for centuries, and you can sample one of the wines from an increasing number of local vineyards.

ⓘ Buckhurst Lane

FOR HISTORY BUFFS

The 'Heart of Kent' was formerly a vast forest, and the abundance of oak in medieval times gave rise to the characteristic timber-framed and half-timbered houses of the area. The houses often included a central hall and projecting upper storeys. Many fine examples survive, notably in Leicester Square, Penshurst and at Chiddingstone.

7 Forstal Farm will fascinate both children and adults alike. Situated on the A262, just ¼ mile (½km) off the A21 near Lamberhurst, this **Model Museum and Craft Village** is the result of 10 years' work by one man. There are model scenes which light up and can be brought to life at the touch of a button. Nursery scenes, Victorian London, World War II, science fiction and many other subjects are represented in a unique collection. In addition to the models there are shops and houses lining an old-fashioned village street. You can take a stroll round the nature trail or enjoy a home-made cake in the Oast Tea Rooms.

7 South of Goudhurst, is Bedgebury Pinetum, an attractive place to visit at any time of the year. It is set in a big park surrounding a Louis XIV-style mansion.

Rhododendrons and azaleas are specialities, but there are numerous varieties of fungi and, of course, the conifers. The mansion is now a girls' school, but most of the park is open and you can enjoy the freedom of wandering about or following the waymarked trail. The Pinetum contains a nationally important collection of pine trees – several of the plants came originally from Kew Gardens, but the Forestry Commission now manages these woodlands. Birdwatchers are lured to Bedgebury, especially during the winter months, by the possibility of finding interesting species such as hawfinch, crossbill and firecrest.

Churchill's country home until his death, Chartwell now houses a Churchill museum. Some of his paintings are on view, as is his studio and a wealth of Churchilliana

Leave Sevenoaks on the A225, and rejoin the A25 to Ightham.

Ightham, Kent

5 Visiting Ightham is like stepping back in time. **Ightham Mote** is an unspoilt, medieval, moated manor house surrounded by beautiful Wealden scenery. Undisturbed by time, the great hall, chapel and crypt have survived in fine condition. There are many fine old half-timbered medieval buildings in the village, including an **oast house** and the **Old Coaching Inn**. The **Church of St Peter** is mainly 14th- and 15th-century and contains some splendid stained glass and several brasses and sculptures.

Continue west on the A25, which joins and becomes the A20. Turn south on to the B2016 to the turning east for Mereworth.

Mereworth, Kent

6 This is the heart of the 'Garden of England'. The unusual **church** was rebuilt in 18th-century neo-Classical style, like nearby **Mereworth Castle**, and has a remarkable large steeple. The castle was built in the early 18th century as a copy of the Villa La Rotunda, near Vicenza in Italy. It has the appearance of an ancient temple, and contains some impressive ceiling paintings, as well as period furniture designed by William Kent. The present village was built by Lord Westmoreland, who destroyed the

original in order to use the site for the extravagant and exotic castle. On the road to Lamberhurst you will pass the **Whitbread Hop Farm** at Beltring, well worth a visit. The farm has the finest collection of Victorian oast houses in the world, now turned into craftsmen's workshops and a **hop museum**, recapturing the life of hop farmers in the past.

From Mereworth return to the B2016 via the A26. Continue south on the B2016, B2015, B2160 and A21 for 14 miles (23km) to Lamberhurst.

Lamberhurst, Kent

7 This village was the centre of the Wealden iron industry and at one time produced railings for St Paul's Cathedral in London. The **Owl House** is a small half-timbered, tile-hung house which was a noted haunt of wool smugglers. It stands in the middle of beautiful grounds and gardens of azaleas, roses and camellias. **Bayham Abbey**, 2 miles (3km) west of the village, is said to be the most impressive group of monastic remains in Kent, with church, monastery and a former gatehouse all well preserved. **Scotney Castle**, south of Lamberhurst, is a ruined 14th-century castle with a moat. It is set in fine gardens.

Continue southeast on the A21, taking the unclassified road on the left after 1½ miles (2km), through Kilndown to the A262 and Goudhurst. About 1½ miles (2km) after Goudhurst, turn right on to the B2085, then left to Cranbrook on meeting the A229.

Cranbrook, Kent

8 Cranbrook is a pleasant town with many 18th-century buildings. In the centre of town is **Union Mill**, the finest working smock windmill in England. Often called the 'Capital of the Weald', Cranbrook only has 6,000 inhabitants, and was built from the profits of the wool trade in the 15th century. The fine medieval **church**, 'the Cathedral of the Weald', has a porch built in 1291, and the local **museum** recaptures much of the history of the area. Three miles (5km) from the town is **Sissinghurst Castle**. The popular and colourful gardens were created in the 1930s by Vita Sackville-West and her husband, Sir Harold Nicolson. Derelict buildings and wild vegetation were transformed into this beautiful series of gardens with orchards, herbs and the famous 'white garden' where only white or grey flowers grow. Visitors can look at the quaint tower room where the authoress wrote her novels.

i Vestry Hall, Stone Street, Cranbrook

*Continue on the **A262**, then the **A28** for 9 miles (14km) to Tenterden.*

Tenterden, Kent

9 Described as the 'Jewel of the Weald', the centre of this Wealden market town is dominated by the marble tower of **St Mildred's Church**, which is chiefly built of the local sandstone. It is worth the climb up the tower because of the fine views across the Weald and, on a clear day, as far as France. The high street has shops and houses, many with original Georgian fronts. William Caxton, the father of English printing, is believed to have been born in Tenterden, and at the western edge of the town is the **William Caxton Inn**. Pub signs are often quite revealing about the past, and near the church is the **Woolpack Inn**, a reminder that much of the town's wealth came from sheep during the 15th and 16th centuries. Woollen cloth was traded overseas, using Smallhythe as a port. It is difficult to visualise this countryside location, now far removed from the sea, as a thriving port and shipbuilding centre. Dame Ellen Terry lived in **Smallhythe Place**, an early 16th-century timbered harbour master's house, from 1899 until she died in 1928, and the house is open to visitors during the summer months. **Spots Farm**, at Smallhythe, has 20 acres (8 hectares) of vineyards you can walk through, as well as an amazing herb garden containing over 500 varieties, possibly the largest collection in the UK; the aroma is overwhelming.

i Town Hall, High Street

*Follow the **A28** for 8 miles (13km) to Northiam.*

Northiam, East Sussex

10 The gnarled old oak tree on the village green achieved fame when Elizabeth I dined beneath it in 1573, while on her way to Rye. She is said to have taken her shoes off during the occasion and left them to the villagers when she continued her journey. **Great Dixter**, half-a-mile (1km) away, is a large 15th-century manor house with a half-timbered and plastered front. The house was enlarged and restored by Sir Edward Lutyens in 1910. Its gardens are specially noted for their clematis.

Return towards the main road, taking the narrow road, first on the right, and follow country lanes to Bodiam.

SPECIAL TO...

9 Tenterden is the main station for the **Kent and East Sussex Steam Railway**, and it handles thousands of passengers every year. A stretch of the line from Tenterden through the beautiful Rother Valley was reopened in 1974 by volunteer steam enthusiasts. An extension was opened to Northiam in 1990, making a total journey of 7 miles (11km), but the highlight for steam lovers will still be the thrill of the engine working hard to climb the steep hill into Tenterden.

Weather-boarded buildings are a distinctive feature of Tenterden

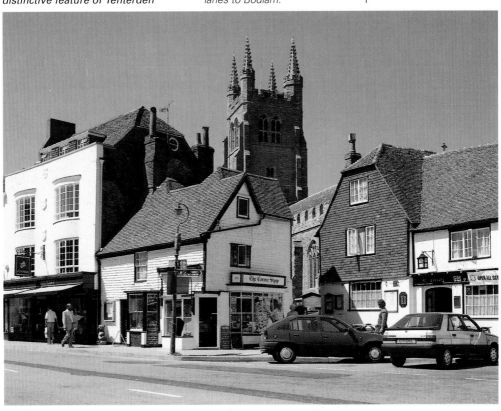

Even the moat could not protect Bodiam from Cromwell's army

Bodiam, East Sussex

11 Bodiam Castle, on the edge of the village, is a magnificent moated fortress, built in the 1380s to stop French raiders coming up the Rother Valley. The castle survived the French, who did not attack, but could not survive Cromwell's armies, who destroyed it. The outside walls are still intact, but it is now an empty shell. Life in a medieval castle is shown on a video, and there are 'Activity Days', when school children can dress up in medieval costumes for living history lessons. It was voted one of the top six castles for children in 1989, and in May it hosts a longbow competition. Five miles (8km) southwest of Bodiam is Robertsbridge. Its half-timbered and weather-boarded cottages, a feature of the area, line the High Street, and it is the home of Gray-Nicolls, makers of cricket bats since 1875. A mile (1.6km) east, a no-through road leads to the ruins of a Cistercian **abbey**, founded in 1176.

Follow the unclassified road past the station to Etchingham, then the A265 to Burwash.

Burwash, East Sussex

12 Burwash is an outstandingly attractive village of 16th- and 17th-century houses. Inside **St Bartholomew's Church** is a cast-iron grave slab which is thought to be the oldest in the country. **Bateman's**, half-a-mile (1km) away, was the home of Rudyard Kipling from 1902 until 1936, providing the inspiration for much of his work. His study has been kept as it was during his lifetime, and the enormous 10-foot (3m) long desk has a few untidy pieces left standing on it. Much of the neighbourhood is featured in his novel *Puck of Pook's Hill*. Upstream there is a **watermill** which has been restored to working order, and near by is the waterdriven turbine Kipling had installed in 1902 to provide his house with electricity.

Take the A265, turning right on to the A267 past Heathfield. Turn left on to unclassified roads shortly after Five Ashes and follow signs to Rotherfield.

Rotherfield, East Sussex

13 On the edge of the Ashdown Forest, Rotherfield sits in the heart of beautiful countryside. It is a delightful place to stop off and walk about. There is a fine **church** dedicated to St Denys, which contains 13th-century wall-paintings including Doom, and St Michael weighing souls, and in the east window is some splendid stained glass by Edward Burne-Jones and William Morris.

Return via unclassified roads to the A26. Turn right and return to Tunbridge Wells.

Royal Tunbridge Wells – Penshurst 7 (11)
Penshurst – Hever 6 (10)
Hever – Limpsfield 10 (16)
Limpsfield – Sevenoaks 9 (14)
Sevenoaks – Ightham 6 (10)
Ightham – Mereworth 6 (10)
Mereworth – Lamberhurst 14 (23)
Lamberhurst – Cranbrook 10 (16)
Cranbrook – Tenterden 11 (18)
Tenterden – Northiam 8 (13)
Northiam – Bodiam 5 (8)
Bodiam – Burwash 10 (16)
Burwash – Rotherfield 13 (21)
Rotherfield – Royal Tunbridge Wells 7 (11)

SCENIC ROUTES

Most of the tour is through striking scenery, but the roads leading into Mereworth, Lamberhurst, Scotney and Bodiam are particularly memorable. The combination of villages, old Wealden buildings, hills, valleys and woods create a picturesque landscape. Villages such as Ightham are very photogenic, as are the North Downs, which can be seen clearly from the **A25**.

Picturesque, timbered Chilham is in the heart of medieval Kent

ℹ 34 St Margaret's Street, Canterbury

Take the A28 for 4 miles (6km) to Chartham.

Chartham, Kent

1 The valley of the Great Stour, with gravel pits and small lakes, is noted for fishing and bird life, and Chartham is a well-known angling centre. **St Mary's Church** dates from the 13th century and has one of the oldest sets of bells in the country. **Chartham Hatch Craft Centre** is just down the road, set in delightful countryside. Further along is Chilham, where the village square is set at the gateway to **Chilham Castle**, built for Henry II in 1174. The castle is not open to the public, but you can visit the gardens. There are usually medieval jousting tournaments on Sundays and Bank Holidays. The **church** has a stone and flint tower, and the largely unspoilt houses around the square are of Tudor and Jacobean style.

From Chilham return to the A28, travel south for 2 miles (3km) then turn off on to unclassified roads to Wye.

Wye, Kent

2 This village, in its rural setting, is the location of the famous **Agriculture School of London University**, housed in a college first set up in the mid-15th century by John Kempe, a native of the town, who became Archbishop of Canterbury. The town also has a

FROM CATHEDRAL TO CLIFFS

Canterbury • Chartham • Wye • Ashford • Rye New Romney • Lympne • Folkestone • Hawkinge Dover • St Margaret's at Cliffe • Walmer • Sandwich Wingham • Canterbury

Cathedral and castles, steep cliffs and miles of flat marshes are part of this drive, which also takes in green countryside, old oast houses and thatched cottages, with a new view every few minutes. Quiet villages and noisy, bustling holiday resorts add further variety to the tour.

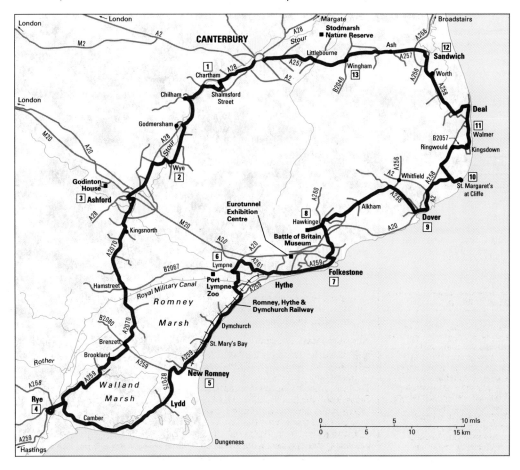

BACK TO NATURE

Stodmarsh National Nature Reserve lies a few miles to the east of Canterbury beside the course of the River Stour. Vast reedbeds and areas of open water attract huge numbers of wildfowl. Reed warblers, Cetti's warblers and bearded tits can be found in the winter, sometimes in the company of short-eared owls. On the coast, **Sandwich Bay** is a large area of sand dunes – much of which is covered by the famous golf course – and mudflats. The area boasts some excellent examples of dune flora.

FOR HISTORY BUFFS

5 There are as many as 74 Martello towers along the south coast, and a noted survivor is at Dymchurch, near New Romney. Martello towers were built to resist an invasion by Napoleon which never happened, but many were used to control smuggling, a common practice in the 19th century because of high import taxes. The Dymchurch tower has been fully restored and has one of the original 24-pounder guns on the roof.

FOR CHILDREN

7 The Rotunda Amusement Park in Folkestone is open seven days a week throughout summer and has added a few new attractions to its old established favourites. Ride on the southeast's only log flume or have a gentle round of crazy golf. There are indoor amusements for rainy days, and on Sundays there is a huge outdoor market full of bargains.

racecourse, a Georgian **mill house** and 18th-century **Olantigh**.

Return to the A28 for 5 miles (8km) to Ashford.

Ashford, Kent

3 This old market centre for Romney Marsh and the Weald of Kent is now a thriving shopping and touring centre. Medieval, Tudor and Georgian houses still survive and the 14th- and 15th-century **parish church** retains much of its old character. **Godington House**, northwest of town, was built in the 17th century. The rooms are full of Chippendale and Sheraton furniture, and there is fine topiary work in the 18th- and 19th-century garden.

ⓘ 18 The Churchyard

Follow the A2070, then the A259 across Romney Marsh for 20 miles (32km) to Rye.

Rye, East Sussex

4 Rye is one of the Cinque Ports, a group of maritime towns which were originally responsible for providing ships and men to guard against invasion. At one time Rye was almost encircled by the sea, but the harbour silted up in the 16th century and the water receded. In the winter, when mists roll in across the countryside, Romney Marsh can be sinister and mysterious – a fitting background to tales of the infamous parson and smuggler, Dr Syn. E F Benson, creator of the *Lucia* novels, was Mayor of Rye from 1934–37.

ⓘ The Heritage Centre, Strand Quay

Head back on the A259 to East Guldeford, then take an unclassified road through Camber to Lydd to join the B2075 to New Romney.

New Romney, Kent

5 Another ancient Cinque Port, now inland from the sea, New Romney

The Mermaid Inn in Rye first opened its doors to guests in 1420

was destroyed in 1287 by a violent storm which changed the course of the River Rother. The **Romney, Hythe and Dymchurch narrow gauge railway** opened in 1927, with locomotives and carriages which are one-third full size. Toys and models can be seen in the exhibition room at New Romney station.

ⓘ Light Railway Car Park, 2 Littlestone Road

Take the A259 again, then unclassified roads for 9 miles (14km) to Lympne, then via the B2067 to the A261 which leads eastwards to Hythe.

Lympne, Kent

6 The 11th-century **castle** at Lympne (pronounced *Lim*) stands on top of a cliff which was once a coastline. Views from here extend across the Channel to the French coast on a clear day. From the castle towers, the remains of a Roman fort can be seen.

Just outside town is **Port Lympne Zoo Park**, set in 300 acres (121 hectares) of gardens surrounding a mansion. East of Lympne is **Hythe**, another Cinque Port which is now a popular seaside resort and the terminus for the Romney, Hythe and Dymchurch Railway. The town has several historic buildings and summer boating along the old **Royal Military Canal**.

ⓘ Prospect Road Car Park, Hythe

Follow the A259 from Hythe to Folkestone.

Folkestone, Kent

7 The harbour of this resort handles cross-Channel ferries, and still has a fishing fleet and a fish market. A **Museum and Art Gallery** in Grace Hill has displays on the town's maritime history, and the **Eurotunnel Exhibition Centre** explains, with the use of videos, models and displays, this huge project which has been talked about for 200 years. **Spade House** was, the former home of the author H G Wells. The Leas, a wide grassy promenade along the cliff top, has fine views and provides an excellent walk through wooded slopes down to the beach.

ⓘ Harbour Street

Head inland along the A260 as far as Hawkinge.

Hawkinge, Kent

8 Set in the heart of the Downland west of Hawkinge is the **Kent Battle of Britain Museum**, which conjures up visions of World War II. It houses the largest collection of fragments of British and German aircraft involved in the fighting.

Take unclassified roads eastwards from Hawkinge, eventually running south on to the A256 for Dover.

Dover, Kent

9 Dover, famous for its White Cliffs, was the chief Cinque Port. It was known to the Romans as *Dubris*, and the **Painted House**, discovered in 1970, dates from about AD200. Among the paintings are several ref-

St Margaret's Bay is a popular start for cross-Channel swimmers!

erences to the theme of Bacchus, the god of wine. More recent is the **Old Town Gaol**, which has been restored to show the dismal conditions of Victorian prison life. On Snargate Street you can see the **Grand Shaft**, a 140-foot (43m) staircase cut into the white cliffs, built in Napoleonic times as a short cut to the town for troops stationed on the Western Heights. The views across to France can be best seen from **Dover Castle**, which overlooks the town. The **Pharos**, a Roman lighthouse, stands within its walls near the fine Saxon **Church of St Mary de Castro**.

☐ Townwall Street

Take the A258, then an unclassified road to St Margaret's at Cliffe.

St Margaret's at Cliffe, Kent

10 The flint-faced church in the upper part of this village is typical of chalkland buildings. Massive chalk cliffs dominate the scene, and sheltered beneath them is the **Pines Garden**, created in the 1970s with trees, shrubs, a lake and waterfall, and a statue of Sir Winston Churchill. Three miles (5km) further is Ringwould, where yet another fine **church** can be seen, with an attractive 17th-century tower. Several Bronze Age **barrows** can be seen at nearby Free Down, and at Kingsdown there is a lot of flint, both on the buildings and on the shore.

Rejoin the A258, then take the B2057 from Ringwould to Walmer.

Walmer, Kent

11 Henry VIII built the **castle** here, along with over 20 other forts to defend the coast of southeast England. This fine coastal fortress, shaped like a Tudor rose, has been transformed into an elegant stately home with beautiful gardens, and is the official residence of the Lord Warden of the Cinque Ports. Lord Wellington was Warden from 1829 to 1852, and his famous boots are on display. Further on, **Deal Castle**, also built by Henry VIII, is in the shape of a six-petalled flower, and tells the full story of the Tudor castles in the exhibition room. The **Timeball Tower**, which used to give time signals to shipping is a unique four-storey museum of time and maritime communication on the sea front. The **museum** in St George's Street has a collection of old photographs, model sailing ships and maps.

☐ Town Hall, High Street, Deal

Take the A258 to Sandwich.

Sandwich, Kent

12 The oldest of the medieval Cinque Ports, Sandwich is separated from the sea by 2 miles (3km) of sand dunes. Its **white windmill** is a smock mill dating from about 1760, which now houses a **folk museum** with domestic and farming exhibits.

Sandwich Golf Course, between the town and Sandwich Bay, is a world-class championship course.

☐ St Peter's Church, Market Street

Follow the A257 for 6 miles (10km) to Wingham.

Wingham, Kent

13 This picturesque village contains a magnificent **church** with a green spire, caused by oxidisation. The **Bird Park** has cockatoos, macaws, owls and waterfowl, all with plenty of flying space, as well as rare farm animals and pets. Valuable research work takes place here to help endangered species, and to overcome man's destruction of natural habitats. A little further out of town is the village of Littlebourne. Fruit and hops are grown around here, and there is an ancient **thatched barn** near the flint-faced **church**.

Continue along the A257 for the return to Canterbury.

Canterbury – Chartham 4 (6)
Chartham – Wye 8 (13)
Wye – Ashford 5 (8)
Ashford – Rye 20 (32)
Rye – New Romney 13 (21)
New Romney – Lympne 9 (14)
Lympne – Folkestone 8 (13)
Folkestone – Hawkinge 3 (5)
Hawkinge – Dover 9 (14)
Dover – St Margaret's at Cliffe 4 (6)
St Margaret's at Cliffe – Walmer 6 (10)
Walmer – Sandwich 6 (10)
Sandwich – Wingham 6 (10)
Wingham – Canterbury 6 (10)

1/2 days – 99 miles (158km)

THE DOWNS & VALLEYS OF HAMPSHIRE

Winchester • Stockbridge • Middle Wallop • Mottisfont Abbey
Romsey • Marwell Zoo • Bishop's Waltham • Portsdown Hill
Hambledon • Queen Elizabeth Country Park
New Alresford • Winchester

The Hampshire Downs provide a gentle interlude between the harsh sandy heaths nearer London and the valleys of the Southwest. From the ancient capital of Wessex this tour takes you from downlands through lush valleys to panoramic views of where battle fleets throughout history set sail.

The quintessence of Englishness: a garden of colour and abundance at Hillier Arboretum

i The Guildhall, The Broadway, Winchester

Leave Winchester on the A272 heading west for 9 miles (14km) to Stockbridge.

Stockbridge, Hampshire

1 A curious 'one-horse' town unique in Hampshire, Stockbridge has a straight main street backed by water-meadows. Before the railways, Welsh cattlemen stopped here with their herds on the way to the great fairs at Farnham and Maidstone. On the north side of High Street, beyond the distinctive porch of the **Grosvenor Hotel**, is a charming **Edwardian garage**, relic of the days of running boards and red flags. Outside the town, Stockbridge Down above your road of entry is home to many rare flowers and butterflies, and **Marsh Court**, on the back road to King's Somborne, was designed by Lutyens and is partly built of chalk blocks. Stockbridge has several good antique shops, and exceptional crafts and fishing shops.

Leave Stockbridge by the A30, then turn right signed Danebury Hillfort and in 2½ miles (4km) turn left on to the A343 for Middle Wallop.

Middle Wallop, Hampshire

2 The Wallops, Over, Middle and Nether, take their name from the brook which links these three pretty villages. Built as a wartime RAF base, where 'Cat's Eyes' Cunningham led his nightfighters into battle, the airfield is now the home of the Army Air Corps, and pilots train here in attack, reconnaissance and transport. Inside

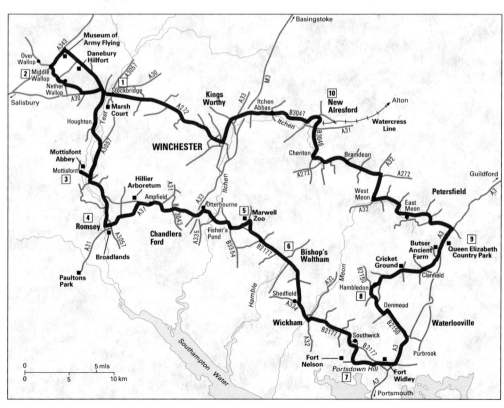

the modern **Museum of Army Flying** are many aircraft and ancient balloons, the world's first helicopter, a Tiger Moth and airworthy Sopwiths from World War I, as well as cockpits to clamber into, videos and displays.

From Middle Wallop take the road through Nether Wallop to join the A30 heading back towards Stockbridge. Just before Stockbridge turn right and follow the unclassified road through Houghton to Mottisfont.

Mottisfont Abbey, Hampshire

3 You will find no abbey here, but there is an elegant National Trust property in tree-lined grounds by the River Test; the original priory was converted after the Dissolution. Of special note is Rex Whistler's blue drawing room, with its visual tricks. Gardeners will appreciate the fine old roses here, and it is worth seeking out the 'font', a tamed spring of clear water. If this gives you a thirst, have lunch or tea at the village **post office**, where you can sit outside under the spreading walnut tree. This is the heartland of the trout-fishing for which the Test is world-famous, and the area is jealously guarded, with barbed-wire fences protecting anglers' huts and benches by private manicured paths.

Return to the A3057 and drive for 3 miles (5km) to Romsey.

Romsey, Hampshire

4 A few years ago, travellers here were greeted at every turn by notices reading 'You're in the Strong Country'. Strong's brewery is no more: the waft of hops last drifted here in 1981, and the **malthouse** you

Alfred's capital and a seat of learning since ancient times, Winchester boasts one of Europe's loveliest cathedrals

see ahead awaits other uses, but lots of good things survive in this lively little place. Its greatest treasure is the 12th-century **abbey**, a fine unspoiled Norman church, which only escaped the ravages of the Dissolution when the townspeople bought it for £100. Buried within is Earl Mountbatten of Burma, who lived at **Broadlands**. This imposing 18th-century mansion gives on to Capability Brown lawns sweeping down to the Test. Another former owner, Lord Palmerston, still keeps an eye on Romsey from his perch in Market Square. Traffic is poorly managed here, so it is worth parking at Broadlands and walking into town. Children should enjoy the **Rapids leisure pool**, with its giant flume and swirling water; and if you visit in November, go to **Saddler's Mill**, where Test Valley salmon perform gymnastic feats to reach their spawning grounds upstream.

[i] Bus Station Car Park, Broadwater Road

Leave Romsey on the A31 heading east. Shortly after Ampfield, turn right at the Potters Heron signed Chandlers Ford. Cross the B3043 and drive along Hocombe Road. At a T-junction turn left over the flyover towards Otterbourne. On entering the village turn right on to an unclassified road, cross the River Itchen and the A335 (dogleg right and left) and proceed along Church Lane, turning at its end on to the B3354. Turn right on to the B2177, then left for Marwell.

BACK TO NATURE

4 The **Hillier Gardens and Arboretum** is a unique array of hardy plants, trees and shrubs from all over the world, situated just off the **A31** between Ampfield and Braishfield near Romsey. The famous nursery firm founded by Sir Harold Hillier is based at **Ampfield House** near by, and for a small charge members of the public can enjoy a quiet and gentle stroll in beautiful surroundings. The rhododendrons and azaleas are particularly spectacular in season.

FOR CHILDREN

4 **Paultons Park**, off the **A31** at Ower near Romsey, is a family leisure park offering a wealth of entertainment and activity for children. Opened just a few years ago and set in 140 acres (56 hectares) of beautiful parkland, Paultons grows every year as features are added; it is now the second-largest attraction in the South. A giant adventure playground, an astra glide, bumper boats, train rides and a pets' corner are just a few of the experiences to be had, along with a trip to Captain Blood's cavern.

Marwell Zoo, Hampshire

5 Set in the 100-acre (40-hectare) park of a Tudor hall, this is one of the biggest zoos in Britain. The approach here is modern, and the animals enjoy considerable freedom. Marwell's biggest claim to fame is the work done here for animal conservation – rescuing threatened species, breeding from them and returning them to the wild. You might bump into a scimitar-horned oryx or perhaps a Przewalski's horse, both snatched from imminent extinction. Children will particularly enjoy patting pot-bellied pigs in their own farmyard! Also recommended are Marwell's Wonderful Railway and the licensed Treetops restaurant.

[i] Marwell Zoo Park, Colden Common

Return to the B2177 and continue to Bishop's Waltham.

Bishop's Waltham, Hampshire

6 As you approach, tall flint ruins on the right give a clue as to how the town got its name. For 400 years, Bishops of Winchester lived here in a splendid palace, built in 1135, and all but destroyed by Cromwell's troops. Little remains but the walls of the great hall, but the site is open to the public. In the town centre, shops and houses span eight centuries of architecture, many hiding salvaged palace beams. Look out for the Bishop's Mitre in the Square, last remnant of the Market Hall. The town's history is charted in the small **museum** in Brook Street. Four miles (6km) to the south, on the **A334**, is the elegant Georgian town of Wickham, birthplace of William of Wykeham, founder of Winchester College. As you leave on Bridge Street, watch for the **Chesapeake Mill**, built in 1820 from a captured American Man o' War. Peaceful Southwick, further on, is where Eisenhower made his 1944 headquarters at **Southwick House**. In the village he and Montgomery met world leaders and planned the world's greatest seaborne invasion.

From Southwick take the Porchester road to Portsdown Hill.

Portsdown Hill, Hampshire

7 The view from Portsdown's chalk heights is one of the finest in Britain. Ahead is Portsmouth and its spreading harbour, home of the Royal Navy, and beyond is the Isle of Wight. In between lies Spithead, where naval fleet reviews take place and, further west, the Solent, now a yachtsman's paradise. Portchester's Roman castle, Nelson's flagship, Victoria's beloved Osborne House and the homes of Dickens and Tennyson are all within sight of Portsdown. For a fascinating look at history, trek down the tunnels in one of **'Palmerston's follies'**. These were giant forts built by the Prime Minister in the 1850s to guard the Solent against the French. **Fort Nelson** is open to the public.

From Portsdown Hill take the A3 heading northwards, and at Waterlooville turn on to the B2150 through Denmead to Hambledon.

Hambledon, Hampshire

8 The cause of Hambledon's world-wide fame lies 2 miles (3km) from its pretty Georgian centre on the Clanfield road. In front of the **Bat and Ball** pub, a granite monument stands near a thatched hut and beautifully mown sward of grass. For sporting people the world over, this is a shrine, for it was here on Broadhalfpenny Down that Hambledon got its title 'the cradle of cricket'. It was in Sussex that shepherds first played the game, but here rules were established and skills honed. Nyren, landlord of the Bat and Ball in 1760, was the manager of the village team which, in its day, beat All England – and his victuals were equally good. Players, we are told, 'struck dismay into a round of beef' and his punch was 'such that would have made a cat speak'!

Leave Hambledon on an unclassified road, passing through Clanfield, then follow Petersfield signs to join the A3. In a mile (1.5km) turn off for Queen Elizabeth Country Park.

The River Test – peerless angler's river – near Romsey

Queen Elizabeth Country Park, Hampshire

9 Set in a deep valley, with steep downland on either side, this is the ideal place to leave the car and stretch your legs. On one side, dense woodland stretches upward; on the other, smooth grassland, speckled with sheep, climbs impressively to the viewpoint on **Butser Hill**. **Butser Ancient Farm** is a reconstruction of real Iron Age farm remains. Here, visitors can walk freely round the huts and pens, finding out for themselves in a unique and graphic way what life was like in the prehistoric age. The **Park Centre**, with café and shop, organises a host of activities – pony trekking, grass skiing and guided walks are daily occurrences, and there are annual 'specials', among them sheep events and in July, the Hampshire Country Fair.

ⓘ Queen Elizabeth Country Park, Gravel Hill, Horndean

*Rejoin the **A3** towards Petersfield, shortly turning left via unclassified roads to East Meon and West Meon. Turn right on to the **A32**, then left at traffic lights on to the **A272** signposted Bramdean. In 4 miles (6km) go right (**B3046**) through Cheriton to New Alresford.*

New Alresford, Hampshire

10 Alresford (pronounced Orlsford) is a town rich in history. Built in the 13th century by the Bishops of Winchester as a wool centre,

The Iron Age reconstructed in the Queen Elizabeth Country Park

Alresford annually played host to 200,000 sheep, from medieval times to as recently as 1972. The best way to sample its charm is to descend picturesque Broad Street, turning left into Ladywell Lane to the ancient **mill** on the River Alre, where woollen cloth was fulled – that is, cleaned and thickened – returning to the town centre via **The Dean**. Alresford's main attraction is its elegance, and everywhere there are small clues to the town's chequered history. For instance, the steep pitch of the tiled roofs hint at previous thatching. The town was ravaged six times by fire, which spread quickly along the thatch, but the practice continued despite an edict from Winchester banning it.

*Leave Alresford on the **B3046** then turn left on to the **B3047**. In 6 miles (10km) cross the **A33** at Kings Worthy and return to Winchester.*

Winchester – Stockbridge 9 (14)
Stockbridge – Middle Wallop 6 (10)
Middle Wallop – Mottisfont 12 (19)
Mottisfont – Romsey 4 (6)
Romsey – Marwell 11 (18)
Marwell – Bishop's Waltham 4 (6)
Bishop's Waltham – Portsdown Hill 10 (16)
Portsdown Hill – Hambledon 10 (16)
Hambledon – Queen Elizabeth Country Park 7 (11)
Queen Elizabeth Country Park – New Alresford 18 (29)
New Alresford – Winchester 8 (13)

SPECIAL TO...

10 Starting from Alresford and running 10 miles (16km) to Alton through peaceful agricultural scenery, the **Watercress Line** is a golden chance to enjoy steam-train travel. Volunteers do most of the restoration work, and West Country Pacific carries out most of the mechanical work on this line. If you want to see how abandoned hulks from Welsh scrapyards are transformed into gleaming and steaming leviathans, stop off at **Ropley**, where the main restoration work is carried out.

SCENIC ROUTES

Two stretches on the route epitomise the English village scene at its best. The Wallop brook idles past the thatched cottages of Middle and Nether Wallop between the **A343** and the **A30**. Cheriton, on the **B3046** south of Alresford, is similarly lovely. Look out as you leave it for some really unusual cottages. Hampshire's gentle valley scenery can be seen to advantage south of Stockbridge. After threading your way from Houghton across the Test's many rippling carrier streams, there are delightful views from the **A3057** across lush water meadows with cornfields and wooded ridges beyond.

1/2 days – 105 miles (168km)

ANCIENT HUNTING GROUND OF KINGS

**Bournemouth • Christchurch • Ringwood
Bolderwood • Rhinefield • Lymington • Bucklers Hard
Exbury Beaulieu • Lyndhurst • Fordingbridge
Wimborne Minster • Bournemouth**

A combination of seashore, downland and forest should satisfy the appetite of those who like their terrain varied but not too rugged. On the way are picturesque towns and villages reflecting 1,500 years of history, peaceful trout streams flowing south to the sea and, at the heart of the tour, the New Forest, an ancient hunting ground of kings now preserved for the people. Within its 100 square miles (259sq km) are walks enough for a lifetime – over open, gorse-covered heath; across sandy ridges; or through dappled, sunlit woods.

The New Forest can be enjoyed at every season of the year

ⓘ Westover Road, Bournemouth

Leave Bournemouth on the A35 and head east for 5 miles (8km) to Christchurch.

Christchurch, Dorset

1 Formerly Twineham, this town was one of Alfred the Great's walled strongholds against the Danes, between the Rivers Avon and Stour. The walls have long gone, and dominating the busy centre now is the fine 12th-century **priory church**, the reason for the town's change of name. Legend has it that a beam, cut too short, was lengthened and positioned overnight by a mystery workman, thought to have been Christ. Within easy reach are the **museum**, **art gallery** and ancient **Place Mill** on the Quay.

ⓘ 23 High Street

Take the B3347 to Ringwood.

Ringwood, Hampshire

2 Upstream on the Avon lies this unassuming bustling market town. The trout fishing is good here, and the town has many attractive Georgian and Queen Anne houses, with a splendid Early English **parish church** near the bypass. Near by, on the A31, is the **Avon Forest Park**, with many acres of contrasting meadow, heath and moorland. From Ringwood you can take in the **New Forest**, which spreads east and north. A narrow road between old gravel pits, converted into reservoirs, brings your first taste of the Forest at **Moyles Court**. The manor house, now a school, was the home of Alice Lisle, who sheltered the rebellious Duke of Monmouth's men, and was sentenced to death by Judge Jeffreys. The route winds through open heaths and lovely woods to high parts of the Forest, past the spot where naturalist Eric Ashby makes his fascinating

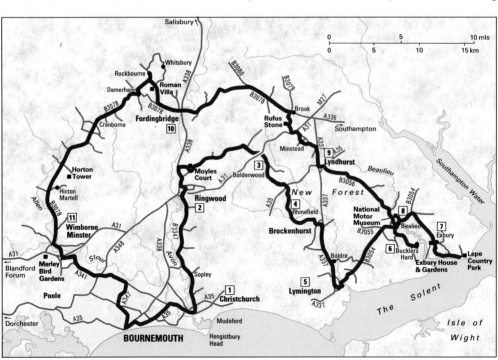

films of the badgers, foxes and other creatures that thrive here. If you want to walk you are spoiled for choice: forest tracks with shafting sunlight to your right, high sandy ridges with panoramic views and open heathland to your left.

ⓘ The Furlong

Leave Ringwood by the A338 signed Salisbury, then turn right in 2 miles (3km) on to an unclassified road and continue east for about 5 miles (8km) before going under the A31 for Bolderwood.

Bolderwood, Hampshire

3 Here, in the heart of the New Forest, the Forestry Commission has created three waymarked walks of different lengths among the trees, which range from native oak and beech to foreign wellingtonia. A leaflet helps you identify them as you walk. There are many deer in the New Forest, but normally only the silent, the patient or the fortunate see them – except at the **Bolderwood Deer Sanctuary**, where a sighting is guaranteed; bring your binoculars. Near by is a memorial among the pines dedicated to Canadian fliers serving at Stony Cross who were killed in the war. The famous ponies which wander in parts of the Forest are not wild, but belong to Commoners, people living in the Forest with rights to graze animals (and to an annual ration of free cordwood for

Boats peacably at anchor at Christchurch, once walled against Danish invaders

their fires). Look out for the brand mark of the owner; every autumn the ponies are rounded up and rebranded, and surplus ponies are sold at the Beaulieu Road sales. Feeding the ponies is illegal.

You might like to stop at the **Knightswood Oak**, reputedly the oldest in the Forest (600 years old) and 21 feet (7m) round. In the snake pit at Holidays Hill (on the **A35**, just east of your crossing point), the less squeamish can get a close-up look at the native vipers and adders.

From Bolderwood follow an unclassified road southeast across the A35 to Rhinefield.

Rhinefield, Hampshire

4 Towering above you are some of the tallest conifers in Britain – Douglas firs, redwoods and spruces – planted in 1859 as an approach to Rhinefield hunting lodge, now demolished. Behind the drive, on either side, are attractive mixed woodlands of oaks, beeches and pines, through which runs the 1½-mile (2km) **Tall Trees nature trail**. **Rhinefield House**, near by, is a hotel housed in a mad Victorian creation that is half-castle, half-house. You can have a meal or afternoon tea here. Brockenhurst is a lively and prosperous village, popular as a centre for New Forest camping and touring. Within the shadow of the Norman/Early English **church** lie the bones of Brusher Mills, New Forest character and killer of snakes.

From Brockenhurst turn right on to the A337 for Lymington.

FOR CHILDREN

1 Try a spot of crab fishing at Mudeford, near Christchurch. You will need some simple equipment – a line or string – and a hook is optional: you can tie the bait on instead. The shops on the quayside should have all the necessities. Station yourself by the rails near the shops and have a go.

RECOMMENDED WALKS

1 One different option from the many forest walks on the tour is to sample the seaside breezes at Mudeford. Take the little ferry across the mouth of the harbour, and walk along the beach to Hengistbury, which rises steadily to over 120 feet (36m) – a gentle round trip of 2 to 3 miles (3 to 5km) with fine views.

BACK TO NATURE

5 Pennington and Keyhaven Marshes are reached by walking along the sea wall from the car park at Keyhaven, a few miles south-west of Lymington. There are good views across the salt-marsh at low tide and over the pools and marshes inland from the wall. Waders and wildfowl are abundant during the winter and, in summer, several species of terns as well as black-headed gulls grace the area.

FOR HISTORY BUFFS

King William II (Rufus or red-haired), son of the Conqueror, was a nasty piece of work – cynical and greedy – and fully deserved the fate which met him while out hunting in the New Forest in August 1100. An arrow, supposedly fired by a companion, missed the stag and mortally wounded William. But questions remain. Was it an accident? Was it Sir Walter Tirel who fired the arrow, and then fled to France? Or was it the mysterious Purkes, who took the body to Winchester? You can visit the site of the king's death, marked by the **Rufus Stone**, (now encased in metal) in a glade just off the **A31** near Minstead.

Lymington, Hampshire

5 Signs of Lymington's early prosperity as a salt town, spa and seaport can still be seen in the charming houses which line the quay and the wide High Street climbing the hill. The town enjoys a different sort of maritime wealth these days: it has become a popular yachting centre. The Isle of Wight car ferry snakes down the Lymington River through serried masts of luxury yachts. Two buildings of particular note here are **Pressgang Cottage**, by the quay; and Georgian **St Thomas's Church** at the top of High street, unusual for its cupola.

ⓘ St Thomas Street Car Park

Leave Lymington by the B3054 signed Beaulieu and in 6 miles (10km), just before Beaulieu, turn right for Bucklers Hard.

Bucklers Hard, Hampshire

6 When you leave your car on the edge of Bucklers Hard, prepare to step back in time. Little has changed here since 1800, when this was one of Britain's shipbuilding centres. Three of the ships which fought under Nelson at Trafalgar were built here. Twin rows of shipbuilders' cottages, carefully preserved, slope down to the water, where the slipways were. Some are open for the public to view, and a **Maritime Museum** tells the story of this unique place.

From Bucklers Hard turn right for Exbury.

Exbury, Hampshire

7 The name of de Rothschild is synonymous with wealth, and at **Exbury House**, home of the banking family, no expense was spared to create the magnificent 200-acre (81-hectare) woodland garden, which is open to the public. Crowning glories here are the displays of rhododen-drons and azaleas, best seen in late spring. Beside the waters of the Solent, **Lepe Country Park** offers a chance to picnic or walk the shore, with lovely views across to the Isle of Wight. To the east is the Spithead shore near Portsmouth; ahead, Cowes and Osborne, Queen Victoria's final home; and to the west, Yarmouth, Hurst Castle and the open sea. Half a mile (1km) of crumbling concrete marks the point where D-Day's Mulberry Harbour was made. Evenings can be particularly lovely here, and big ships describe wide arcs as they follow the deep water out to sea.

Return to Beaulieu.

Beaulieu, Hampshire

8 Charming Beaulieu, with its pond and river, is the setting for a world-famous museum. The **National Motor Museum** stands in the grounds of 13th-century **Beaulieu Abbey**, home of the Montagus, which retains much beauty despite the destruction wrought after the Dissolution. A monorail winds through the 3rd Baron Montagu's modern showcase for over 250 vintage cars and motorcycles. The collection includes record breakers *Bluebird* and *Thrust 2*, and there are many other attractions in the grounds.

ⓘ John Montagu Building

Take the B3056 for 7 miles (11km) to Lyndhurst.

Lyndhurst, Hampshire

9 Open roads through rolling gorse heathlands bring you to the 'capital' of the New Forest, a busy tourist town in the summer. Alice Hargreaves (née Liddell), the original Alice of Lewis

The bridge over the Avon at Fordingbridge, in Hampshire

Carroll's *Alice in Wonderland*, is buried in Lyndhurst churchyard. At **Queen's House** the Verderers, guardians since Norman times of Commoners' rights, hold their bi-monthly ancient court on Mondays. They employ agisters to patrol the forest daily, often on horseback, to supervise and control animals grazing on the 90,000 acres (36,423 hectares). Forest ponies have their tails cut specially to indicate their own agister. The **New Forest Museum** offers an insight into the fascinating history and traditions of the popular area.

Wimborne Minster, Dorset

11 On the way to Wimborne Minster, you pass through the charming village of **Rockbourne**, with its pretty Tudor and Georgian cottages by a stream. To the south of the village is the excavated site of a **Roman villa**, open to the public. Wimborne Minster itself, though medieval in its street pattern, is no sorry relic of a bygone age. This busy town on the River Stour has a **Town Trail** which

The uniquely patterned façade of historic Wimborne Minster

SCENIC ROUTES

Between Moyles Court and Bolderwood there is a chance to sample the New Forest's dual personality – dense woodland and treeless valleys and ridges. The B3078, between Brook and Fordingbridge, also offers lovely open vistas. For an equally impressive seascape, take the Inchmery road from Exbury to Lepe, which will take you to within a stone's throw of the Solent's edge.

[i] New Forest Museum and Visitor Centre

Leave Lyndhurst on the A337 signposted Cadnam. In 2 miles (3km) turn left through Minstead, then left, immediately left and immediately right to cross the A31 to Brook (1½ miles, 2km), then keep left on the B3078 for Fordingbridge (8 miles, 13km).

Fordingbridge, Hampshire

10 Fordingbridge had a quiet time in the '70s and '80s, but is now coming to life again, with new shops opening and industries arriving. Stand on the **old bridge** and look for trout or pike. On this spot, during the time of William the Conqueror, a guard was posted to arrest New Forest deer poachers on their only escape route to the west. The fine medieval **parish church** stands on the Alderholt road.

Take the B3078 signed Damerham and follow unclassified roads through Rockbourne, rejoining the B3078 to Cranborne, and on to Wimborne Minster.

will help you explore its rich heritage of fine medieval and Georgian buildings – details obtainable from the Information Bureau. Central to it all is the Minster, of Saxon origin and curiously chequered in grey and brown stone. After all the history, you might want to browse through the hundreds of stalls at Wimborne's huge weekend market, or visit the **model town** on King Street.

[i] 29 High Street

Leave by the B3078 crossing the A31 and immediately bear left via Canford Magna to join the A341 and the A347 to Bournemouth.

Bournemouth – Christchurch	5 (8)
Christchurch – Ringwood	10 (16)
Ringwood – Bolderwood	10 (16)
Bolderwood – Rhinefield	4 (6)
Rhinefield – Lymington	8 (13)
Lymington – Bucklers Hard	8 (13)
Bucklers Hard – Exbury	6 (10)
Exbury – Beaulieu	4 (6)
Beaulieu – Lyndhurst	7 (11)
Lyndhurst – Fordingbridge	14 (23)
Fordingbridge – Wimborne Minster	20 (32)
Wimborne Minster – Bournemouth	9 (14)

SPECIAL TO...

11 Every generation seems to have its favourite racehorse – Golden Miller, Arkle, Red Rum, to name a few. The horse that captured the public's interest in the late '80s and early '90s was the grey, Desert Orchid, a truly great steeplechaser and star of many meetings – particularly Cheltenham. 'Desi' was trained at Whitsbury near Rockbourne. A short loop to your tour starting opposite the Rockbourne Roman Villa will take you through the downland where Desert Orchid trains and past the immaculately kept stables of his trainer.

WALES &
THE MARCHES

Wales is a small country of great beauty. Few parts of the world can contain as much varied scenery in such a restricted area. North Wales has the nation's highest peaks, in the Snowdon area, but there are dramatic mountain ranges in central and southern Wales, too. The Brecon Beacons, which are a dividing line between the south and the rural midlands, form one of the Welsh National Parks, the others being Snowdonia and the old county of Pembrokeshire. Here, in the narrow strip of land around the coastline, is the Pembroke Coastal National Park, which winds its way round inlets and coves, cliffs and beaches, and is marked by a long distance footpath. Even in the industrial parts of Wales, especially in the south where the coal valleys are world famous, there is fine hill scenery just a few miles from the old mining towns. The hills contribute to a wet climate, but the frequent rains create a lush green landscape, with rivers, foaming waterfalls and an abundance of lakes, some of which are man-made sources of water for thirsty towns, as well as being scenic attractions or centres for water sports.

Wales is also a land of railways and castles. There are a few main line railways along the north and south coasts and a scenic cross-country route to Aberystwyth, but there are several small, privately or voluntarily operated lines, such as at Ffestiniog, Bala or Llanberis.

Wales has a long history of rebellion and conflict, and centuries of struggle against English rule have left a legacy of imposing fortresses. Caernarfon is probably the outstanding example, built to mark Edward I's conquest of the north. Penrhyn, near Bangor, is really a stately home, providing an ornate illustration of the wealth generated by the North Wales slate industries – for a few, at least. Medieval castles dotted along the borders recall this area's turbulent past, notably Chepstow, Monmouth, White, Chirk and Rhuddlan.

The Welsh coastline has several popular resorts with sandy beaches, but for quieter attractions venture inland, where the wild landscape is sparsely populated. If you stop for a picnic in one of the more isolated parts you may find that the noise of the wind and of the sheep is the greatest disturbance to your tranquillity. Wales is a walkers' paradise, and wherever you are you will find walks of all distances to suit all tastes. You should leave the car whenever possible, to enable you to appreciate the landscape to the full.

Chepstow
This is a border town which has grown up at a crossing point of the River Wye and is now located conveniently close to the M4. There was an Iron Age as well as a Roman settlement near here, but the town was really created by the Normans. They began to build the castle in 1067, and it still dominates the town from its site over the River Wye. The museum opposite the castle describes the history of the town throughout the ages, and St Mary's parish church is worth a visit.

Tenby
Described as 'the Jewel in the Crown of the Welsh Riviera', Tenby's narrow streets and tiny shops are huddled within medieval town walls. This is one of Britain's finest historic towns, containing over 300 buildings of special architectural or historic interest. The picturesque harbour has long been a hub of activity, and there are regular sailings to Caldy Island. Fine sandy beaches and excellent walking provide an abundance of holiday entertainment for young and old.

Aberystwyth

The largest town and principal shopping centre of mid Wales is set in the middle of the glorious Cardigan Bay. The ruined castle, built by Edward I, overlooks the small harbour in the Rheidol Estuary, and on a hill above the town is the modern campus of the University College of Wales, which includes the National Library of Wales, housing early Welsh manuscripts. The narrow gauge Vale of Rheidol Railway line runs to the deep gorge of Devil's Bridge, and at the northern end of the beach and promenade the longest electric cliff railway in Britain climbs to the top of Constitution Hill.

Barmouth

Situated where the mountains meet the sea, this is one of the most picturesque resorts on Cardigan Bay. It has a fine golden beach and a small harbour busy with pleasure craft and fishing boats. Visit the Royal National Life-boat Institution Museum and two other buildings which recreate the history of this area: Tŷ Gwyn, the old lock-up for drunken seamen, and Tŷ Gwyn y

Above: Autumn colours in the Elan Valley, Wales's drowned valley. Right: Pen-y-Fan, Brecon, encircled by green hills

Bermo, a restored 15th-century building. After exploring the town you could take a walk alongside the estuary to take in the lovely coastal scenery all around.

Bangor

This ancient town, surrounded by water and high mountains in an area of great natural beauty, is a long-established religious centre: the present cathedral was built on the site of a monastery founded in AD525 – earlier than the cathedral in Canterbury. The northern college of the University of Wales is based here, on a high ridge overlooking the city. Bangor sits on the Menai Strait, and you can see the island of Anglesey from its restored pier, or cross the Strait on Telford's Menai Bridge or the later Britannia Bridge. The Museum of Welsh Antiquities traces life in Wales from prehistoric times; and on the outskirts of town is the magnificent Penrhyn Castle.

2/3 days – 172 miles (277km)

CASTLES ON THE WELSH MARCHES

Chepstow • Monmouth • Symonds Yat
Goodrich • Ross-on-Wye • Skenfrith • Grosmont
Hay-on-Wye • Bronllys • Brecon • Pontsticill
Talybont-on-Usk • Crickhowell • Abergavenny
Raglan • Usk • Caerleon • Penhow • Chepstow

This route passes through the Wye and Usk Valleys. The castles built along the Welsh borders are testaments to a turbulent age, when this was an area of constant fighting between the Normans and the Welsh.

The first of the great Norman castles in Wales was built here at Chepstow, circa 1070

i The Castle Car Park, Chepstow

Drive north for 16 miles (26km) on the A466 to Monmouth.

Monmouth, Gwent

1 Monmouth was an old Roman settlement, but its main growth came after 1066, and in 1673 the 1st Duke of Beaufort built **Great Castle House** on the site of the old Norman castle. Near Agincourt Square, dominated by the 18th-century **Shire Hall**, is a statue of C S Rolls, of Rolls Royce fame, whose family lived near here. East of town is **Kymin Hill**, where the **Naval Temple** commemorates British admirals. The walk up to it from town follows the line of **Offa's Dyke Long Distance Footpath**.

i Shire Hall

Take the A4136, then turn left on to the B4228 about 2 miles (3km) past Staunton. Bear left on to the B4332 after a further ½ mile (1km) to Symonds Yat.

Symonds Yat, Hereford and Worcester

2 The scenery of the Wye Valley is among the finest in Britain and Symonds Yat is a particularly impressive beauty spot, above the deep gorge. The river flows for 4 miles (6km) in a large meander before returning to within 400 yards (365m) of the same point. An **AA viewpoint** on the summit at 473 feet (144m) affords magnificent views.

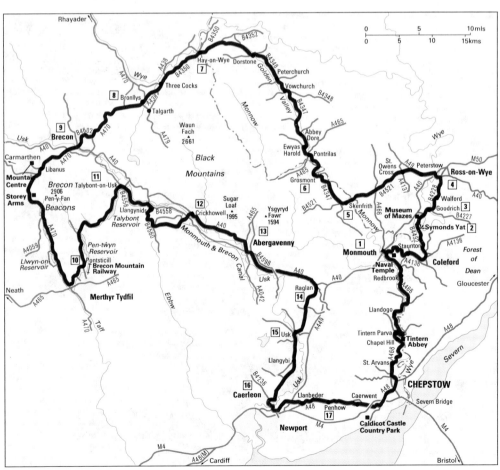

Continue north via an unclassified road, turning right on to the B4227 to Goodrich.

Goodrich, Hereford and Worcester

3 Imposing **Goodrich Castle** is a red sandstone ruin which Cromwell lost to the Royalists during the Civil War, but then battered with a mortar which fired 200lb (90kg) shots. This dramatically situated castle had a moat which was excavated from solid rock, and you can still look down the 168-foot (51km) well in the courtyard.

Cross the River Wye and take the B4228 on to Ross-on-Wye.

Ross-on-Wye, Hereford and Worcester

4 The splendid 208-foot (63m) spire of **St Mary's Church** rises high above the roofs of this attractive town. Interesting old streets spread out from the market place, with its 17th-century red sandstone **Market Hall**. Notable features include several ancient alms houses and 16th-century **Wilton Bridge**.

i 20 Broad Street

Leave on the A49, then the B4521 Abergavenny road to Skenfrith.

Skenfrith, Gwent

5 Skenfrith Castle was built as one of a group of three castles, along with Grosmont and White, to guard the Marches against Welsh uprisings. Its remains include a central keep enclosed by a four-sided curtain wall and a moat. A small stone village clusters round the castle, with a quaint little 13th-century **church** and a **mill** with a working water wheel.

Continue along the B4521 for a short distance then turn north on to the B4347 to Grosmont.

Grosmont, Gwent

6 Set on a hillside by the River Monnow, Grosmont is the site of another Norman fortress, taken and re-taken several times during the Welsh uprisings of the 13th to 15th centuries. The **castle ruins** can be reached by footpath from the town. Grosmont's 13th-century **parish church** is noted for its huge but crude effigy of an armoured knight.

At Abbey Dore, further along the road, the abbey remains include a vast, atmospheric church, tucked away in the Golden Valley.

Follow the B4347, then the B4348 through the Golden Valley and on to Hay-on-Wye.

Hay-on-Wye, Powys

7 Hay stands high above the southern bank of the River Wye. Folk hero Owain Glyndwr destroyed its **castle** during the 15th century, but the keep, parts of the walls and a gateway remain. The town's cinema has become the biggest **second-hand book shop** in the world; in fact the whole town seems to be taken up with second-hand books.

i The Car Park

Head southwest for 8 miles (13km) along the B4350 and A438 to Bronllys.

Bronllys, Powys

8 From Bronllys there are clear views of the **Brecon Beacons** ahead and the **Black Mountains**, which dominate the scenery to the left. The 12th-century church, now rebuilt, has a very odd detached tower, and a stone-built **Malt House** is still in excellent condition and contains its original equipment. **Bronllys Castle** is half a mile (1km) along the **A479**.

From Bronllys take the A438, the A470 and the B4602 to Brecon

Brecon, Powys

9 Brecon is a pure delight, encircled by hills at the meeting point of the Rivers Usk and Honddu. The cathedral, originally the church of a Benedictine priory, dates mainly from the 13th and 14th centuries, and **Brecon Castle** is now in the grounds of the Castle Hotel. The County Hall houses the **Brecknock Museum**, with its wealth of local history, and the **South Wales Borderers Army Museum** has relics ranging from the Zulu War in 1879 to World War II and later. East of town is the terminus of the **Monmouth and Brecon Canal**, and to the south is the **Brecon Beacons National Park**. The **Mountain Centre**, off the A470, west of the little village of Libanus, is an ideal starting point for exploring the Park.

i Cattle Market Car Park; The Mountain Centre, Libanus

Continue southwards along the A470 then take unclassified roads northwards to Pontsticill.

Pontsticill, Mid Glamorgan

10 Walking and boating are major attractions in this area; or you could have a journey on the steam train of the **Brecon Mountain Railway**,

---

Working a lock on the Brecon and Monmouth Canal

FOR HISTORY BUFFS

1 Tintern Abbey, just off the road to Monmouth in the Wye Valley, was a Cistercian foundation in 1131 which survived until the Dissolution of the Monasteries under Henry VIII. The abbey church has survived almost intact, and the ruins of many monastic buildings can still be seen.

FOR CHILDREN

2 As you enter the **Jubilee Maze** at the **Museum of Mazes** in Symonds Yat, you will be met by a maze man, wearing Victorian boating costume. There are 12 routes to the centre, where the Temple of Diana awaits you. Evening illuminations create a labyrinth of eerie shadows. The museum tells the history of mazes, and of magic spells and witchcraft.

RECOMMENDED WALKS

9 A good starting point for walking on the **Brecon Beacons** is at Storey Arms on the A470, which is at 1,425 feet (427m) above sea level and gives the shortest route to **Pen y Fan**, the highest point in the Beacons. Be sure to take an OS map, food supplies and weatherproof clothes, even in fine weather.

SPECIAL TO...

9 Brecon's **Brecknock Museum** has a superb display of Welsh lovespoons, traditional gifts of betrothal which were carved out of single pieces of wood. From the 17th to the 19th centuries the lovespoon developed into complex and intricate works of art, with keys, bells and other motifs worked into the design.

The River Wye as seen from the vantage point of Symonds Yat

Raglan, Gwent

14 One of Britain's finest ruins is 15th-century **Raglan Castle** which was actually built as a fortified manor. The keep is outside the main castle and Parliamentary troops overcame the Royalists here during the Civil War, by approaching from the opposite side. The castle houses an exhibition on the history of Raglan.

Follow an unclassified road south to Usk.

Usk, Gwent

15 Usk is a small market town on the site of an ancient roman settlement, *Burrium*. Visit the church to see the remarkable restored Tudor rood screen; and, at the other end of the town, the **Gwent Rural Life Museum**, in an old stone malt barn, which is crammed with exhibits about life in the area. **Usk Castle** is privately owned but you can visit the ruins of the **Priory** next to the church.

Cross the river and continue along unclassified roads for 8 miles (13km) to Caerleon.

Caerleon, Gwent

16 One of the four permanent Roman legions in Britain was based here, and parts of the Roman city of Isca are displayed in an excellent new exhibition room. The major find has been the **amphitheatre** outside the city walls. This oval earth mound, 184 feet (56m) long and 136 feet (41m) wide, seated 5,000 people, and is the only excavated amphitheatre in Britain. The **Legionary Museum** has more information and relics from the barracks.

Take the B4236, then an unclassified road to join the A48 for Penhow.

Penhow, Gwent

17 The oldest inhabited castle in Wales in **Penhow Castle**, which is perched on a hillside above the main road. Now privately owned, it is open to the public and is an excellent example of the smaller type of fortified manor house. Three miles (5km) further is Caerwent, on the site of *Venta Silurium*, the only walled Roman civilian town in Wales. Remnants of the wall and mosaic pavements can still be seen. **Caldicot Castle Country Park**, 2 miles (3km) away, surrounds the 12th-century **castle**.

Continue straight along the A48 for 8 miles (13km) to Chepstow.

BACK TO NATURE

The **Forest of Dean** is an excellent area for the birdwatcher. Woodpeckers, tits and nuthatches can be see, and pied flycatchers are often spotted at the RSPB's **Nagshead reserve**, where nest boxes encourage the species.

---

which runs for 4 miles (6km) down the valley, through splendid scenery.

Take unclassified roads to Talybont-on-Usk.

Talybont-on-Usk, Powys

11 This delightful little village is now a tourist centre, especially for walkers and outdoor activities; there is an **Outdoor Pursuits Centre** in the old railway station. The 18th-century **Monmouth and Brecon Canal**, which passes through the village, was built to carry coal and iron ore. It eventually closed in 1962, but was reopened by volunteers in 1970 for use by pleasure craft.

Follow the B4558 to Llangynidr, then the B4560 and an unclassified road to Crickhowell.

Crickhowell, Powys

12 The name of this little market town is derived from the Iron Age fort Crug Hywel (Howell's Cairn). The town grew up around **Alisby's Castle**, which was captured and destroyed in 1403 by Owain Glyndŵr, and is now a picturesque ruin. The River Usk is crossed by an old **bridge**, dating from the 17th century, which appears to have 13 arches on one side but only 12 on the other – the result of 19th-century alterations.

Take the A40 for 7 miles (11km) to Abergavenny.

Abergavenny, Gwent

13 At the edge of the Brecon Beacons National Park Abergavenny, the 'Gateway to the Vale of Usk', is overlooked by the **Sugar Loaf** mountain, 1,955 feet (596m) high, and **Ysgyryd (Skirrid) Fawr**, 1,595 feet (486m). Its ruined **castle** was founded in 1090. Impressive buildings in the town include the stone **tythe barn**, and the red sandstone Lloyds Bank. **St Mary's Church** is built on the site of a former Benedictine priory.

ⓘ Swan Meadow, Cross Street

Continue along the A40 to Raglan.

SCENIC ROUTES

The **A466** along the Wye Valley from Chepstow to Monmouth is a series of beautiful and sometimes dramatic views. Driving along the **A470** from Brecon reveals hills, open moorland and forest and lakes, and the southern margins of the Brecon Beacons take in delightful scenery.

Tenby's broad and sandy beaches make it the essence of carefree holiday memories

ℹ The Croft, Tenby

Leave Tenby on the A4139 and then turn left on to the B4585 to Manorbier.

Manorbier, Dyfed

1 The medieval traveller and scholar, Gerald of Wales (Giraldus Cambrensis), was born here in 1147 and described it as the 'pleasantest spot in Wales'. There is a **castle** dating from Gerald's time, which gives an impressive view out to sea from the ramparts. The sandy beach has some rocky pools, and is a perfect playground for the children.

Return to the A4139 for 5 miles (8km) to Lamphey.

Lamphey, Dyfed

2 The romantic ruins of a 13th-century **Bishop's Palace** lie to the northeast of Lamphey. The Palace, with its ornate parapets, fishponds and notable 16th-century chapel, was built as a country retreat for the Bishops of St David's. At **Herberts Moor Open Farm** you can wander round the nature trail, as well as seeing the farmyard animals and pets.

Continue for another 2 miles (3km) along the A4139 to Pembroke.

Pembroke, Dyfed

3 This ancient town was built around the great fortress of **Pembroke Castle**, the largest castle in the area, and the birthplace of Henry Tudor. It still has its fine round keep, and beneath the castle is a huge natural cavern known as **The Wogan**. A more modern building is the **Power**

ROUND THE PEMBROKE COAST NATIONAL PARK

Tenby • Manorbier • Lamphey • Pembroke
Haverfordwest • Solva • St David's • Mathry • Fishguard
Newport • Cardigan • Drefach Felindre • Carmarthen
Laugharne • Pendine • Saundersfoot • Tenby

The old county of Pembrokeshire has a magnificent coastline. The inland scenery, though less dramatic, is enhanced by pretty villages and several fine castles.

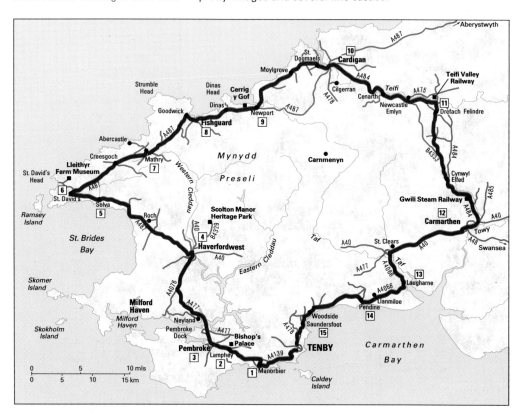

FOR CHILDREN

4Scolton Manor, 4 miles (6km) northeast of Haverfordwest, is set in magnificent grounds where there is plenty to keep children occupied: nature trails, guided walks, an adventure playground and play area, exhibitions and, in the summer months, a vintage car rally and model aircraft show.

BACK TO NATURE

6St David's Head has some superb coastal scenery and a wonderful display of coastal heathland flowers. Look for ling, bell heather and dwarf gorse growing alongside thrift and sea campion. For the best views of seabirds, visit **Stackpole**, or better still **Skomer Island**, a few miles off the coast and reached by ferry from Martin's Haven. Puffins, razorbills, kittiwakes, lesser black-backed gulls and choughs all put on a fine display.

SPECIAL TO...

6A boat trip around Pembrokeshire's offshore islands with the Thousand Islands Company at St David's takes you on a 50-mile (80km) voyage past the highest sea cliffs in Wales, the longest sea caves and the largest grey seal colony, on **Ramsey Island**. The boat speeds over strong tidal currents in the narrows between the islands, including the notorious Bitches of Ramsey Sound, with its 20mph tidal current.

Station, which runs guided tours throughout the summer months. Pembroke still retains some of its original town wall, and has an interesting **Museum of the Home**.

ⅈ The Commons Road

Take the A477, then join the A4076 to Haverfordwest – 11 miles (18km).

Haverfordwest, Dyfed

4The castle here now houses the museum and art gallery. St Mary's Church has exquisite Early English-style lancet windows and the mutilated effigy of a pilgrim with scallops on his satchel. The town is cut in two by the River Cleddau.

ⅈ Old Bridge

Head northwest along the A487 for 13 miles (21km) to Solva.

Solva, Dyfed

5Solva's old port still has warehouses and a restored lime kiln, and is a favourite sailing spot. The tiny, beautiful bay set on a coastline of cliffs is now also noted for the tropical butterfly farm or **Nectarium**, where you can see butterflies close up, as well as caterpillars, locusts and spiders.

Keep on along the A487 for 3 miles (5km) to St David's.

St David's, Dyfed

6The city of St David's – the smallest in Britain – was founded on the site of an early Christian community, and is dominated by the **cathedral** and the graceful, walled **Bishop's Palace**. Also in the city is the **Oceanarium**, a purpose-built sea aquarium, and the **Marine Life Centre**, where over 70 species of local marine creatures can be seen. The outdoor rural life of the past can be seen in the **Lleithyr Farm Museum**, which has one of the largest Welsh collections of agricultural implements.

ⅈ City Hall

Turn northeastwards, still on the A487 to Mathry.

St David was the descendant of Welsh kings, and he is buried here in the city which bears his name

Mathry, Dyfed

7This little village overlooks the Western Cleddau source stream. Mountain bikes can be hired here, for rides into the **Preseli Hills**, where 33 dolerite stones were gathered for transportation to Stonehenge. Northwest of Mathry is Abercastle, where there is a **burial chamber** with a 16-foot (5m) capstone resting on three of its original seven supports.

Continue along the A487 to Fishguard.

Fishguard, Dyfed

8Fishguard has two parts. Upper Fishguard stands back from the sea, and from it the road falls steeply to Lower Fishguard, a quaint and largely unspoilt town. There are many ancient links with boating here, and also with textiles. **Tregwynt Mill** draws on centuries of skill and craftsmanship to produce quality woollen goods. The July **Fishguard Music Festival** is another attraction. For a windblown and bracing day, take a return trip on the ferry to Rosslare, across the Irish Sea.

ⅈ 4 Hamilton Street

Head east to Newport, still travelling on the A487.

Newport, Dyfed

9Just outside the town is the **Cilgwyn Candle Workshop**, where you can see hand-made candles being produced, and the **Mini Museum**, next door, has displays on the history of candle making. The remains of Newport's 12th-century castle can still be seen and the owners, the Baronry of Cemaes, still have the power to appoint the Mayor. One and a half miles (2.5km) west of town is **Cerrig y Gof**, a group of burial chambers forming a circle, an arrangement unique to Wales.

Turn left along unclassified roads through Moylgrove and St Dogmael's, then take the B4546 to Cardigan.

Cardigan, Dyfed

10St Dogmael's Abbey, just outside Cardigan, was founded in 1115, and the ruins include large fragments

The Boathouse at Laugharne, where Dylan Thomas lived and wrote

of the north and west walls standing almost to their original height. One of Cardigan's most striking architectural features is the **ancient bridge**, which spans the River Teifi, but little now remains of **Cardigan Castle**, where the first National Eisteddfod took place in 1176. The magnificent towers of **Cilgerran Castle**, best reached from along the **A484**, overlook the gorge of the Teifi just upstream from the town. Watch out for the coracle demonstrations to be seen in the **Cardigan Wildlife Park**, and there is a **coracle centre** and **mill** at Cenarth, a few miles along the **A484**.

ⓘ Theatr Mwldan,
  Bath House Road

  Follow the A484, then turn right along an unclassified road to Drefach Felindre.

Drefach Felindre, Dyfed

11 Just before the turning to Drefach Felindre, a left turn leads to the **Teifi Valley Railway** at Henllan, where tiny engines pull the trains along a narrow-gauge railway. The Teifi valley has long been a woollen producing area, and the **Museum of the Welsh Woollen Industry** is in the town near a large **leisure centre**. There are still a few small mills in the area where you can see the cloth being made, often using wool from the local sheep. The original mill building houses an exhibition showing the processes involved in making the cloth, and there are demonstrations of spinning and weaving.

  Continue south along unclassified roads to join the B4333, then the A484 for 15 miles (24km) to Carmarthen.

Carmarthen, Dyfed

12 Carmarthen is believed to be the oldest town in Wales, and the birthplace of Merlin. Remains of Roman occupation include an **amphitheatre** site. The **Gwili Steam Railway**, opened in 1860, but closed in 1973 when the milk traffic was transferred to road tankers, was reopened by volunteers in 1978 and now operates for 1.6 miles (2.5km) from Bronwydd Arms to Llwyfan Cerrig, following the course of the River Gwili. A nature trail has been developed at Llwyfan Cerrig and there is also a children's activity area.

ⓘ Lammas Street

  Go west along the A40, turning left at St Clears to join the A4066 for Laugharne.

Laugharne, Dyfed

13 This picturesque village had a strong influence on Dylan Thomas, and the **Town Hall, Clock Tower** and many of the people became part of *Under Milk Wood*. Thomas moved into the **Boathouse** with his family in 1949 and along the path to it is '**The Shack**', which became his workshop. The Boathouse is now a **museum**, Dylan Thomas is buried in the local church-

yard and there is a festival of his work every third year in July. The castle on the edge of the sea was built in the 12th century, but the present building is mainly Tudor.

  Continue along the A4066 to Pendine.

Pendine, Dyfed

14 Pendine is best noted for its 6 miles (9km) of golden sand, on which Sir Malcolm Campbell and others made land speed record attempts. It was here that, in 1927, Parry Thomas was killed when he crashed his car 'Babs', which was buried in the sand until 1969, when it was dug out and restored. Amy Johnson took off from here in 1933 for the start of her epic transatlantic flight. Nowadays the beach is used for bathing and some fishing, and there are beautiful cliff walks near by.

  Take the B4314, then unclassified roads following the coast to Saundersfoot.

Saundersfoot, Dyfed

15 This 19th-century fishing port and coal port has become a family holiday centre with three sandy beaches, rock pools and a sheltered harbour. Boats are available for fishing and pleasure trips. The village is in a sheltered valley, and there are good walks along the coast.

ⓘ The Harbour

  Drive south along the B4316 and then the A478 for the 4 miles (6km) back to Tenby.

Tenby – Manorbier 6 (10)
Manorbier – Lamphey 5 (8)
Lamphey – Pembroke 2 (3)
Pembroke – Haverfordwest 11 (18)
Haverfordwest – Solva 13 (21)
Solva – St David's 3 (5)
St David's – Mathry 9 (14)
Mathry – Fishguard 7 (11)
Fishguard – Newport 8 (13)
Newport – Cardigan 11 (18)
Cardigan – Drefach Felindre 15 (24)
Drefach Felindre – Carmarthen 15 (24)
Carmarthen – Laugharne 13 (21)
Laugharne – Pendine 6 (9)
Pendine – Saundersfoot 9 (14)
Saundersfoot –Tenby 4 (6)

RECOMMENDED WALKS

Any walk along the **Coastal Path** will provide tremendous views. Take care, though: parts of the path run alongside sheer drops into the sea.

6 Walk from St David's cathedral to the coast at **Whitesand Bay**. If you wish to add 2 miles (3km) and double the length of this walk, go northwards and do a round tour of **St David's Head**.

SCENIC ROUTES

There are superb views of the coastline on the route from Pendine to Saundersfoot and along the road to Solva. The Teifi valley, from Cardigan, is a green and rural landscape which makes a pleasant drive.

FOR HISTORY BUFFS

Ancient settlements were numerous in the Preseli Hills and elsewhere in southwest Wales; among the important Bronze Age relics are those at **Carnmenyn**. An ancient route known as the Great West Road passes a pile of rocks called **Mynachlog Ddu**; the bluestone which is also found at Stonehenge.

2 days – 134 miles (216km)

LAND OF RIVERS & MOUNTAINS

**Aberystwyth • Borth • Machynlleth • Llyn Clywedog
Rhayader • Newbridge on Wye • Builth Wells
Llanwrtyd Wells • Abergwesyn • Tregaron • Pontrhydygroes
Devil's Bridge • Ponterwyd • Aberystwyth**

From the sandy beach of Borth and the muddy estuary of the Dyfi, this drive takes you through the man-made scenery of Llyn Clywedog – a striking contrast with the wild hills all around. There are rivers and waterfalls, wooded valleys and rolling hills, before the return to Aberystwyth's seaside bustle.

Abergwesyn boasts some of the most memorable Welsh scenery

ℹ Terrace Road, Aberystwyth

Follow the coast northwards for 6 miles (10km) along the A487 and the B4572 to Borth.

Borth, Dyfed

1 Three miles (5km) of sand can be found just to the north of this small village, which consists mainly of one street of cottages. **Brynllys Farm** near by demonstrates organic farming methods; there are nature walks here, and an information centre explains the farm's policies. Strong boots or wellingtons are advisable.

Head inland along the B4353, then turn left on to the A487 at Tre'r Ddol and follow it through to Machynlleth.

Machynlleth, Powys

2 On the journey to Machynlleth, pause to visit the old Wesleyan chapel at Tre'r Ddol which is now a museum of religious life in Wales; further along the road, Eglwysfach has a recently restored **waterwheel** near the old **Dyfi** furnace. Machynlleth itself is the chief market town of the Dyfi Valley and gained fame in the 15th century as the seat of Owain Glyndŵr's short-lived Welsh parliament. The **Owain Glyndŵr Centre** houses an exhibition of his campaigns. The **Centre for Alternative Technology**, to the north of the town, is a fascinating place to visit. Here you can see a whole Green Community at work, using windmills, solar panels and water-driven machinery. There is an ecological maze to explore, a restaurant and children's play area. You can see a

SCENIC ROUTES

Just before descending into Borth there are fine views of the sandy coast with the estuary and hills beyond. There are magnificent hill views all around Clywedog; as well as on the minor roads near Abergwesyn and the B4574 near Cwmystwyth.

SPECIAL TO...

1 Ynslas is the area of sand dunes to the north of Borth which block off much of the Dyfi estuary from the sea. Behind the dune is an expanse of reclaimed marsh; this area is now a major nature reserve managed by the Nature Conservancy Council, together with the West Wales Naturalists Trust. Ferries used to run across the estuary to Aberdyfi, and remains of a refuge tower can still be seen, where passengers could wait if they became stranded by the incoming tide.

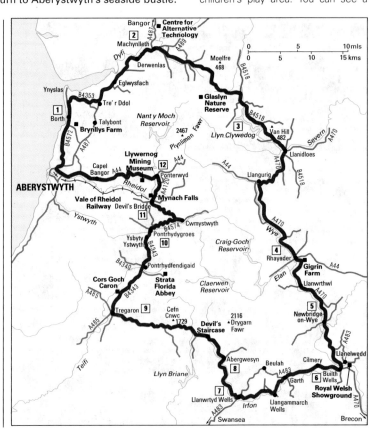

traditional form of energy at **Felin Crewi**, just outside the town, one of Wales' last working water mills.

ⓘ Canolfan Owain Glydnwr

Leave on the A489, then take the unclassified road southeastwards to join the B4518 and on to Llyn Clywedog.

Llyn Clywedog, Powys

3 This reservoir, built between 1964 and 1968, has the highest concrete dam of its kind in Britain – 237 feet (72m) high – and holds up to 11,000 million gallons (50,000 million litres) of water behind it. There are excellent views of the surrounding hill country from the dam and Glyndŵr's Way and other waymarked walks follow the Clywedog valley. Four miles (6km) further is Llanidloes, the first town on the River Severn, and there are several interesting buildings along its tree-lined streets. The most famous is the 16th-century half-timbered **Market Hall**, with its open ground floor – one of the last of its kind in Wales; the upper floor now houses a museum.

ⓘ Longbridge Street

Drive southwards along the A470 from Llanidloes for 21 miles (34km) to Rhayader.

Rhayader, Powys

4 This small market town on the River Wye is an ideal centre for visiting the 'Lakeland of Wales'. The lakes are the reservoirs of the Elan valley, which provide Birmingham with its water supply. Pony trekking and angling are particularly popular here. Although Rhayader is now a peaceful little town, it has had its share of excitement in the past. The 19th-century Rebecca riots, protesting against toll gate impositions, centred around the town, and the **castle** was destroyed during the Civil War. At the **Welsh Royal Crystal Glass Factory** you can watch the art of glass-blowing, and there are numerous craft shops and a pottery. **Gigrin Farm**, ½ mile (1km) to the south, offers a farm trail of nearly 2 miles (3km) in beautiful surroundings, and there are pets and a children's playground.

ⓘ Leisure Centre, North Street

Follow the A470 for another 8 miles (13km) to Newbridge on Wye.

Newbridge on Wye, Powys

5 The 'new' bridge of the town's name was built in 1910 to replace an old wooden structure. The **church** was founded in the late 19th century by the Venables-Llewellyn family, who own **Llysdinam Hall**. There is a **Field Study Centre** in the Hall's grounds belonging to the University of Wales' Institute of Science and Technology.

Continue southwards for a further 6 miles (10km) on the A470 to Builth Wells.

Builth Wells, Powys

6 Builth Wells was one of a string of Welsh spa towns which drew crowds of health-seeking Victorians,

but it was an important centre long before that. The **castle** was built in Norman times by James de San George, who was also responsible for Harlech, Caernarfon, Beaumaris and Conwy castles. The **Wyeside Arts Centre** provides a fine selection of entertainment throughout the summer with films, exhibitions and theatre. Just outside town, in the village of Llanelwedd, is the **Royal Welsh Showground**, which hosts the Royal Welsh Agricultural Show in July.

ⓘ Groe Car Park

Take the A483, then turn left along unclassified roads at Garth to Llanwrtyd Wells.

Builth Wells, popular Victorian spa and modern cultural centre

Llanwrtyd Wells, Powys

7 Featured in the Guiness Book of Records as the smallest town in Britain, Llanwrtyd Wells is situated on the River Irfon. There are still traces of Victorian grandeur recalling the town's heyday, when travellers flocked here to sample its sulphur water – which can still be smelt along the river. The **Abergwesyn Pass**, which leads over the mountain from Llanwrtyd, has some of the finest scenery in Wales. On the A483 is the **Cambrian Factory**, where you can see traditional Welsh tweed being spun and woven.

Drive northwards into the hills along an unclassified road to Abergwesyn.

Abergwesyn, Powys

8 The mountain road from Abergwesyn to Tregaron is one of Britain's most spectacular roads. It

A stream on its way to join the spectacular falls at Devil's Bridge

FOR HISTORY BUFFS

9 On the road from Tregaron to Pontrhydygroes you will pass the ruins of the Cistercian **Strata Florida Abbey**, founded in 1164. It was here, in 1238, that Llywelyn the Great gathered all the Welsh princes to swear allegiance to his son Dafydd. The abbey fell into disrepair after the Dissolution, but the magnificent Norman arch still remains.

FOR CHILDREN

12 Gold, silver, lead and copper were mined from the rocks of the Cambrian Mountains in former centuries, and many of the relics of these days can still be seen. The **Llywernog Silver-Lead Mine** near Ponterwyd has many old machines, some of which have been restored to make a fascinating working museum. You can try your hand at panning for gold and working the hand pumps, and visit the underground drift mine, with its floodlit cavern.

was originally a drovers' route, used to take cattle to the Midlands and London in the 18th and 19th centuries, and there are amazing views near the **Devil's Staircase**, a steep and tortuous zig-zag section of the road.

Take the mountain road to Tregaron.

Tregaron, Dyfed

9 At the foot of steep hills, and at the southern end of a great expanse of bog, Tregaron is a popular pony trekking centre. The often bleak and misty marshland, **Cors Goch Caron**, was formerly a lake fed by the River Teifi, and is now a National Nature Reserve, with restricted public access. Tregaron is a small, Welsh-speaking community, famous as the birthplace of outlaw Twm Sion Catti, and of Henry Richard, the 'Apostle of Peace' who founded the Peace Union, forerunner of the League of Nations.

*Follow the **B4343** for 10 miles (16km) to Pontrhydygroes and the **B4574** to Cwmystwyth, 4 miles (6km) further.*

Pontrhydygroes, Dyfed

10 The village of Pontrhydygroes grew around the lead-mining industry and is now a quiet community set among wooded hills. The surrounding area was part of the Hafod estate in the 18th century, where Thomas Johnes began the task of afforesting the land. Further along, Cwmystwyth is another old mining settlement; the mines here were once worked by the Romans and the monks of Strata Florida Abbey.

Head northwest along the B4574 for another 4 miles (6km) to Devil's Bridge.

Devil's Bridge, Dyfed

11 The River Mynach meets the River Rheidol here to create spectacular falls over 300 feet (91m) high. Three bridges were built across the chasm, one above the other, and Devil's Bridge is the earliest one, probably the 12th-century work of the monks from nearby Strata Florida Abbey. The higher bridges date from 1753 and the early 20th century. Ninety-one steep steps, called **Jacob's Ladder**, lead down to the river. The narrow-gauge **Vale of Rheidol Railway** climbs 680 feet (207m) in the 12 miles (19km) from Aberystwyth along a breathtakingly scenic route to terminate at Devil's Bridge Station.

*Take the **A4120** northwards to Ponterwyd.*

Ponterwyd, Dyfed

12 This small cluster of houses round a craggy gorge featured in the writings of 19th-century traveller George Borrow, whose book *Wild Wales* relates his stay at the village inn, now the **Borrow Arms**. A mile west of the village is the **Llwernog Silver-Lead Mine** and there are fine views stretching to Cardigan Bay from Bwlch Nant-yr-Arian Visitor Centre, further along the road.

*Head east along the **A44** back to Aberystwyth.*

Majestic Cader Idris, seen here from Lake Talyllyn. The lake is known for its sizeable trout, whilst Cader Idris is a nature reserve

ⓘ The Old Library, Barmouth

From Barmouth follow the A496 north to Llanbedr.

Llanbedr, Gwynedd

1 At Llanfair, just to the north of Llanbedr on the A496, are the exciting old slate caverns, where you can walk through the old workings and see the enormous Cathedral cavern, but be sure to wear warm clothing, as the temperature inside is normally 10°C (50°F) or below.

Continue along the A496 for a further 3 miles (5km) to Harlech.

Harlech, Gwynedd

2 Harlech Castle is one of the most magnificently sited of Welsh castles, looking out over Cardigan Bay. It was built in the 13th century by Edward I to subdue the Welsh but was captured by Owain Glyndŵr in 1404. Harlech's **theatre** presents a varied programme throughout the year and there are plenty of interesting craft shops in town.

ⓘ High Street

Keep on along the A496, then turn off right on to the A487 for 2 miles (3km) before joining the A470 for Trawsfynydd.

Trawsfynydd, Gwynedd

3 The lake here is a man-made reservoir providing cooling water for the nuclear power station which dominates the scenery. Nature trails have been created around the lake, and there is excellent fishing. To the south along the A470 is the **Rhiw Goch Ski Centre** at Bronaber, where all-year skiing is possible for novices as well as experienced skiers.

2 days – 150 miles (244km)

WATER, WATER EVERYWHERE

Barmouth • Llanbedr • Harlech • Trawsfynydd • Bala Lake Vyrnwy • Dinas Mawddwy • Corris • Aberdyfi • Tywyn Abergynolwyn • Fairbourne • Dolgellau • Barmouth

Follow the magnificent coastline with glorious sandy beaches before turning inland and heading into the hills. Tumbling rivers and large lakes are constant companions from Trawsfynydd as far as Corris, and man-made features include dams and a huge nuclear power station.

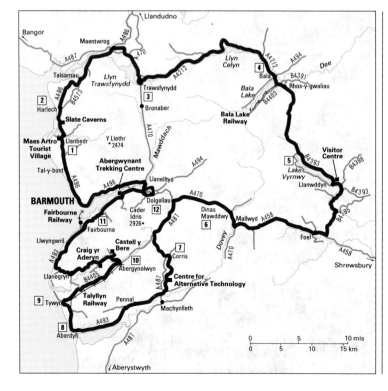

BACK TO NATURE

1 **Shell Island**, also known as Mochras, near Llanbedr is not really an island but a peninsula with sand dunes and sandy beaches covered with shells – more than 200 varieties are believed to have been found. It is a great place for birds, including terns and shelduck, and waders such as sandpipers, dunlin, oyster-catchers and gulls, and there is a great selection of flowers – over 170 species have been seen in the summer, including a few orchids.

FOR CHILDREN

1 Maes Artro Village, an old wartime RAF camp, has been converted and now offers a range of exhibitions, displays and activities, with museums, an aquarium and a Log Fort playground. Old farm implements, a 'Village of Yesteryear' and an air raid shelter, which has been restored with light and sound effects, add to the fun.

RECOMMENDED WALKS

1 Stroll through Llanbedr village from Maes Artro Craft Village and then follow the north side of the Artro estuary to the coast at **Llandanwg**, where there is a small medieval church which is often half covered with wind-blown sand.

12 A gentle walk of 4½ miles (7km) can be taken along the estuary from Arthog to Penmaenpool, following the line of the old dismantled railway.

SCENIC ROUTES

Driving north along the coast road (**A496**) there are spectacular views of the sea, the coastline, the estuary and the hills of Snowdonia beyond. Following the **A4212** takes you through wild countryside and past a huge lake which softens the scenery. The unclassified road from Bala follows a beautiful valley with a tumbling stream, before climbing up through deciduous woods and coniferous forests out on to the open moorland. There can be no finer variety of scenery in such a short distance anywhere in Wales.

Drive into the hills along the A4212 for 18 miles (29km) to Bala.

Bala, Gwynedd

4 Situated at the top of **Bala Lake**, or Llyn Tegid, as it is known in Welsh, the largest natural lake in Wales, Bala has become a great water sports centre. Sailing, windsurfing, fishing and canoeing all take place on the River Tryweryn, where international slalom and whitewater championships have been held. The other big lake near by is **Llyn Celyn**, a man-made reservoir, which supplies Liverpool with some of its water and is a popular trout-fishing lake. The **Bala Lake Narrow Gauge Scenic Railway** runs 4½ miles (7km) to Llanuwchllyn through splendid scenery. Bala was the home of the Methodist cause and has retained much of its Welsh character and culture.

i High Street

Leave Bala on the B4391, then follow the unclassified road southwards over the hills and on to the B4393 for 15 miles (24km) to Lake Vyrnwy.

Lake Vyrnwy, Gwynedd

5 This vast reservoir was created in the late 19th century to supply Liverpool with water; the village of Llanwddyn was levelled to make way for it and rebuilt on higher ground. The lake and the surrounding woodlands which clothe the valley sides are now a reserve of the RSPB. There is a small visitor centre, and nature trails and hides are

The controversial skyline of Trawsfynydd Nuclear Power Station above the natural beauty of Gwynedd

provided to enable you to view the wildlife in the area, which includes red squirrels, polecats and badgers.

Continue along the B4393, then turn right on to a minor road to join the B4395. Turn right again on to the A458 through Mallwyd, then head north on the A470 to Dinas Mawddwy.

Dinas Mawddwy, Gwynedd

6 This pretty little village is an ideal base for outdoor holidays in the area. At the old railway station is **Meirion Mill**, a large working woollen mill open to visitors in the summer. Pottery and slate goods are available as well as woollens, and the old railway line is a good place for a stroll.

From Dinas Mawddwy continue along the A470 and then left on the A487 for 14 miles (23km) to Corris.

Corris, Gwynedd

7 Corris is an old mining village with a new centre for traditional industries, where tourists can watch craftsmen at work. There is also a **Railway Museum** and, to the south, at the disused Llwyngwern Quarry, is the **Centre for Alternative Technology** (see page 52).

i Craft Centre

Drive southwards along the unclassified road on the eastern side of the river through Esgairgeiliog. Turn right on to the B4404, join the A487 for a short distance, then turn right on the A493 to Aberdyfi.

Aberdyfi, Gwynedd

8 Sailing boats have now replaced the cargo ships that once traded at this harbour on the sheltered Dyfi Estuary. There is a fine sandy beach along the coast, and you can take a ferry trip across to **Ynyslas**, with its vast expanse of sand dunes and marshland. The town achieved fame in the song *The Bells of Aberdyfi*; ghostly church bells are said to ring from an ancient town which was completely flooded by the sea.

ⓘ The Wharf

Drive north along the A493 for 5 miles (8km) to Tywyn.

Tywyn, Gwynedd

9 There are miles of golden sandy beaches at this popular seaside resort which is excellent for surfing and sailing. **St Cadfan's Church** dates back to Norman times and houses **St Cadfan's Stone**, a 7-foot (2m) monument some 1300 years old. The inscriptions on it are thought to be the oldest known writing in Welsh. Tywyn is famous for the **Talyllyn Railway**, which runs inland for 7 miles (11km) past spectacular scenery.

ⓘ High Street

Leave Tywyn on the A493, but turn inland along the B4405 to Abergynolwyn.

Abergynolwyn, Gwynedd

10 Two miles (3km) west of Abergynolwyn, along an unclassified road, is the romantic ruin of **Castell y Bere**, built by Llywelyn the Great in the 13th century, and further still is the huge crag of **Craig yr Aderyn** (Bird Rock), thought to be the only inland nesting place of cormorants in Britain, but also the home for choughs, kestrels and feral goats.

Take an unclassified road heading westwards through Llanegryn back to the coast, then the A493 to Fairbourne.

Fairbourne, Gwynedd

11 Fairbourne is a popular holiday base with a sandy beach and miles of safe swimming, where windsurfing is a great attraction. So, too, is the narrow-gauge **Fairbourne Railway** which was built in the 1890s as a horse-drawn tramway. It was later converted to steam and now runs 1½ miles from Fairbourne to the end of the peninsula. The main line Cambrian coast railway also runs through here.

Rejoin and continue along the A493 for 9 miles (15km) to Dolgellau.

Dolgellau, Gwynedd

12 In a romantic setting at the foot of Cader Idris, Dolgellau has always been a major route centre and is still an important regional capital and mar-ket centre. Tourism has completely replaced Dolgellau's main industry, flannel-weaving, and all that remains of this former occupation are the ruins of the **fulling mills** on the banks of the River Aran. Pony trekking is popular in this area, and ponies can be hired at the **Abergwynant Trekking Centre**, 3 miles (5km) west of town. Walking is also popular, and there are strenuous walks up to the summit of Cader Idris, as well as more gentle strolls. A delightful route near by is the **Torrent Walk**, from Brithdir to the falls of the Afon Clywedog.

ⓘ Ty Meirion, Eldon Square

Join the A470 to Llanilltyd, then turn left on to the A496 back to Barmouth.

Barmouth – Llanbedr 8 (13)
Llanbedr – Harlech 3 (5)
Harlech – Trawsfynydd 14 (23)
Trawsfynydd – Bala 18 (29)
Bala – Lake Vyrnwy 15 (24)
Lake Vyrnwy – Dinas Mawddwy 19 (31)
Dinas Mawddwy – Corris 14 (23)
Corris – Aberdyfi 14 (23)
Aberdyfi – Tywyn 5 (8)
Tywyn – Abergynolwyn 7 (11)
Abergynolwyn – Fairbourne 14 (23)
Fairbourne – Dolgellau 9 (15)
Dolgellau – Barmouth 10 (16)

The Talyllyn Railway caters for railway children of all ages

SPECIAL TO...

10 The Talyllyn Railway, which runs inland from Tywyn to Nant Gwernol, was built in 1865 to handle slate traffic. This was the first railway in the world to be taken over by a voluntary preservation society, and it is now operated as a tourist attraction. It runs through most beautiful scenery in a steep glaciated valley, and a Railway Museum traces its history.

FOR HISTORY BUFFS

12 The stone-built town of Dolgellau is on the site of an ancient settlement among green hills. Three Roman roads met here, and it remained an important centre for the Welsh people through-out the Middle Ages. The Welsh leader Owain Glyndŵr signed his alliance with Charles VI, the King of France, here. Later, in more peaceful days, this became the main town for the Meirionnydd wool and flannel trade, and is still closely linked with sheep and wool.

2 days - 113 miles (180km)

QUARRIES, CASTLES & RAILWAYS

Bangor • Menai Bridge • Caernarfon • Llanrug
Llanberis • Beddgelert • Porthmadog • Portmeirion
Blaenau Ffestiniog • Betws-y-Coed • Llanrwst • Tal-y-Cafn
Colwyn Bay • Llandudno • Conwy • Llanfairfechan • Bangor

From Bangor make a brief visit to the island of Anglesey before heading down the coast to Caernarfon and then inland to Snowdonia. The hills are scarred with quarries in places, but still create an overpoweringly beautiful backdrop, as the tour circles round the edge of the Snowdonia National Park on the way to the seaside at Colwyn Bay and back along the north coast.

The Pont y Pair Bridge at Betws-y-Coed, one of that town's many picturesque bridges

i Theatr Qwynedd, Bangor

Drive on the A5122 for 3 miles (5km) to Menai Bridge.

Menai Bridge, Gwynedd

1 Menai Bridge, known in Welsh as Porthaethwy, takes its name from the **suspension bridge** built by Telford between 1819 and 1826 high above the Menai Strait. Nowadays, traffic on the busy **A5** uses Stephenson's Britannia Bridge, whose original tubular structure was rebuilt after a fire in 1970, with a road deck above the railway. From a lay-by on the **A545** beyond Menai Bridge, there are superb views of both bridges, with the mountains of Snowdonia beyond. In Menai Bridge itself is the **Tegfryn Art Gallery**, which features the work of contemporary Welsh artists and is set in pleasant gardens.

Follow the A4080 to the A5, recross the Menai Strait on the Britannia Bridge, then on to the A487 to Caernarfon.

Caernarfon, Gwynedd

2 The airport south of Caenarfon is a great all-weather attraction. It used to be an RAF camp during World War II, and is now a hands-on museum, where you can climb into exhibits, touch the controls and use a flight simulator. You can also have a flight over **Caernarfon Castle** or round Snowdon. In 1969, Prince Charles was invested in the castle, following a tradition set by Edward I, whose first-born son was presented to the people as the Prince of Wales. Inside the castle you can see the investiture robes with a description of the ceremony, and an expla-

nation of the history of the castle and surrounding area, as well as the **Museum of the Royal Welch Fusiliers**. Just outside the town, at **Segontium**, are the remains of a fine Roman fort which served as an important outpost of the Empire for three centuries.

☐ Oriel Pendeitsh

Take the A4086 eastwards and turn on to an unclassified road to Llanrug.

Llanrug, Gwynedd

3 The lived-in castle at **Bryn Bras**, to the south of Llanrug, has spacious lawns, tranquil woodland walks and excellent mountain views. This neo-Norman building on the fringe of Snowdonia was built in the 1830s on the site of an earlier castle, and the majestic gardens are worth visiting in their own right.

Return to and continue along the A4086 for a further 4 miles (6km) to Llanberis.

Llanberis, Gwynedd

4 At Llanberis you can take a 40-minute trip in a narrow-gauge train along the shores of Llyn Padarn, which is in the **Padarn Country Park**. The famed modern pump storage hydro scheme is close by at **Dinorwic**. **Dolbadarn Castle** is in the town, and less than a mile (1.6km) from the High Street is **Ceunant Mawr**, one of the most impressive waterfalls in Wales. The most popular footpath up Snowdon starts here, as does the **Snowdon Mountain Railway**, the only public rack-and-pinion railway, which climbs 3,000 feet (915m) to the summit in less than 5 miles (8km). Each train can take a

Palace as well as fortress, Edward I founded Caernarfon in 1283 on the site of an earlier castle

maximum of 59 passengers and will normally not run with fewer than 25. Services depend on demand and weather conditions, which can be very harsh at the top of Snowdon, even when Llanberis is pleasant and sunny. The views can be superb, both from the train and from the summit, where there is a restaurant.

☐ Amgueddfa'r Gogledd Museum of the North

Leave on the A4086, then turn right on to the A498 for 14 miles (23km) to Beddgelert.

Beddgelert, Gwynedd

5 The **grave of Gelert** is one of the saddest memorials you are likely to see. According to legend, which may actually be a 19th-century invention, Gelert was a faithful wolfhound killed by Prince Llywelyn, who thought it had killed his son, when in fact the dog had saved him from a wolf. Just outside this small town is the award-winning **Sygun Copper mine**, where you can explore the tunnels of a 19th-century mine which was once one of the world's major copper producers. A guided tour will take you past veins of ore containing gold, silver and other metals. From Beddgelert the drive takes you through the picturesque **Pass of Aberglaslyn**.

☐ Llewelyn Cottage

Follow the A498 southwards to Porthmadog.

Porthmadog, Gwynedd

6 Porthmadog was the creation of William Alexander Madocks, who hoped to benefit from the tourist traffic to Ireland; in fact, the town made its money from slate. The **Ffestiniog Railway**, which runs through magnificent scenery to Blaenau Ffestiniog, once carried the slate here to be shipped abroad, and is now a major tourist attraction. It

uses horseshoe bends and a complete spiral at one point to gain height. Porthmadog also has the little **Welsh Highland Railway**, and a **Motor Museum** next to the **Porthmadog Pottery**.

i High Street

Drive along the A487 before turning right on to an unclassified road to Portmeirion.

Portmeirion, Gwynedd

7 This Italianate garden village, surrounded by woods and beaches, was created by the Welsh architect Sir Clough Williams-Ellis to show that development is possible without destroying a beautiful site. Portmeirion was used as the setting for the 1960s cult television series *The Prisoner*, and now produces a distinctive range of colourful pottery.

Return to and take the A487 eastwards, turning left on to the A496 at Maentwrog. Shortly turn right on to the B4391 which joins the A470 at Ffestiniog. Turn left on to the A470 and continue to Blaenau Ffestiniog.

The exotic style of Portmeirion, unique and intriguing

Blaenau Ffestiniog, Gwynedd

8 Slate is all around this town, which depended for its livelihood on the quarries, until demand for slate fell away. Now visitors can get first-hand experience of the slate miners' working conditions at the **Llechwedd Slate Caverns**, where the Deep Mine tour will take you down on Britain's steepest passenger incline. Just above the town is the world's largest slate mine at **Gloddfa Ganol**, where you can walk into the mine and see craftsmen at work. A modern industry is established at Tanygrisiau, where hydro electricity is produced in a pumped storage scheme. Drive up the mountain road to the **Stwlan**

Dam for the remarkable view along the Vale of Ffestiniog. The **Ffestiniog Railway** runs through 13½ (22km) scenic miles to Porthmadog, (see page 59), and the more energetic can visit the **Rhiwgoch dry ski slope** at Trawsfynydd Holiday Village.

i High Street

Continue along the A470 to Betws-y-Coed.

Betws-y-Coed, Gwynedd

9 Betws-y-Coed is a popular inland resort set among forested land and magnificent mountains. The River Conwy is met by three tributaries here, and there are numerous bridges, waterfalls, and river pools with walks and play areas for children. Upstream are the **Swallow Falls**, one of the most famous of all tourist attractions in North Wales, and downstream is **Fairy Glen**, a much photographed and painted beauty spot. Back in the centre of the small town, there are many interesting shops and a craft centre. The 14th-century **Church of St Mary** has a Norman font and an effigy of the great-nephew of Llywelyn the Great. There is also a **Motor Museum** here.

i Royal Oak Stables

Leave Betws-y-Coed on the A5, shortly turning right on to the B5106 and follow it north for 4 miles (6km) to Llanrwst.

Llanrwst, Gwynedd

10 This historic market town is set in a delightful landscape of hills, forests, rivers and lakes. The **bridge** was designed by Inigo Jones in 1636, and the **Gwydir Chapel** contains the coffin of Llywelyn, Prince of Wales. Take a tour around the **Trefriw Wells Roman Spa**, where the water has been used as an aid to healthy living since Roman times, and is said to ease rheumatism and nervous tension. At the **Trefriw Woollen Mills**, you can see bedspreads and tweeds being manufactured, using electricity generated from the River Crafnant.

Continue along the A470 to Tal-y-Cafn.

Tal-y-Cafn, Gwynedd

11 The 80-acre (32-hectare) garden at **Bodnant** is claimed to be one of the finest gardens in the world. Now owned by the National Trust, it is located in the beautiful Conwy Valley, with views out to the Snowdon mountains. Throughout the year visitors can find much of interest, with native and exotic trees and flowers, and there is a nursery where plants are propagated.

Keep going along the A470 and then the A547 to Colwyn Bay.

Colwyn Bay, Clwyd

12 Colwyn Bay is a lively seaside town, which grew in the late 19th century as a result of the arrival of the railway, and the pier, promenade and many hotels and shops date from this period. The town is famous for its parks and gardens and has often been the winner of the 'Wales in Bloom' competition. The **Welsh**

The route to Snowdon starts here, at the Llanberis Pass

Mountain Zoo has chimpanzees, free-flying eagles, a sealion display and jungle adventure land. Other wild animals, though less lively, can be seen in the **Dinosaur World** in Eirias Park, which contains the largest collection of model dinosaurs in the British Isles.

ⓘ Station Road

Follow the B5115 coast road for 6 miles (10km) to Llandudno.

Llandudno, Gwynedd

13 St Tudno gave his name to the town in the 5th century, and a church still stands on the site of his cell. The town is the largest holiday resort in Wales, with two excellent sandy beaches situated between the headlands of Great and Little Orme. The **Great Orme Country Park** can be reached on the **Great Orme Tramway**, which has been taking passengers up to the top of the 679-foot (207m) summit since 1902. The energetic can enjoy the **artificial ski slope** and the 2,300-foot (700m) **toboggan run**, and there are fun rides for the children. A purpose-built resort, Llandudno retains some of its Victorian elegance while catering for modern visitors. Lewis Carroll was an early visitor and Alice Liddell for whom he wrote *Alice in Wonderland*, stayed here at her family's summer residence. A White Rabbit statue recalls Carroll's connections with the town, and there is an Alice exhibition in **The Rabbit Hole**, on Trinity Square.

ⓘ Chapel Street

Drive south along the A546 for 5 miles (8km) to Conwy.

Conwy, Gwynedd

14 The distinctive **castle** of Conwy, with its cluster of towers, dominates the town, and inside it is a model of the castle and town as they were in the 14th century. This ancient city still has its complete medieval walls, and you can take a pleasant stroll along the ramparts. There are three remarkable bridges crossing the river, including the **Conwy Suspension Bridge**, designed and built by Thomas Telford in 1826 and renovated in 1990. The **smallest house in Britain**, a mere 6 feet (2m) wide and 10 feet (3m) high, stands on the quay. Nature lovers might enjoy a visit to the **Butterfly House** in Bodlodeb Park, where exotic varieties fly freely around in a natural environment.

ⓘ Conwy Castle Visitor Centre

Head west along the A55 to Penmaenmawr and further along to Llanfairfechan.

Llanfairfechan, Gwynedd

15 Penmaenmawr has one of the finest beaches in North Wales, stretching between two granite headlands, and this is a fun holiday centre for the children. Further along, at Llanfairfechan, there is a sandy beach and beautiful inland scenery. There are excellent walks near by, notably up to the **Aber Falls**, 3 miles (5km) west of the town. The village of Aber was once the location of the palace of the Welsh king, Llywelyn the Great.

Keep on along the A55 before turning right on to the A5122 passing Penrhyn Castle on the return to Bangor.

Bangor – Menai Bridge 3 (5)
Menai Bridge – Caernarfon 9 (14)
Caernarfon – Llanrug 4 (6)
Llanrug – Llanberis 4 (6)
Llanberis – Beddgelert 14 (23)
Beddgelert – Porthmadog 8 (13)
Porthmadog – Portmeirion 3 (5)
Portmeirion – Blaenau Ffestiniog 12 (19)
Blaenau Ffestiniog – Betws-y-Coed 12 (19)
Betws-y-Coed - Llanrwst 4 (6)
Llanrwst – Tal-y-Cafn 7 (11)
Tal-y-Cafn – Colwyn Bay 7 (11)
Colwyn Bay – Llandudno 6 (10)
Llandudno – Conwy 5 (8)
Conwy – Llanfairfechan 7 (11)
Llanfairfechan – Bangor 8 (13)

SPECIAL TO...

'Perhaps in the whole world there is no region more picturesquely beautiful than Snowdonia,' said George Borrow in his book Wild Wales, written after his travels through Wales in the 1850s. It certainly is a special place, contained in the 840 square miles (2,175sq km) of the **Snowdonia National Park**. There are mountain peaks over 3,000 feet (915m) high, as well as miles of coastline and sandy beaches, and old mines and quarries, museums, castles and railways add further interest to this remarkable area.

SCENIC ROUTES

The view from **Menai Bridge** takes in Anglesey, a delightful blend of sea and landscape, while just outside Beddgelert is the **Aberglaslyn Pass**, a mixture of steep slopes, rocky outcrops and a turbulent, tumbling stream partially hidden beneath trees.

CENTRAL ENGLAND & EAST ANGLIA

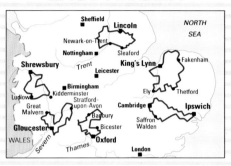

This large area of England stretches from the Welsh Borders to the North Sea, and covers a great variety of scenery: volcanic peaks in Shropshire; the steep scarp of the Cotswolds; the lowlands of East Anglia, and the flat Fens near King's Lynn.

The Fens and East Anglia are rich agricultural lands, growing potatoes, sugar beet and flowers and large expanses of prairie-like wheat fields. Further west, in the cattle country of Shropshire and Gloucestershire, the climate is wetter and the countryside takes on a patchwork appearance – in marked contrast to the open landscapes of Norfolk, Suffolk and Lincolnshire. On the higher lands of the Cotswolds, a golden, mellow stone is used to build walls and houses, giving a gentle beauty to farmland, villages and towns. Grand mansions such as Blenheim Palace and imposing churches have been built out of the Cotswold limestone, as have some of the Oxford colleges.

Fine churches are characteristic of this area and are generally the result of wealth earned from sheep farming and the sale of wool.

The Cambridge colleges include some of the most impressive buildings in England, but perhaps the most dramatic sight on this flat landscape is Ely cathedral, which can be seen from many miles away.

Other striking landmarks on the fenlands are the windmills, which were once vitally important means of pumping away surplus water.

From Lincoln the landscape changes as the tour moves into Robin Hood country, where a considerable expanse of forest has survived. There are also areas of forest to be seen on the Shrewsbury tour which follows the trail of industrial development, visiting Ironbridge, the birthplace of the 'industrial revolution'. After tracing the achievements of industry you can celebrate a literary genius at Stratford, on the Gloucester tour, where visitors from all over the world make their pilgrimage to the birthplace of William Shakespeare.

Lincoln

Lincoln's triple-towered cathedral dominates the city and the surrounding countryside, from its site on a limestone ridge overlooking the River Witham. A fascinating collection of old buildings can be seen in the cathedral close, including the old tithe barn and the Bishop's Palace and the 11th-century castle sits high on the city's steep hill. Other attractions include the Museum of Lincolnshire Life and the City and County Museum.

King's Lynn

This historic port and market town grew up in the 'Lin', a marshy area alongside the River Ouse along which ships travelled, bringing wealth into the town. Warehouses and merchants' houses are seen today, but particularly notable features include the amalgam of buildings forming the Guildhall; the 1683 Custom House, standing alone alongside the quay; and the 12th-century St Margaret's Church.

The Fenland beauty of Hemingford Grey on the River Ouse

One of Norfolk's glorious windmills at Cley-next-the-Sea

Ipswich

There shas been a settlement here since the Stone Age, but the port's real development started with Anglo-Saxon settlers in the 7th century. Cardinal Wolsey was born here in 1475. Industry has contributed much to the growth of this important regional and shopping centre, and there are some fine old buildings, such as the 16th-century Ancient House and the Custom House. The Ipswich Museum and the Wolsey Art Gallery are both worth a visit.

Oxford

Oxford is a captivating place. Its ancient university buildings in their mellow stone have a tranquil dignity, despite being within walking distance of the busy shopping centre. Magdalene, built in the 15th century, is a particularly beautiful college. The 17th-century Ashmolean is Britain's oldest museum and the Bodleian Library, begun in 1598, contains over 5 million books. There are countless other collections and museums and a walk through the streets or along the Cherwell or Thames will convey the city's unique charm.

Gloucester

The Romans built the fortified port of Glevum here to aid their attack on Wales; a small part of the wall survives, and there are many more relics to be seen in the City Museum. Gloucester's cathedral is one of the finest in the world, with a massive nave and 14th- to early 15th-century cloisters. The port has declined in recent years, but be sure to visit the National Waterways Museum in the Llanthony Warehouse.

Shrewsbury

Shrewsbury, on the River Severn is bordered by parkland and crossed by many bridges. The red sandstone castle guards a narrow strip of land leading into the original town, where there are many fascinating buildings including Rawley's Mansion and the Lion Coaching Inn, as well as a good selection of modern shops. The famous Shrewsbury School, where Charles Darwin was a pupil, looks down on the town and the river.

2 days – 122 miles (196km)

THROUGH FEN, FOREST & FARMLAND

Lincoln • Bardney • Woodhall Spa • Heckington
Sleaford • Leadenham • Newark-on-Trent • Southwell
Edwinstowe • North Leverton • Dunham Bridge • Lincoln

This is a tour through history and legend, visiting the land of Robin Hood, one of England's most famous folk heroes. It crosses the edge of the fenland region of Britain, taking in the great ducal estates of Nottinghamshire – Clumber Park, Thoresby Hall and Welbeck Abbey – as well as the ancient woodlands of Sherwood Forest.

Sherwood Forest, forever the home of the Robin Hood legends

i 9 Castle Hill; 21 Cornhill, Lincoln

From Lincoln take the B1190 east for 10 miles (16km) to Bardney.

Bardney, Lincolnshire

1 A small fen town on the River Witham, Bardney is dominated by its sugar beet factory, which was opened in 1927. The town's appearance is more practical than beautiful, but there are some fine examples of Georgian buildings to be seen among the Victorian houses. **Bardney Abbey**, dating from the 7th century, was destroyed by Vikings and refounded in 1087. Ethelred the Unready built **Tupholme Abbey**, 2 miles (3km) beyond the river bridge, and restoration work is being carried out here.

Continue along the B1190, then just after Bucknall turn south on to unclassified roads to Woodhall Spa.

Woodhall Spa, Lincolnshire

2 This inland watering place was once famous for its natural springs and has a pump room built in the 19th century after the discovery of medicinal waters. Today it is best known for its championship **golf course**. The 60-foot (18m) **Tower on the Moor** is thought to have been erected by the builders of **Tattershall Castle**, further south, whose fine keep is a relic of the castle built in 1440 by Ralph Cromwell, one of the richest men in the kingdom. He also built a magnificent collegiate church, in which perpetual prayers for his soul were to be said. There are excellent views from the castle looking across the low countryside as far as Lincoln and Boston. The only working fen steam engine in the country is at near by **Dogdyke Pumping Station**, worth a visit.

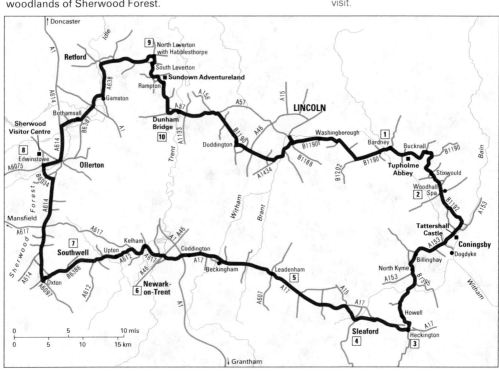

Heckington Windmill, restored to use on an original site

From Tattershall take the A153, the B1395 at North Kyme, and in a short distance turn right on to an unclassified road, crossing the A17 into Heckington.

Heckington, Lincolnshire

3 The flat, exposed landscape round Heckington is an ideal location for a windmill, and there has been one on the same site since 1830. The Friends of **Heckington Windmill** have fully restored the present mill, which is the only eight-sailed windmill still working in the country, and was used for drainage as well as grinding corn. The Information Centre next door to it is in the **Pea Room**, which until the 1960s was used for sorting pea seeds. One of the pubs in the village, the **Nag's Head**, claims that Dick Turpin, the infamous highwayman, once stayed there. The magnificent decorated cruciform **church** dates from the 14th century.

ⓘ The Pearoom Craft Centre, Station Yard

Follow the B1394, then the A17 for 5 miles (8km) to Sleaford, entering the town on the B1394.

Sleaford, Lincolnshire

4 Sleaford is a small town set on the River Slea and the partly navigable **Sleaford Canal. St Denys' Church**, which dominates the town, has a 144-foot (44m) solid stone spire, one of the oldest in the country, and its window tracery is exceptionally fine. The **Black Bull Inn**'s sign dates from 1689 and illustrates the old sport of bull-baiting, which continued in these parts until 1807. The mounds beside **Castle Causeway** are all that remains of the 12th-century castle, where King John was taken ill with a fatal fever on the night after losing his crown jewels while crossing the Wash.

ⓘ Money's Yard, Carre Street

Take the A15 north to rejoin the A17 and continue to Leadenham.

Leadenham, Lincolnshire

5 This little village grew up along the line of limestone hills called Lincoln Cliff, which stretches from near Humberside as far south as Grantham. It is worth visiting just for the lovely **church spire**, but there are many attractive stone houses and the **Old Hall** is built entirely of golden-coloured stone.

Follow the A17 for a further 10 miles (16km) to Newark-on-Trent.

Newark-on-Trent, Nottinghamshire

6 The sign on the edge of the town reads 'Historic Newark-on-Trent', and this is certainly a treasure house of history. The ruined 12th-century **castle** is where King John died in 1216, and stands opposite the **Ossington Coffee Tavern**, a Victorian flight of fancy. Travellers have been passing through the town for centuries: the Roman Fosse Way and

the Great North Road intersect near by, and the River Trent has been canalised here. The cobblestoned market place, the scene of Prime Minister William Gladstone's first major political speech, still survives, and you cannot miss the massive 252-foot (77m) spire of **St Mary Magdalen**, which is 30 feet (9m) higher than the total length of the church.

ⓘ The Gilstrap Centre, Castlegate

Take the A617 and the A612 west for 8 miles (13km) to Southwell.

Southwell, Nottinghamshire

7 Visitors to this market town are taken by surprise as the spires of the magnificent **Minster** suddenly come into view above the rolling countryside. This 12th- and 13th-century building, with a Romanesque nave and transept, is the mother church of Nottinghamshire and replaced an earlier Saxon church. Charles I spent his last few hours of freedom at the **Saracen's Head Inn**, just along the road, and another famous visitor, the poet Lord Byron, often stayed at **Burgage Manor** near by – Byron wrote the well-known epitaph for the local carrier, John Adams, who died of drunkenness:
John Adams lies here, of the parish of Southwell,
A carrier who carried his can to his mouth well,
He carried too much, and he carried so fast,
He could carry no more – and so was carried at last.

BACK TO NATURE

1 **Chamber's Wood**, near Bardney, is a Forestry Commission oak woodland which is particularly good for the birdwatcher, especially in the spring when everything is singing. Look for several species of tits as well as chaffinches, woodpeckers, nuthatches and treecreepers. Interesting flowers include giant bellflower and lily of the valley.

RECOMMENDED WALKS

4 Pleasant walks in the Sleaford area include the **Culverthorpe Walk**, starting from a lakeside picnic site southwest of Sleaford, and the **Blankney Walk** to the north of Sleaford, near the B1188.

FOR HISTORY BUFFS

6 Lady Godiva of Coventry fame and wife of Earl Leofric of Mercia, was the first official owner of the town of Newark, and presented it to the monastery of Stow, further down the River Trent. In the next century Newark was owned by the Bishop of Lincoln, who used the stone to rebuild the wooden castle. The new version was destroyed by Oliver Cromwell's troops.

SPECIAL TO...

7 The spires of Southwell's Norman **Minster** are visible for miles around. It was built during the 12th century and contains early English Gothic as well as Norman architecture, which has survived turbulent times: during the Civil War, Cromwell's soldiers stabled their horses in the nave. The octagonal Chapter House is a unique feature, dating from the 13th century, with twin Norman towers.

SCENIC ROUTES

On the approach to Lincoln along the **B1190** there is a striking view of its towers and spires. The flat countryside means that the main views are of settlements, but the landscape seen from the Lincoln cliff is picturesque.

FOR CHILDREN

9 Sundown Adventureland is a children's theme park on the road from North Leverton to Rampton. Its many attractions include a pirate ship, Noah's ark and a sleeping dragon. There are secret passages to explore in a Tudor village and you might come across bank raiders on a Western street, or Goldilocks and Red Riding Hood. There is also a miniature farm with pets and farm animals.

Take the B6386 to Oxton, then the A6097 north which becomes the A614, and finally turn left on to the B6034 to Edwinstowe.

Edwinstowe, Nottinghamshire

8 Edwinstowe, in the Sherwood Forest area, is an old colliery village, and it was at St Mary's Church that Maid Marian is said to have married Robin Hood. The massive and ancient **Major Oak**, named after Major Rooke, a local 18th-century antiquary, is claimed to be the oldest tree in the forest. It is 40 feet (12m) round its base, but needs a bit of propping up nowadays. Near by is the **Sherwood Visitor Centre**, where there are walks, nature trails, exhibitions and amusements. **Sherwood Forest Village**, just down the road, is a holiday complex with indoor facilities.

i Sherwood Information Centre, Church Street

Return via the A6075 to the A614 heading north then turn right on to unclassified roads passing Bothamsall, then along the B6387 crossing the A1 to the A638 to Retford. Take unclassified roads east from Retford to North Leverton and on to Rampton.

North Leverton, Nottinghamshire

9 Dutch-style houses give this village a flavour of Holland, which fits in well with the flat, fenland landscape. A **windmill**, three storeys high and

A surfeit of food and drink caused King John's death at Newark in 1216!

still in working order, stands above the plain, but is dwarfed by the vast cooling towers of the power station to the north along the Trent valley. Further south is the village of Rampton, surrounded by rich farmland criss-crossed with drainage ditches, used to reclaim the area from marshland.

Continue south along unclassified roads then join the A57 to Dunham Bridge.

Dunham Bridge, Nottinghamshire

10 Prepare to pay when you cross the River Trent, as a toll is levied here – a rare occurrence on British roads. The A57 out of Dunham runs alongside a major drainage ditch which dates from Roman times. Further along, Doddington brings you back into Lincolnshire. The landscape round here has been drained and cultivated for hundreds of years, and this delightful village has a fine Elizabethan hall as its focal point, with impressive ceramics and a medieval scold's bridle is among many other curiosities.

Return to Lincoln on the B1190.

Norfolk's largest seaside resort is at Hunstanton

ℹ The Old Gaol House, Saturday Market Place, King's Lynn

Take the A47 for 14 miles (22km) to Wisbech, entering the town via the B198.

Wisbech, Cambridgeshire

1 Wisbech is at the centre of a rich flower- and fruit-growing area. It was once only 4 miles (6km) from the sea, but due to land reclamation is now 11 miles (17km) inland. The **Wisbech and Fenland Museum** illustrates local history. Near by is the **Aviation Museum**, containing an interesting but rather morbid exhibition of aircraft equipment recovered from crashes in the area. The **church** has two naves, and a Braille Plan for blind visitors in the garden. The **Brinks**, two rows of houses along the River Neme, are among the finest examples of Georgian architecture in England, and **Peckover House** contains fine panelling and furniture; in its garden is the ginkgo, or maidenhair tree – the tallest in the land until a storm took away the top.

ℹ District Library, Ely Place

Follow the A1101, then the A1122 to Downham Market for 13 miles (21km).

Downham Market, Norfolk

2 There has been a settlement in this area since Roman times. **Denver Sluice**, 2 miles (3km) away, is where the River Great Ouse and the Old and New Bedford Rivers are regulated in order to prevent flood-

FEN, FARM & COAST

King's Lynn • Wisbech • Downham Market • Ely
Weeting • Thetford • East Dereham • Fakenham
Houghton St Giles • Wells-next-the-Sea • Holkham
Burnham Market • Hunstanton • Sandringham • King's Lynn

Through flat fields and across the fenland, you are drawn to the magnificence of Ely's cathedral, then on to the undulating ground of rural Norfolk. The farming landscape continues to the coast, before ending with lavender and a royal residence.

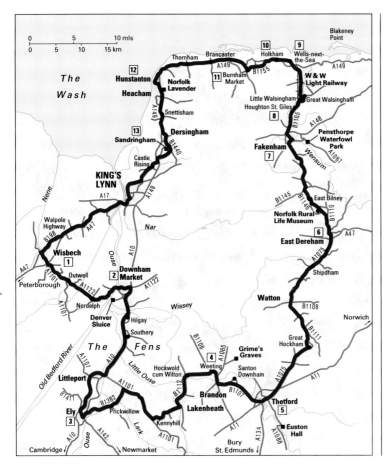

SCENIC ROUTES

Driving anywhere near Ely, the tower of the cathedral will draw you towards it like a magnet. Near Thetford, dark forests dominate the scene, but there are still a few patches of open heathland. In August the golden fields of wheat make a delightful sight, and an incomparable treat is to be had near Heacham when all the lavender fields are in flower.

The broads near Downham Market, eternally popular with visitors

4 Grime's Graves, named after the Anglo-Saxon god Grim, are situated on a patch of common land in Breckland. These grassy hollows are about 4,000 years old, and this is the largest known group of flint mines in Britain. You can climb down one on an iron ladder to see where the miners worked with wooden tools or deer antlers.

9 East of Wells-next-the-Sea, much of the coastline is owned by the National Trust, and there are several miles of nature reserves. The sand and shingle spit of Blakeney Point can be reached by foot from Cley, or by boat from Blakeney or Morston Quay. Common and sandwich terns nest on the spit, together with waders such as ringed plover and oystercatcher, and several species of duck. The Norfolk Naturalists' Trust reserve at Cley has hides overlooking pools and reedbeds. Bitterns, spoonbills, bearded tits and grey herons are regularly seen and a wide range of waders can be found during migration times.

ing. The most interesting building in the town is the Church of St Edmund, with its Early English tower.

Leave Downham Market eastwards to join the A10 then turn south and follow to Ely.

Ely, Cambridgeshire

3 Ely ('Eel Island') refers to the staple diet of the Saxons who once lived here. The Fens cathedral city is still a small market centre with ancient buildings and medieval gateways but has a busy quayside. It was founded as a religious community in the 7th century, and during the Norman Invasion was the centre of Anglo-Saxon resistance under Hereward the Wake. Ely also has a parish church, St Mary's, and the vicarage was the home of Oliver Cromwell for 11 years. Nine hundred-year-old Ely Cathedral's greatest glory is its unique octagon, designed by Alan de Walsingham after the earlier tower had collapsed in 1322.

ⓘ Oliver Cromwell's House, 29 St Mary's Street

Leave Ely on the B1382 through Prickwillow, then take the A1101 to Kennyhill, turning left on to an unclassified road to Lakenheath. Pick up the B1112 as far as Hockwold cum Wilton, and finally another unclassified road to Weeting.

Weeting, Norfolk

4 Weeting is a good centre for exploring Breckland, a region of heathland that straddles the Suffolk and Norfolk border. Grime's Graves are and Thetford Forest Park is at Santon Downham. There are deer and red squirrels in the forest, and a rich variety of trees. Weeting Heath is the place to see the classic Breckland bird, the stone curlew.

Follow the B1106 and A1065 to Brandon, then the B1107 for the remaining 8 miles (13km) to Thetford.

Thetford, Norfolk

5 Formerly the capital of the region, Thetford is a cathedral city and contained as many as five monasteries. Some of the oldest fragments are the remains of the 12th-century Cluniac priory, Castle Hill, the site of Iron Age earthworks, and a Norman castle mound. You should find time to visit Euston Hall, the 18th-century home of the Duke and Duchess of Grafton, which has fine paintings by Stubbs, Van Dyck and Lely. The 15th-century timber-framed Ancient House Museum has beautifully carved beam ceilings and exhibits on local history.

Leave Thetford on the A1075 heading northwards to East Dereham.

East Dereham, Norfolk

6 St Withburga founded a nunnery here in the 7th century, and St Withburga's Well is in the churchyard of St Nicholas's Church. The town has some fine Georgian buildings, and Bishop Bonner's Cottage has attractive pargeting. At Gressenhall, on the road north to Fakenham, is the Norfolk Rural Life Museum and Union Farm, which has rare breeds of sheep, cattle, pigs and poultry, and a museum on farming.

From East Dereham continue northwards on the B1110, then the B1146 to Fakenham.

Fakenham, Norfolk

7 Fakenham is a delightful small market town which dates from Saxon times. Its parish church has a commanding 15th-century tower, and the two old coaching inns in the Market Place have traces of earlier architecture behind their Georgian façades. The fascinating Gas Museum, which is open on occasional days throughout the summer, explains how gas was made and contains the only complete gasworks in England. Just a mile away is the Pensthorpe Waterfowl Park, which houses a large selection of birds, and aims to protect waterfowl and wetland habitats.

ⓘ Red Lion House, 37 Market Place

Cross the A148 and follow the B1105 for 4 miles (6km) to Houghton St Giles.

Houghton St Giles, Norfolk

8 The attractive village of Houghton St Giles has old links with Walsingham, including a small chapel on the old Walsingham Way, known as the **Slipper Chapel** because pilgrims would remove their shoes before completing their journey barefoot to Little Walsingham, which has been a Christian shrine since 1061. The **Anglican Shrine** and the **Roman Catholic Shrine** are at either end of the **Holy Mile**, and a ruined abbey stands in pleasant gardens. Great Walsingham, just a few minutes along the **B1388** from Little Walsingham, is noted for its textile centre, where you can watch the screen-printing process.

ⓘ Shire Hall Museum, Common Place, Little Walsingham

Return to the B1105 from Great Walsingham and follow to Wells-next-the-Sea.

Wells-next-the-Sea, Norfolk

9 The **Wells and Walsingham Light Railway** runs through 4 miles (6km) of countryside to the famous pilgrimage villages of Walsingham, and is the longest 10¼-inch (26cm) narrow-gauge steam railway in the world. The town of Wells still has many of its 18th- and 19th-century houses, set in a network of alleys and yards near the small quay, which first started trading in wool over 600 years ago.

ⓘ Staithe Street

Follow the A149, west for 2 miles (3km) to Holkham.

Holkham, Norfolk

10 In a beautiful deer park with a lake landscaped by Capability Brown, is the 18th-century mansion of **Holkham Hall**, just south of the village of Holkham. Its art collection includes work by Rubens, Van Dyck and Gainsborough and there is an amazing marble hall. In the **Bygones Collection**, over 4,000 items have been assembled from kitchens, dairies and cars.

Continue further along the A149 then left on to the B1155 to Burnham Market.

Burnham Market, Norfolk

11 Burnham Market is the main village in a group of seven Burnhams, clustered closely together, and has a handsome, wide green surrounded by 18th-century houses. The Burnhams were made famous by Horatio Nelson, who probably learned to sail on the muddy creeks of the coast before being sent away to sea at the age of 12. He was born in 1758 at **Burnham Thorpe**, where his father was the rector, and the lectern in the church is made from timbers from his ship, the *Victory*.

Unique among East Anglian coastal towns, Hunstanton faces west

Return to the A149 for 12 miles (19km) to Hunstanton.

Hunstanton, Norfolk

12 Hunstanton developed as a seaside resort in the 19th century, and is famous for its red-and-white striped chalk cliffs and excellent beaches. At the **Sea Life Centre** fish, seals and crabs are all around as you walk through varied marine settings. England's only lavender farm, **Norfolk Lavender**, is just south of town, at Heacham. A national collection of lavender plants is being assembled here, and there is a herb garden with over 50 varieties of culinary and decorative plants.

ⓘ The Green

Head south on the A149, then the B1440 from Dersingham to Sandringham, and further south to Castle Rising.

Sandringham, Norfolk

13 The royal estate of Sandringham covers 20,000 acres (8,094 hectares) and was bought by Queen Victoria for the Prince of Wales in 1862. The extensive grounds contain the parish **Church of St Mary Magdalene**, a museum, nature trails and an adventure playground. A former royal residence can be seen at **Castle Rising**, where the castle was built in the 12 century for the Earls of Sussex but subsequently belonged to the Earls of Norfolk. Set within huge earthworks, the shell of the Great Hall is still impressive.

Take the B1439 back to rejoin the A149, then an unclassified road back to King's Lynn.

King's Lynn – Wisbech 14 (22)
Wisbech – Downham Market 13 (21)
Downham Market – Ely 14 (22)
Ely – Weeting 23 (37)
Weeting – Thetford 8 (13)
Thetford – East Dereham 22 (36)
East Dereham – Fakenham 13 (21)
Fakenham – Houghton St Giles 4 (6)
Houghton St Giles – Wells-next-the-Sea 6 (10)
Wells-next-the-Sea – Holkham 2 (3)
Holkham – Burnham Market 4 (6)
Burnham Market – Hunstanton 12 (19)
Hunstanton – Sandringham 8 (13)
Sandringham – King's Lynn 8 (13)

RECOMMENDED WALKS

12 Both the Norfolk Coastal Path and the Peddar's Way can be walked from Hunstanton, the one along the coast and the other through the heart of rural west Norfolk. Wherever you are on this tour of west Norfolk you will find a selection of gentle walks along rivers, across heathland, in the forests or along the coast.

FOR CHILDREN

12 For an active day out Hunstanton is an ideal place to take the children, with its sandy beach, rock pools and endless entertainment; and the **Oasis** all-weather leisure centre offers swirl pools, a toddlers' pool and a variety of indoor sports.

SPECIAL TO...

12 Hunstanton cliffs were laid down on the bed of the sea between 135 and 70 million years ago, in what geologists call the Cretaceous period. Different colours mark the layers of rock. The carstone is reddish or brown, and is often used locally as a building stone, and most of the chalk is white. It is in the chalk that fossils are found: bivalves similar to those found on the beach today, as well as brachiopods, belemnites and ammonites.

2 days – 143 miles (229km)

EAST ANGLIA'S CHURCHES & COLLEGES

Ipswich • East Bergholt • Sudbury • Castle Hedingham
Finchingfield • Thaxted • Saffron Walden • Duxford
Grantchester • Cambridge • Lode • Newmarket • Clare
Long Melford • Lavenham • Hadleigh • Ipswich

Thatch, stone and brick are major features of the villages in this rural area, but dominating the countryside are the churches and their spires. This gentle landscape, covered with colourful fields of rape in spring and wheat in summer, provided the inspiration for Constable's paintings and Brooke's poetry.

SCENIC ROUTES

The **Dick Turpin Heritage Route** passes through Saffron Walden and Thaxted, as well as other attractive villages, historic sites and open countryside. On the approach to Thaxted on the **B1051**, the church and the windmill add variety to the rural charm of the rich farmland.

ⓘ St Stephen's Church, St Stephen's Lane, Ipswich

*Take the **A137** from Ipswich, then right on to the **B1070** shortly after Brantham and finally an unclassified road via Flatford to East Bergholt.*

East Bergholt, Suffolk

1 The artist John Constable was born here in 1776 and said of the area: 'These scenes made me a painter'.

King's College Chapel

Clustered round the 15th-century **Church of St Mary**, with its unfinished tower and remarkable bell house, are Elizabethan cottages set in beautiful gardens. **Flatford Mill** now used as a Field Study Centre. **Willy Lott's Cottage**, an early 18th-century mill-house which appears in Constable's *The Hay Wain*, still stands beside the mill stream.

*Leave on an unclassified road, and cross the **A12** on to the **B1068** and **A134** to Sudbury.*

Sudbury, Suffolk

2 Charles Dickens used this ancient cloth and market town on the River Stour as the model for 'Eatanswill' in *Pickwick Papers*. There is a bronze statue to Thomas Gainsborough, the artist, who was born here in 1727, in an elegant Georgian town house now containing many of his paintings. The town was formerly a river port, and one of the old warehouses has been turned into the **Quay Theatre**. St Peter's Church has fine painted screen panels and a splendid piece of 15th-century embroidery on velvet, the 'Alderman's Pall'.

ⓘ Sudbury Town Hall, Market Hill

*Leave Sudbury on the **A131**, turning right on to the **B1058** to Castle Hedingham.*

Castle Hedingham, Essex

3 The De Vere family, Earls of Oxford, built **Hedingham Castle** on the hilltop in about 1140, and the banqueting hall with its minstrel gallery still survives. The keep overlooks medieval houses, which cluster round the Norman **Church of St Nicholas**. There are many reminders of the town's prosperous days in the 15th-century **Moot Hall** and the elegant Georgian houses of the wealthy wool merchants. Just outside the village is the **Colne Valley Railway**, where there are restored steam engines and carriages.

*Join the **A604** south for a short distance, then take unclassified roads on the right via Wethersfield, then right on to the **B1053** to Finchingfield.*

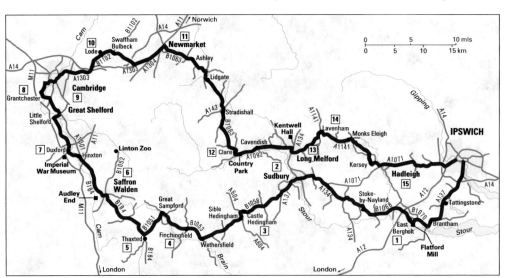

Finchingfield, Essex

4 Finchingfield's charm has survived in spite of its great popularity. One of its many fine buildings is the gabled and barge-boarded **Hill House**, set opposite a row of 16th-century cottages and Georgian houses. The **Church of St John the Baptist** has a Norman tower and Georgian-style bell-cote.

Continue on the B1053 to Great Sampford, then turn left on to the B1051 to Thaxted.

Thaxted, Essex

5 Thaxted's 14th-century, cathedral-like **flint church** is one of the largest in Essex, with a thin, graceful spire rising 181 feet (55m). Another tall building, the **tower windmill**, was built in 1804, and now houses a small rural museum; and the 15th-century **Guildhall** is built of local wood and plaster, on a foundation of flint. Composer Gustav Holst once lived in Thaxted, and Sir John Betjeman wrote of it: 'There are few places in England to equal the beauty, compactness and juxtaposition of medieval and Georgian architecture'.

Head northwest on the B184 to Saffron Walden.

Saffron Walden, Essex

6 Saffron Walden's **flint church** rivals that of Thaxted in magnificence and size; 200 feet (61m) long and nearly as high. Its spire was added in 1831. Wool was a major industry here, but the town also prospered from growing saffron for medicine and dyes. There are delightful old narrow streets to explore, and the **museum** has exhibitions of furniture, ceramics and toys. Jacobean **Audley End House**, near by, is in grounds landscaped by Capability Brown. Elizabeth I stayed here with the poet, Sir Philip Sidney, in 1578, and the rooms have been laid out to give a 'lived in' feeling.

ⓘ 1 Market Place

Continue on the B184 taking the A1301 at M11 junction and, in a

short distance, turn left on to an unclassified road through Hinxton to Duxford.

Duxford, Cambridgeshire

7 Duxford is a small village with a low, squat church and attractive thatched pub, the **John Barley Corn**. It is famous for the **Imperial War Museum** at Duxford Airfield, a former Battle of Britain fighter station.

Continue along unclassified roads through Little Shelford to Great Shelford, then left on to the A1301 and finally left on to unclassified roads again to Grantchester.

Grantchester, Cambridgeshire

8 Grantchester was immortalised in a poem written by Rupert Brooke in 1912 about the **Old Vicarage**, where he lived. The village has a characteristic low **church**, with a small spire protruding.

Head north for 3 miles (5km) to Cambridge.

Cambridge, Cambridgeshire

9 Cambridge became famous as a seat of learning when the University was established early in the 13th century, and its elegant colleges and chapels of mellow stone give this beautiful city a stately air. But this is an important market centre and a leader in high technology industries, as well as a university city, and there are many fine buildings and riverside parklands. **King's College Chapel** and the **Bridge of Sighs** are musts for all visitors, and in summer you can punt along the River Cam that flows around the city. No visit would be complete without seeing the **Fitzwilliam Museum**, with its priceless collections of porcelain, antiquities, paintings and armour.

ⓘ Wheeler Street

Take the A1303 east, then turn north on to the B1102 to Lode.

The quintessential English village: Finchingfield with its duckpond

SPECIAL TO...

1 Dedham, near East Bergholt, is proud of its connections with the artist John Constable. As a boy he went to school here and the beautiful scenery of Dedham Vale is now the area referred to as Constable Country. The **Art and Craft Centre** is on three floors of a converted congregational church, and prints, paintings and various crafts are on display and for sale. There is also a working pottery and a toy museum.

FOR CHILDREN

6 Linton Zoo, north of Saffron Walden on the B1052, was created by the Simmons family and opened in 1972. This is the **Cambridgeshire Wildlife Breeding Centre**, which focuses on conservation and education. Set in beautiful gardens, the centre has lions, pumas, snakes, owls, spiders and many others, as well as a

BACK TO NATURE

9 The Fowlmere RSPB Reserve lies just off the Royston to Cambridge road (A10) near the village of Fowlmere. It comprises an area of reed-bed with open water, and attracts breeding birds including sedge and reed warblers. In the winter, look for water rails, kingfishers and bearded tits.

Lode, Cambridgeshire

10 The small village of Lode is famous for the Augustinian priory known as **Anglesey Abbey**, founded in the 12th century and converted into a house in about 1600. The estate was bought by Huttleston Broughton, who created 100 acres (40 hectares) of gardens. A vast collection of paintings, sculpture and *objets d'art* has been assembled inside amid sumptuous furnishings. **Lode Watermill**, across the lode, or canal, that skirts the gardens, has been restored and grinds corn on the first Sunday of each month.

From Lode follow the B1102 to Swaffham Bulbeck, then follow an unclassified road to the A1303 to Newmarket.

The fine detail of window and wall on a house in Clare

Newmarket, Suffolk

11 Newmarket has been the headquarters of horse racing in Britain since the 17th century, and the **National Stud** and many training stables are located on the surrounding heath. Guided tours of the Stud, where you can see some of racing's superstars, are possible by appointment. The **National Horse Racing Museum** takes you back to the origins of racing. The famous **Rowley Mile** is named after a horse owned by Charles II, and the **Rutland Arms**, parts of which date back to his day, has kept some of its rooms in the style of the 1850s.

Follow the B1063 for 17 miles (27km) to Clare, then eastwards to Cavendish along the A1092.

Clare, Suffolk

12 This ancient little market town has excellent examples of parget-ing – fine plasterwork – such as those seen on the 15th-century **Priest's House** or **Ancient House**, now the local museum. The church, which has a most unusual design, is well worth visiting. Norman **Clare Castle** was built in 1090 and stands high on a 100-foot (30m) mound. At **Clare Castle Country Park** there is a butterfly garden, and you can take a

pleasant walk along the old railway track. Three miles (5km) east is Cavendish, the ancestral village of the Dukes of Devonshire, and its attractions include a 16th-century **farmhouse** near the church, and philanthropist Sue Ryder's 16th-century **rectory**, which contains memorabilia and photographs explaining the origins and aims of her work.

Continue east on the A1092, then turn south on to the A134 to Long Melford.

Long Melford, Suffolk

13 Long Melford is another of Suffolk's lovely villages, with fine wool merchants' houses. At the end of the mile-long main street is the **Church of the Holy Trinity**, one of the finest in the country, exhibiting a superb display of flushwork – ornate decoration in flint. The village green is overlooked by Elizabethan **Long Melford Hall**, a turreted Tudor mansion with tall chimneys. One mile (1.6km) north of the village is **Kentwell Hall**, a moated Elizabethan mansion with a brickpaved mosaic maze in the shape of a Tudor rose.

Follow unclassified roads northeast for 5 miles (8km) to Lavenham.

Lavenham, Suffolk

14 Lavenham's remarkable church, the **Church of St Peter and St Paul**, has a flint tower 140 feet (43m) high, and the **Guildhall**, an early 16th-century timber-framed building, contains a display of local history. The **Swan Inn** is a famous hostelry which has been carefully preserved. Some of the black-and-white buildings have been painted pink to add to the colour of this pretty village.

i Lady Street

Follow the A1141, turning right to pass through Kersey, then on to Hadleigh.

Hadleigh, Suffolk

15 Before reaching Hadleigh, enjoy the rural charm of Kersey, with its old priory, ducks paddling in the ford and thatched cottages. In Hadleigh itself, the **Guildhall** and **Deanery tower** are listed buildings dating from the 15th century. Interesting marks on the side of the 1813 **Corn Exchange** show where the brickwork was used by schoolchildren for sharpening back their slate pencils as they went to school.

i Toppesfield Hall

Return to Ipswich on the A1071.

Edward I built the first Banbury cross to mark a resting-place of his wife's coffin en route to London

ⓘ St Aldates, Oxford

Leave Oxford on the A44 and turn left along an unclassified road towards Cassington. Turn right to Bladon on the A4095 then left on the A44 to Woodstock.

Woodstock, Oxfordshire

1 You can stop off in Bladon, to visit the churchyard where Sir Winston Churchill and his wife and parents are buried, before continuing along the road to Blenheim, where he was born. **Blenheim Palace** was given to the Marlborough family by Queen Anne as a reward for a major victory by the 1st Duke of Marlborough over the French at Blenheim in 1704. Just outside the park is the old town of Woodstock, with its mellow stone buildings. Kings of England used to come here for the excellent hunting in the Forest of Wychwood, but modern visitors have gentler interests. A quiet hour can be spent in the **Oxfordshire County Museum**, in the town centre, where the history of the people and the changing landscape is conveyed in exhibitions which range from the Stone Age to the present time.

ⓘ Hensington Road

From Woodstock take the A44 turning left on to the B4437 to Charlbury and then the B4026 to Chipping Norton.

Chipping Norton, Oxfordshire

2 Gateway to the Cotswolds and historic market town, this was the market for the sheep farmers of the area, and the wide main street is a relic of those days (the name 'chipping' means market). There are many fine old stone buildings, including the **church**, **market hall**, pubs and big houses, but it is the fine **wool church** which dominates the town, one of over 40 in the Cotswolds. Paid for by the proceeds from sheep farming, it is mainly 14th- and 15th-century, but much of its stonework has been restored. Another of the town's landmarks is the chimney of **Bliss Tweed Mill** which is an important reminder of local history.

ⓘ 5 Middle Row

Take the B4026, then go north along the A3400 for just over a mile (1.6km) and turn left along an unclassified road signed Little Rollright.

Rollright Stones, Oxfordshire

3 This Bronze Age circle, which dates from earlier than 1000BC, was nearly as important as Stonehenge in the Neolithic period. Nicknamed the 'King's Men', it measures a full 100 feet (30m) across. Over the road is the **King Stone**, a monolith, and near by, just along the road, is the group of stones called the **Whispering Knights**, at the site of a prehistoric burial chamber. The surrounding countryside is patterned with stone walls of weathered limestone.

COTSWOLD WOOL & STONE

Oxford • Woodstock • Chipping Norton • Rollright Stones
Broughton • Banbury • Sulgrave • Aynho • Deddington
Steeple Aston • Bicester • Boarstall • Oxford

This is mainly a circuit of Cotswold countryside – a landscape of stone walls surrounding fertile fields and distinctive village architecture. The stone-built villages contain many fine churches, but the best known structure by far is the cross in the centre of Banbury. The family homes of two great men can be seen; one Englishman in Blenheim and one American in Sulgrave, both of whom influenced the world in their time.

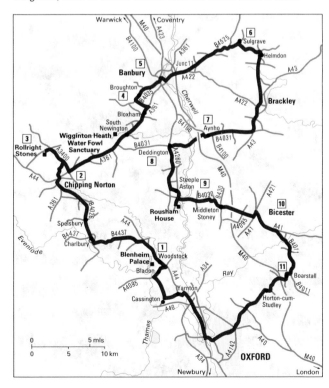

Return to the A3400 and turn south before branching left on to the A361, then turn left in Bloxham along unclassified roads to Broughton.

Broughton, Oxfordshire

4 Broughton Castle is a fortified manor rather than a castle, turned into an Elizabethan house of style by the Fiennes family in about 1600. Surrounded by a great moat lake, it is set in gorgeous parkland, and has a stone church near by. The present owners, Lord and Lady Saye and Sele, are descendants of the family that has lived here for centuries. Celia Fiennes, the 17th-century traveller and diarist, was a member of this family. William de Wykeham, founder of Winchester School and New College, Oxford, acquired the manor and converted the manor house into a castle. The medieval Great Hall is the most impressive room, and suits of armour from the Civil War are on show.

Drive 3 miles (5km) east along the B4035 to Banbury.

Banbury, Oxfordshire

5 Banbury is a town of charm and character, with its interesting buildings and narrow medieval streets. Famous for the nursery rhyme 'Ride a cock horse to Banbury Cross', the town is also known for its spice cakes, which have been made here since the 16th century. The unusual church with its round tower replaced an older one demolished in the 18th century. There is still a weekly street market, which has been held regularly for over 800 years, and there used to be a livestock market, too, but nowadays the animals are taken to a permanent site on the edge of town, Europe's largest cattle market.

The Rollright Stones, a Bronze Age circle of stones whose function remains shrouded in mystery

ⓘ Banbury Museum, 8 Horsefair

Head eastwards along the A422, turning left after 2 miles (3km) on to the B4525 to Sulgrave.

Sulgrave, Northamptonshire

6 The old manor in this attractive stone village was the home of ancestors of George Washington from 1539 to 1659, having been bought by Lawrence Washington, wool merchant and twice Mayor of Northampton. Not to be missed is the family coat of arms with its stars and stripes carved above the entrance porch, and the most treasured possession inside is an original oil painting of George Washington.

Take the unclassified road through Helmdon, heading south to Brackley to join the A43 and in a short distance right on to the B4031 to Aynho.

Aynho, Northamptonshire

7 This limestone village contains apricot trees from which, legend has it, fruit was paid as a toll to the Cartwrights, Lords of the Manor. They lived in the mansion in **Aynhoe Park**, and there are several memorials to them, including a Victorian marble cross in the church.

From Aynho go west along the B4031 to Deddington.

Deddington, Oxfordshire

8 Dominating this village, which is built out of the honey-coloured local stone, is the church, with each of its eight pinnacles topped with gilded vanes. **Castle House**, adjacent to the church, was formerly the rectory, and parts of the building date from the 14th century. The area has many links with the days of the Civil War, and Charles I is believed to have slept at the 16th-century **Castle Farm** near by.

*Drive southwards for 5 miles (8km) along the **A4260** and then left on to an unclassified road to Steeple Aston.*

Steeple Aston, Oxfordshire

9 Steeple Aston was winner of the Oxfordshire Best Kept Village Award in 1981 and 1983, and is still an eye-catching village. The village inn, **Hopcroft's Holt**, had associations with Claude Duval, a French highwayman who worked in these parts, and ended up on the Tyburn gallows. Just beyond Steeple Aston is the Jacobean mansion of **Rousham House**, built by Sir Robert Dormer in 1635 and still owned by the same family. William Kent improved the house in the 18th century by adding the wings and stable block. In the magnificent garden, the complete Kent layout has survived. There is a fine herd of rare Long Horn cattle in the park, and you should be sure not to miss the walled garden.

*Another unclassified road leads south on to the **B4030** in turn leading to the **A4095** for the 9 miles (14km) to Bicester.*

Bicester, Oxfordshire

10 Little can be seen of the Roman town at **Alchester**, to the south of Bicester, but excavations show

Broughton Castle is a fine example of a gracious Elizabethan manor

that people lived here from about the middle of the 1st century AD until the late Roman period. Bicester itself is a market town with many old streets. Its **church** contains elements of a 13th-century building, and there was once a 12th-century priory near by. The Bicester Hunt is based here, and several roads have wide verges for the horseriders to avoid traffic.

*Take the **A41** following the line of an old Roman road and then the **B4011** towards Thame before turning sharp right to Boarstall.*

Boarstall, Buckinghamshire

11 This tiny hamlet is the location of **Boarstall Tower**, an amazing stone gatehouse which was originally part of a massive fortified house. It dates from the 14th century and is now looked after by the National Trust, who also own **Boarstall Duck Decoy**. This 18th-century decoy is in 13 acres (5 hectares) of natural old woodland. Attractions include a small exhibition hall, nature trail and bird hide.

Take unclassified roads via Horton-cum-Studley along the edge of Otmoor for the return to Oxford.

Oxford – Woodstock 10 (16)
Woodstock – Chipping Norton 13 (21)
Chipping Norton – Rollright Stones 5 (8)
Rollright Stones – Broughton 14 (23)
Broughton – Banbury 3 (5)
Banbury – Sulgrave 7 (11)
Sulgrave – Aynho 13 (21)
Aynho – Deddington 3 (5)
Deddington – Steeple Aston 5 (8)
Steeple Aston – Bicester 9 (14)
Bicester – Boarstall 7 (11)
Boarstall – Oxford 10 (16)

2 days – 128 miles (207km)

THE RURAL HEART OF ENGLAND

Gloucester • Ledbury • Great Malvern • Tewkesbury
Bredon • Evesham • Alcester • Wilmcote
Stratford-upon-Avon • Chipping Campden • Buckland
Winchcombe • Cheltenham • Painswick • Gloucester

Across the Severn plain, through a gap in the Malvern Hills and into the Avon valley, this route eventually climbs up on to the hills of the Cotswolds, cut by winding rivers, where stone-built villages have become part of the countryside.

The unpretentious simplicity of Mary Arden's home, at Wilmcote

i St Michael's Tower, The Cross, Gloucester

Take the A417 for 17 miles (27km) to Ledbury.

Ledbury, Hereford and Worcester

1 This unspoilt market town of half-timbered buildings has many literary links: Browning and Wordsworth used to visit, and John Masefield was born here. Elizabeth Barrett Browning spent her childhood at **Hope End**, just out of town, and her father lies buried in the north aisle of **St Michael's Church**. One of the most attractive buildings is the 16th-century **Feathers Inn**, and **Ledbury Park** is the house Prince Rupert used as his headquarters during the Civil War. Nineteenth-century **Eastnor Castle** is surrounded by a beautiful park.

i 1 Church Lane

Follow the A449 through Wynds Gap and Malvern Wells to Great Malvern, 8 miles (13km).

Great Malvern, Hereford and Worcester

2 Pure spring water from the Malvern Hills made this a popular spa town in Victorian days. A steep flight of steps by the Mount Pleasant Hotel leads up to **St Anne's Well**, the source of this water. The town is centred round its greatest treasure, the **Priory Church of St Mary and St Michael**,

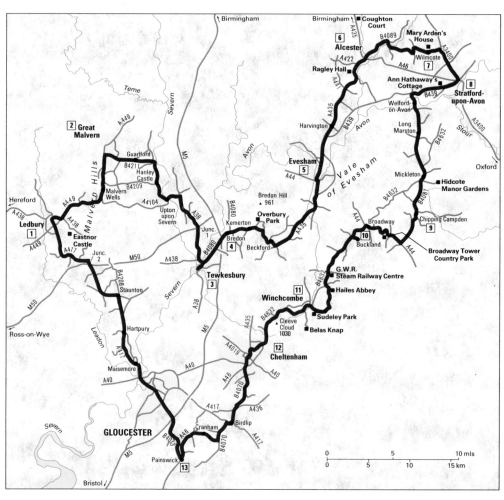

which contains exquisite 15th- and 16th-century stained glass and beautiful tiles. **Malvern Museum** portrays the town through the ages, and there is an elegant Victorian **bandstand** where bands play on Sunday afternoons in summer.

ⓘ Winter Gardens, Grange Road

Take the B4211 to Upton upon Severn, turning left on to the A4104, and in 1 mile (1.6km) on to the A38 to Tewkesbury.

Tewkesbury, Gloucestershire

3 Almost all Tewkesbury's buildings are old timber-framed structures, notably the **Bell Inn**, and the **Royal Hop Pole Inn** is mentioned in *The Pickwick Papers* by Charles Dickens. Tewkesbury Abbey is one of the finest Norman abbeys in the country and contains several medieval stained-glass windows.

ⓘ The Museum, 64 Barton Street

Return on the A38 for a short distance, then take the B4080 to Bredon.

Bredon, Hereford and Worcester

4 Bredon, alongside the River Avon, at the foot of Bredon Hill, is a picturebook village. Its impressive Norman church has a graceful spire which soars 160 feet (48m) high, and the **tithe barn** dates from the 14th century. A mile (1.6km) east is the village of Kemerton, with its fine church. **Overbury Park**, just outside the village, leads to Bredon Hill, which rises to 961 feet (293m). It has a fine Gothic **folly** on its slopes and the remains of prehistoric and Roman **earthworks** on its summit.

Continue along an unclassified road through Kemerton and Beckford, then take the A435 for 7 miles (11km) to Evesham.

Evesham, Hereford and Worcester

5 Evesham is a market town in the heart of the Vale of Evesham, noted for its fruit blossom in spring. A 15th-century half-timbered **gateway** in the market place is one of the few remains of **Evesham Abbey**. At the centre of town is the 110-foot (33m) high **Bell Tower**, which was built in 1539. There are two fine churches: 12th-century **All Saints' Church** and the **Church of St Lawrence**. A plaque near the river marks the burial spot of Simon de Montfort, the 'father of the English parliament', who led barons in revolt against Henry III and was killed at the Battle of Evesham in 1265.

ⓘ The Almonry Museum, Abbey Gate

Take the A435 for another 10 miles (16km) to Alcester.

Alcester, Warwickshire

6 Pronounced 'Olster', this former Roman town contains many old streets and houses, notably Malt Mill Lane, which is lined with ancient houses. **Coughton Court**, 2 miles (3km) to the north, is the family home

of the Throckmortons, who were implicated in the Gunpowder Plot to blow up Parliament in 1605. The house contains the 'Throckmorton coat', which was made in 1811 to prove that it was possible to take the wool off a sheep and produce a coat from it in one day! Southwest of town is **Ragley Hall**, a Jacobean mansion whose great hall is decorated with exquisite rococo plasterwork.

Follow the B4089, then unclassified roads east to Wilmcote.

Wilmcote, Warwickshire

7 This sprawling village is best known for the lovely timbered **farmhouse** which was the home of Mary Arden, Shakespeare's mother. It is now a **museum** of furniture and the farm buildings contain exhibitions of agricultural implements and country bygones, including man traps which were used to catch poachers.

Continue along the unclassified road, then the A3400 for 3 miles (5km) to Stratford-upon-Avon.

Stratford-upon-Avon, Warwickshire

8 Stratford has retained its role as a market town despite being one of the world's most famous tourist centres. **Shakespeare's Birthplace** in Henley Street is now a museum and contains exhibits about the poet's life. Stratford is full of interesting places to visit, including the **Royal Shakespeare Company Gallery** and the **World of Shakespeare**. One of the most ornate timbered houses is **Harvard House**, the former home of the mother of John Harvard, who founded Harvard University in the US. In a house in Greenhill Street, dating from Shakespeares' days, is the **National Teddy Bear Museum** which will appeal to all ages.

ⓘ Bridgefoot

Leave Stratford, going west along the B439 for 4 miles (6km) before turning south along unclassified roads through Welford-on-Avon and Long Marston to the B4632. Turn right and soon left on to the B4081 to Chipping Campden.

SCENIC ROUTES

Cotswold villages and towns are all attractive but the view over Cranham from the unclassified road to Painswick is one of the most exciting. The **Malvern Hills** and the dramatic silhouette of the **Herefordshire Beacon** (the British Camp) are best seen along the A449 from Ledbury.

RECOMMENDED WALKS

Footpaths on this tour range from very easy gentle strolls to much longer and arduous walks. A climb to the top of the **Worcestershire Beacons** in the Malverns will give one of the finest views in England, with the green undulations of Hereford to the west and the flatter Severn valley to the east.

SPECIAL TO...

8 With the exception of London, Shakespeare's Stratford is probably the best known town in England. A tour of selected locations can take you through his life, starting with his birthplace in Henley Street, then on to the 15th-century half-timbered Grammar School in Church Street, which he attended. Most famous of all is Anne Hathaway's cottage, home of the woman he was to marry. New Place, on Chapel Street, was the site of his last home.

The Royal Shakespeare Theatre at the Bard's birthplace, Stratford

The cream of the Cotswolds is to be found in Chipping Campden

Mercia. Its abbey, founded 797, was destroyed during the Dissolution, but the site has been excavated. The **Railway Museum** has many relics of the steam age, and the town hall houses the **Folk Museum** and a **Police Museum**. **Sudeley Park**, reached through the village, was once the house of Catherine Parr, the last of Henry VIII's wives. The magnificent gardens have been developed and renovated. Just east of town on the **B4632**, at the top of the hill at **Cleeve Hill**, are the remnants of a settlement and earthworks, and much good walking, including the **Cotswold Way**, a long distance footpath. **Cleeve Cloud**, 1031 feet (314m), is one of the highest points in the Cotswolds, and the views from its summit are quite spectacular.

[i] Town Hall, High Street

Continue along the B4632 to Cheltenham.

Cheltenham, Gloucestershire

12 Cheltenham started life as a typical Cotswold village, but the discovery of a mineral spring in 1718 turned it into a fashionable spa. The **Promenade**, a wide street with Regency houses, has been described as the most beautiful thoroughfare in Britain. The famous **Pittville Pump Room**, with its colonnade and dome, is a masterpiece of 19th-century Greek revival. There are many other old buildings and museums worth visiting, such as the **Gustav Holst Museum** housed in the composer's birthplace and containing rooms with period furnishing. The town is famous for its two schools, the **College for Boys** and **Cheltenham Ladies' College**.

[i] 77 Promenade

Take the B4070 south to Birdlip and follow the Stroud road until an unclassified road leads through Cranham and on to the A46 to Painswick.

Painswick, Gloucestershire

13 Painswick is an old wool town with many buildings of note, but is dominated by 15th-century **St Mary's Church** and its collection of '99' yew trees. Tradition says that only 99 will grow at any one time – the Devil always kills off the 100th. Among the town's many old houses are **Court House**, with its tall chimneys, and 18th-century **Painswick House**. South of town a few old **cloth mills** have survived on Painswick stream.

[i] Painswick Library, Stroud Road

Return to Gloucester on the B4073.

FOR CHILDREN

10 **Broadway Tower Country Park** is an ideal place to spend the day with the family. The late 18th-century mock castle has an observation room and telescope giving views over 12 counties. Other attractions include an educational display of local geology, an adventure playground, and a collection of rare animals.

FOR HISTORY BUFFS

11 From Winchcombe you can drive to within ¾ mile (1km) of the Bronze Age ancient long barrow at **Belas Knap**, probably the finest example of a false-entrance longbarrow in the Cotswolds. When it was excavated 36 skeletons were found in 10 separate chambers.

BACK TO NATURE

The **Wildfowl Trust** reserve at **Slimbridge**, southwest of Gloucester off the **A38**, is known the world over for its impressive collection of wildfowl. These are seen best in late winter and early spring when the males are in full breeding plumage and are displaying to the females.

Chipping Campden, Gloucestershire

9 Wool made this town rich, and it retains a wealth of beautiful architecture. The Jacobean **Market Hall** in the High Street was built in 1627, and the **Woolstaplers' Hall** is now the town museum. The **Church of St James** is one of the most splendid Cotswold churches. **Hidcote Manor Gardens**, to the northeast have six gardens with winter borders, camellia corners, terraces and walks.

[i] Woolstaplers Museum, High Street

Take the B4081 and the A44 through Broadway, then the B4632 and a minor road to Buckland.

Buckland, Gloucestershire

10 Buckland is a quiet village nestling at the foot of the Cotswolds, whose **rectory** is England's oldest and most complete medieval parsonage. Further along the B4632 is the **GWR Steam Railway Centre** at Toddington, where you can make a 6-mile (9km) round trip. Leave the B4632 to visit **Hailes Abbey**, where the old Cistercian ruins stand alongside the 12th-century parish **church**. In 1270 a small jar of blood, supposedly that of Christ, was given to the abbey, and brought it much fame as a centre of pilgrimage.

Follow the unclassified road to Winchcombe.

Winchcombe, Gloucestershire

11 This attractive town was once the capital of the Kingdom of

OLD VOLCANOES & BRIDGES IN SHROPSHIRE

The poet A E Housman celebrated his native Shropshire – including Much Wenlock – in A Shropshire Lad

ℹ️ The Square, Shrewsbury

Take the A458 as far as the ring road where unclassified roads lead to Cantlop Bridge and Acton Burnell.

Acton Burnell, Shropshire

1 On the edge of this picturesque village, with its timber-framed black-and-white cottages and grey-green stone buildings, is a **cast-iron bridge**, built in 1810 to a design by Thomas Telford. **Acton Burnell Castle** is a red sandstone ruin, which dates from the 13th century; it is said the first English Parliament met here in 1283. The **Church of St Mary** is almost entirely 13th-century, apart from its Victorian tower, and contains memorials to the Burnell family who held the manor in 1183. It also houses memorials to the Lees family, who owned the village in the 17th century and who were ancestors of General Robert E Lee, chief commander of the Southern forces in the American Civil war.

Follow unclassified roads via Frodesley then the A49 to Church Stretton.

Church Stretton, Shropshire

2 Church Stretton is in fact three settlements. All Stretton lies to the north of the main town, and Little Stretton stands 1½ miles (2.5km) south. The town's medieval remains are in the High Street, along with its 18th- and 19th-century buildings. The **Church of St Laurence** is partly 12th-century Norman with a 14th-century roof. In the south transept is a memorial to Sarah Smith, the Victorian novelist who wrote under the name of Hesba Stretton. The town was popular with Victorians who came to sample its natural spring water.

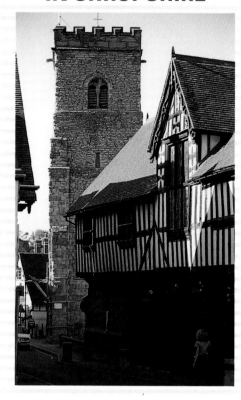

Shrewsbury • Acton Burnell • Church Stretton Craven Arms Ludlow • Cleehill • Bewdley • Bridgnorth Shipton • Much Wenlock • Ironbridge Wroxeter • Shrewbury

The Welsh border counties are among the greenest parts of Britain. Gentle hills and steep-sided volcanic cones add variety to the scenery. The Severn Valley is the birthplace of the industrial revolution, with the world's greatest collection of 19th-century industrial relics.

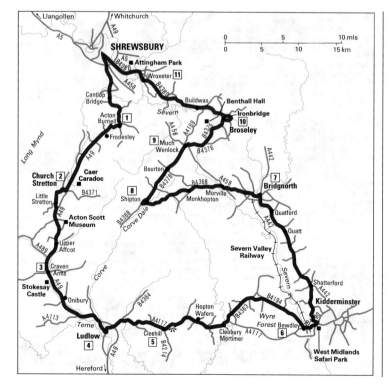

FOR CHILDREN

2 Acton Scott Working Farm Museum, near Church Stretton, shows life on a Shropshire farm before the introduction of the internal combustion engine. This is not just a show place but a going concern, and visitors can even lend a helping hand. The farm is stocked with rare breeds – it is one of the few places you can see the Tamworth pig – and has a fishpool, waymarked nature trail, café and paddocks. Strong boots and warm clothing are recommended.

distance. The strange 'golf ball' on 1,750-foot (533m) **Titterstone Clee Hill**, north of the village, is part of a satellite tracking station. Further along the **A4117**, running east, is Cleobury Mortimer, with its remarkable twisted wooden **church tower**. Hugh de Mortimer built a fortress here in 1160 and its earthworks can still be seen near the church.

Follow the B4363 turning right on to the B4194 through Wyre Forest to Bewdley.

Bewdley, Hereford and Worcester

6 This elegant Georgian town was a major port of England in the 17th and 18th centuries. For many years boats were manhandled up the River Severn by a hardy breed of boatmen called 'bow hauliers'. There are pleasant walks in the Wyre Forest, and the **Severn Valley Railway** runs to Bridgnorth through fields and woods. Near by is **West Midlands Safari Park**, a leisure park with animal reserves and amusements.

ⓘ Load Street

Take the B4190 towards Kidderminster turning left on to unclassified roads towards Shatterford, then turning left on to the A442 to Bridgnorth.

Bridgnorth, Shropshire

7 There are two parts to this historic market centre, connected by a winding main road, a cliff railway and a steep flight of steps. The original settlement was in the High Town, where **Bridgnorth Castle** was built. The only remaining fragment is the leaning tower, which is set at a steeper angle than the Leaning Tower of Pisa. The most graceful building is Italianate **St Mary Magdalene's Church**, built in 1792 by Thomas Telford. For railway enthusiasts there is not only the **Severn Valley Railway**, but also the funicular, linking the upper and lower parts of the town. In Low Town is **Bishop Percy's House**, a fine half-timbered building of 1580.

ⓘ The Library, Listley Street

Leave Bridgnorth on the A458, then after 3 miles (5km) turn left at Morville on to the B4368 to Shipton.

Shipton, Shropshire

8 Set in the heart of Corve Dale, with views of Brown Clee Hill to the south, this small village sits snugly in the midst of the green fields and valley. **Shipton Hall** is the focal point, a beautiful complex of stone buildings dating from 1587. There is an attractive walled garden, medieval dovecote and old parish church, as well as a fine 18th-century stable block.

Take the B4378 to Much Wenlock

Much Wenlock, Shropshire

9 This charming market town has many half-timbered buildings, notably the **Manor House**, the

FOR HISTORY BUFFS

4 Before Catharine of Aragon married Henry VIII she was his brother's bride. Prince Arthur, the eldest son of Henry VII, brought Catharine to Ludlow Castle and had the gardens designed in a series of walks for her. Arthur died at Ludlow and his younger brother Henry became king.

SCENIC ROUTES

In the Shipton area the scenery is gentle and the B4378 to Much Wenlock runs through Corve Dale with fine views of the River Corve. From Acton Burnell to Church Stretton, along the A49 and the unclassified road, the views are spectacular, with Long Mynd to the west and Caer Caradoc Hill, where it is thought the Romans defeated the British leader Caractacus in ad50, to the east.

RECOMMENDED WALKS

The **Shropshire Way** is a long distance walk from Whitchurch through Shrewsbury to Clun and the Clee Hills. There are several walks around Ludlow, notably across the Teme and on to Whitcliffe Common, which was the town's common land in the Middle Ages, and the Forestry Commission have several attractive, clearly marked walks, such as from the Wyre Forest centre near Bewdley.

Continue south along the B4370, joining the A49 to Craven Arms.

Craven Arms, Shropshire

3 This small village was originally the hamlet of Newton, but in the 19th century it developed and was named after a coaching inn. Today it is a centre for livestock auctions, at the foot of Wenlock Edge, a steep out-crop of limestone. **Stokesay Castle**, ½ mile (1km) along the road, is the best preserved and oldest example of a fortified manor house in England.

Keep on with the A49 a further 7 miles (11km) to Ludlow.

Ludlow, Shropshire

4 Ludlow is a pearl in a sea of riches and has been described as 'the perfect historic town', with nearly 500 listed buildings. Two buildings worthy of a visit are **Ludlow Castle**, which dates from Norman times, and the sandstone **Church of St Laurence**. Mainly 15th-century, it is the largest in the county and the ashes of the poet A E Housman lie in its churchyard. Near by are 17th-century **Feathers Hotel**, and the beautiful black-and-white **Reader's House**. **Ludlow Museum**, in Buttercross, tells the story of the town from Norman times, and a major arts festival takes place here in late June and early July.

ⓘ Castle Street

Take the A4117 going east for 6 miles (10km) to Cleehill.

Cleehill, Shropshire

5 East of Cleehill, on the A4117, is an **AA Viewpoint** which offers amazing views over Tenbury and the Teme Valley, towards the hills in the

Guildhall and **Raynald's Mansion**. Ruined **Wenlock Priory** was founded by St Milburga in the 7th century as a convent and destroyed by Danes in the 9th century. It was rebuilt by Lady Godiva and her husband, Leofric, in the 11th century, though it was soon destroyed again by the Normans. **Benthall Hall**, 4 miles (6km) north-east, is a 16th-century house with fine panelling, a carved oak staircase and mullioned windows.

🛈 The Museum, The Square

Leave Much Wenlock on the B4376 turning left on to the B4375. In a short distance turn left on to an unclassified road to Ironbridge.

The delightful township of Ironbridge took a leading role in the Industrial Revolution

Continue for 2 miles (3km) on an unclassified road to take the B4380 to Wroxeter.

Wroxeter, Shropshire

11 Near this quiet little village is the Roman town of *Viroconium*, which was the fourth largest town in Roman Britain. A walk round the site reveals the baths, a market hall and fragments of other buildings. The most impressive relic of the baths is the 20-foot (6m) wall, where a square entrance once had double doors leading to the *frigidarium* or 'cooling off' room. A **museum** displays pottery, painted plaster and coins from the site. Two miles (3km) northwest on the **B4380** is Atcham, where **Attingham Park** features magnificent gardens woodlands and a deer park. The gardens are open throughout the year, and the house

BACK TO NATURE

2 The **Long Mynd**, near Church Stretton, is a rocky plateau covered in moorland. Bracken and bilberry grow on the slopes and boggy areas harbour sundews and butterworts. The open moors are home to red grouse, with ring ouzels and wheatears favouring rocky outcrops.

6 West of Bewdley is **Wyre Forest**, all that remains of a vast royal hunting forest mentioned in the Domesday Book. It is an area of mixed heath, scrub and oak woodland, with plantations of Douglas fir and larch, where fallow deer roam and silver-washed fritillary butterflies glide.

Ironbridge, Shropshire

10 Ironbridge was in the forefront of the Industrial Revolution. Its splendid **iron bridge** over the River Severn, the first of its kind in the world, was built in 1778 by Abraham Darby to enable traffic to pass across the river without interrupting its navigation. West of Ironbridge, the **B4380** brings you to Buildwas, where the bridge over the Severn is a 1906 replacement of Telford's original one. The ruins of nearby 12th-century **Buildwas Abbey**, now roofless and without its aisle walls, are a striking contrast to the enormous cooling towers of the power station downstream. Stone from the ruin was incorporated in the local church.

🛈 The Wharfage

contains a fine collection of early 19th-century English and Italian furniture. Parts of the red sandstone 13th-century **Church of St Eata** were built with stones from the ruins of Viroconium.

Continue along the B4380 to return to Shrewsbury.

Shrewsbury – Acton Burnell 8 (13)
Acton Burnell – Church Stretton 9 (14)
Church Stretton – Craven Arms 8 (13)
Craven Arms – Ludlow 7 (11)
Ludlow – Cleehill 6 (10)
Cleehill – Bewdley 15 (24)
Bewdley – Bridgnorth 14 (23)
Bridgnorth – Shipton 10 (16)
Shipton – Much Wenlock 6 (10)
Much Wenlock – Ironbridge 4 (6)
Ironbridge – Wroxeter 10 (16)
Wroxeter – Shrewsbury 5 (8)

SPECIAL TO...

10 Six miles (9km) of the Severn Valley changed the world as a result of industrial developments in the late 18th and 19th centuries. Here, the past is portrayed in the museums of **Ironbridge**, **Coalbrookdale**, **Jackfield** and **Coalport**. The **Ironbridge Gorge Museum** was one of the first World Heritage Sites in Britain, and one ticket admits you to the bridge, the Darby furnace, Blists Hill, Coalport China Museum, the tile museum, Rosehill House and elsewhere. The ticket is valid indefinitely.

THE NORTH

The North of England is noted for the old industrial towns of Lancashire and Yorkshire, where communities developed in the wake of the coal mining, engineering, woollen and cotton manufacturing industries. They have become modern thriving towns, while retaining much of historical interest, including relics of the industrial revolution. Surrounding these urban areas are some of the finest expanses of British countryside, especially in the Lake District and the Pennines.

Visitors from all over the world are attracted by the scenic beauties of the Lake District, with its mountains, still lakes and villages which seem to have grown out of this rocky landscape. Stone walls can be seen stretching skywards over all but the highest hills, in an area where beauty inspired Wordsworth, bringing walkers and climbers in their droves.

The Lake District villages are generally built of lava or slate, except in Eskdale, to the west, where pink granite is found, but those in the Pennines are quite different: dark and somewhat forbidding in areas of millstone grit, or light and cheery where carboniferous limestone is the local rock. Old quarries and mines are dotted around the hills, and the higher parts of the Pennines became moorland, often bleak and isolated.

Down in the valleys, conditions are kinder to man and animals, and on the lowlands which surround these hill masses there is much rich farming, generally for cattle and sheep, which appreciate the lush grasslands. The larger lowlands, such as the Vale of York, the Lancashire and Cheshire Plain and lowlands of Solway, are where most of the large towns have grown up.

Carlisle

The regional capital of Cumbria is a well-placed city, with the Lake District to the south and Hadrian's wall to the north. Carlisle's castle has been a border fortress since Norman times, and its detailed history is portrayed in an exhibition in the keep. A military museum, dedicated to the Border regiments, is also housed here. The cathedral is one of England's smallest, and has remarkable carved choir stalls. Near by is the Carlisle Cross, where servants were once hired, and where Bonnie Prince Charlie stood to claim the throne of England in 1745.

Morecambe

This Victorian seaside resort overlooks Morecambe Bay, with its miles of sand, and the Lake District hills are clearly visible to the north. Traditionally a holiday centre for visitors from northern England, Morecambe retains its popularity, and the late weeks of the summer season have the added attraction of 'illuminations'. Marineland, with

The meadows and barns of ancient farmland at Gunnerside, Yorks

its displays of marine life and the famous dolphins, was the first oceanarium in Europe.

Ripon

Ripon is a busy little town, dominated by its cathedral, one of the oldest in England. An ancient Saxon crypt, thought to date from AD672, lies beneath the cathedral, and inside the fine features include a 16th-century Gothic nave. Another ancient building is the Wakeman's House, built in the 14th century for the man who would 'set the watch' by blowing a horn at 9pm every evening – a practice which continues today. An inscription on the 19th-century Town Hall reminds residents that 'Except ye Lord keep ye cittie, ye Wakeman waketh in vain'. The Prison and Police Museum is worth a visit.

York

It was the Vikings who established the settlement of Jorvik, which was developed by the Normans as the capital of the north. History lives in every street of this glorious city, which celebrates its 10th-century origins in the time-travelling Jorvik Viking Museum and recreates whole

The spectacular landscape of Langdale and Langdale Pikes

streets from the past in the Castle Museum of Yorkshire Life. But the greatest treasure is York Minster, the largest medieval cathedral in northern Europe, whose grandeur and beauty are unsurpassable. You will need a long stay to see everything of interest in York: medieval houses overhanging the narrow Shambles; the extensive city walls; and the National Railway Museum, a favourite with children and railway buffs, are only a few of its wealth of attractions.

Macclesfield

This old textile town made its name from the manufacture of silk, and there are still some of the 18th- and 19th-century mills on the steep streets overlooking the Bollin Valley. The story of silk can be seen in the award-winning Silk Museum, and you can visit the Paradise Silk Mill, a working mill until 1981. Macclesfield's other outstanding attraction is the church, originally founded in the 13th century, which sits high above the town and can be reached by climbing 108 steps.

2 days – 175 miles (281km)

THE HEART OF LAKELAND

Carlisle • Caldbeck • Bassenthwaite • Buttermere • Keswick
Grasmere • Ambleside • Coniston • Bowness and Windermere
Patterdale • Penrith • Haltwhistle • Carlisle

Leave the soft red sandstones of Carlisle and the Eden Valley to weave through hills of volcanic rocks and lakes carved out during the last Ice Age, before heading into the Pennines, with their different, gentler beauty.

Ashness Bridge, near Derwent Water, was built for packhorses

ℹ️ Old Town Hall, Green Market, Carlisle

Take the B5299 south from Carlisle to Caldbeck.

Caldbeck, Cumbria

1 This stone-built village is set in undulating countryside with the Lake District hills to the south. In the churchyard is the **grave of John Peel**, who was buried here in 1854. The famous huntsman inspired his friend, John Woodcock Graves, to write the song 'D'ye ken John Peel'. There is a plaque outside the house where Graves composed the song, and in 1939 a shelter was erected opposite the church as a memorial to them both.

Continue on the B5299 for 3 miles (5km) before branching left on to unclassified roads through Uldale to Bassenthwaite.

Bassenthwaite, Cumbria

2 Just a tiny hamlet, Bassenthwaite is situated off the **A591**. 'Thwaite' is a Norse word for a clearing in the forest, and is found in many village names in the area. **Bassenthwaite Church**, 3 miles (5km) south, was founded in the 12th or 13th century and retains its Norman chancel arch and many Early English features. Nearby **Lake Bassenthwaite** is a large ice-cut lake, and towering above its western shore is **Skiddaw**, one of only three Lake District hills which reach higher than 3,000 feet (931m).

SCENIC ROUTES

Tarn Hows, near Hawkshead, is claimed by some to be one of the best sights in the Lake District and the rocky land around Honister and on Helvellyn is a rugged contrast.

BACK TO NATURE

A rich variety of birds can be seen on this tour. Specials in the Lake District are the peregrine falcons, which were nearly extinct 20 years ago, but now breed on many of the rocky cliffs. Unique to one valley is the nest of a pair of golden eagles, the only one in England. Purple, golden and starry saxifrages are found in high, inaccessible wet areas, and higher still in rocky places, where sheep cannot reach, are rare alpine plants left from the Ice Age.

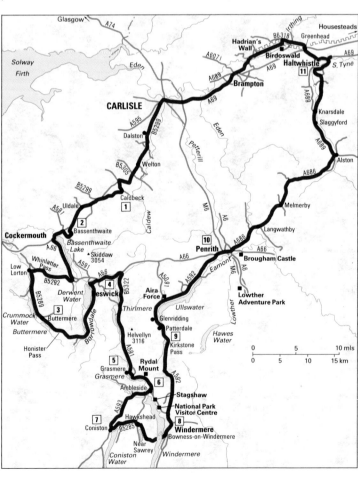

Leave Bassenthwaite on unclassified roads towards the B5291 round the northern shores of the lake, then take the A66 south to Braithwaite. Continue on the B5292 and over Whinlatter Pass to Low Lorton then left on to B5289 to Buttermere.

Buttermere, Cumbria

3 The tiny village of Buttermere stands in the heart of spectacular landscape. A stiff climb to **Whinlatter Pass**, beyond the Forestry Commission's excellent Visitor Centre, takes you on to wild moorland. This is the territory of the native Hardwick Sheep, which survive the cold winters thanks to their exceptionally thick coats. The surrounding hills, Red Pike and High Stile, tower over the flat green valley floor, with impressive waterfalls such as Scale Force. The B5289 takes you through Borrowdale, a valley, which is reached by crossing 1,174-foot (358m) Honister Pass. Dark rocks tower above the skyline and quarries scar the landscape where Borrowdale rock, which was formed by volcanic activity about 500 million years ago, is extracted. This famous rock is used in buildings as far away as Dallas and Hong Kong, and you can buy small souvenirs from many of the local shops. The southern end of the valley is dominated by the summits of 2,560-foot (780m) Glaramara and 2,986-foot (910m) Great End.

The B5289 leads north to Keswick.

Keswick, Cumbria

4 The capital of the northern Lake District now caters for walkers, climbers and holiday-makers, but one of its oldest industries is the manufacture of coloured pencils, which originally used local deposits of graphite. The **Cumberland Pencil Factory** has a museum open to visitors and among its exhibits is the world's largest pencil. On a hill to the east of Keswick is the **Castlerigg Stone Circle**, a prehistoric monument in a setting of magical beauty. Cumbrian folklore claims that the famous great stones were once men who were turned into boulders by witches.

i The Moot Hall, Market Square

Take the A66 for 4 miles (6km), then turn right on to the B5322 through St John's in the Vale and then the A591 south to Grasmere.

Grasmere, Cumbria

5 Grasmere's hills and lakes are a real tourist magnet. William Wordsworth wrote much of his greatest verse here, and his friends Coleridge, de Quincey and Southey were inspired by the location. **Dove Cottage**, where Wordsworth lived with his sister Dorothy, is open to the public and contains relics of his life and times. A few miles further along the **A591** is **Rydal Mount**, where Wordsworth lived from 1813 until his death in 1850. It houses many of the family's belongings and has a beautiful view of tranquil Rydal Water.

Bridge House, Ambleside – visitors are welcome, but in single file!

i Redbank Road

Continue on the A591 to Ambleside.

Ambleside, Cumbria

6 Ambleside is a major Lake District centre at the northern end of Lake Windermere. Its many stone houses include **Bridge House**, the smallest in the Lake District. Built on a tiny bridge over the Stock Ghyll, possibly so that the original owner could avoid paying ground rent, it is now owned by the National Trust and is open to the public, though only a few can get in at a time! In the town library are the various relics excavated from the Roman site of **Galava Fort**, at Borrans Park, and the enchanting woodland gardens of **Stagshaw**, just south of the town, have superb views of the lake.

i The Old Courthouse, Church Street

Leave Ambleside on the A593 to Coniston.

Coniston, Cumbria

7 Coniston Water is known to speed-boat enthusiasts as the place where Donald Campbell set a new world record and later died in 1967. The **Steam Yacht** *Gondola*, an 1859 steam launch, has been restored by the National Trust, and now takes passengers on regular scheduled trips around the lake. A little further on, at Hawkshead, is the **Beatrix Potter Gallery**; at **Hill House**, in Near Sawrey, Beatrix Potter wrote some of her world-famous children's stories. The house is open to the public.

i 16 Yewdale Road

Take the B5285 for 10 miles (16km) to the Windermere ferry.

Bowness and Windermere, Cumbria

8 The ferry across Lake Windermere to Bowness was restored in 1990 and leads to this small town with its narrow streets and 15th-century church, which contains some good examples of stained glass.

SPECIAL TO...

5 For over a hundred years, the celebrated Grasmere gingerbread has been made in the village. The recipe is such a closely guarded secret it has to be kept in the vaults of a local bank! The rush-bearing ceremony, held every year, involves the carrying of elaborately decorated bundles of rushes to the church, after which the bearers are rewarded with a piece of delicious gingerbread.

FOR CHILDREN

8 The **Lake District National Park Visitor Centre** is on the eastern shore of Lake Windermere at Brockhole, northwest of Windermere. As well as providing information about the park, it offers a wide variety of attractions, including special family events during school holidays, lake trips in summer, garden tours from May to September, Teddy Bears' Picnics in spring and summer and a children's Squirrel Nutkin Trail.

RECOMMENDED WALKS

With over 1,800 miles (2,900km) of footpaths in the Lake District National Park, as well as many paths in the Pennines, there is an overwhelming choice.

8 For a gentle walk, follow the footpath opposite the railway station in Windermere to the top of **Orrest Head**, 784 feet (239m), where there are fine views of the lake and Belle Isle.

9 A popular walk leads up Helvellyn from Patterdale, via Striding Edge, to the summit and returns by way of Swirral Edge. On a clear day the whole circle of Lake District summits can be seen.

FOR HISTORY BUFFS

11 Housesteads, to the east of Haltwhistle, just off the B6318, is the best preserved Roman fort on Hadrian's Wall. Excavations have revealed granaries, a commandant's house, military headquarters, a hospital, baths, latrines and barracks. In the opposite direction, on the way back to Carlisle is the ruined fort of **Camboglanna**, occupying a ridge-top site near Birdoswald. It was built to guard the Roman bridge carrying Hadrian's Wall over the river at Willowford.

Windermere, just north of Bowness, is a focal point in the Lake District for sailing and boating. The **Steamboat Museum**, at Rayrigg Road, has a collection of Victorian and Edwardian boats, many of which still float and are in working order. The lake has 14 islands, including **Belle Isle**, a privately owned landscaped estate with a round 18th-century mansion house, which can be visited.

[i] The Glebe, Bowness; The Gateway Centre, Victoria Street, Windermere

Take the A592 north to Patterdale.

Patterdale, Cumbria

9 Patterdale was named after St Patrick, who is said to have walked here after being shipwrecked on Duddon Sands in AD540. **St Patrick's Church**, built in 1853, is notable for its tapestries by embroidress Ann Macbeth, who lived here until her death in 1948. This attractive village is at the head of **Ullswater**, a popular boating lake. A steamer plies from the pier at Glenridding to the opposite end of the lake, and the scenery is dominated by 3,117-foot (950m) **Helvellyn**. At the foot of the sheer eastern slopes is Red Tarn, a corrie lake in a hollow scooped out of solid rock during the Ice Age. Two miles (3km) from Glenridding is **Aira Force**, and it was here that Wordsworth was inspired to write of his 'host of golden daffodils'.

[i] Main Car Park, Glenridding

Take the A592 alongside Ullswater for 14 miles (23km) to Penrith.

Penrith, Cumbria

10 Penrith was the capital of Old Cumbria, and there are remains of buildings suggesting its former importance. The 12th-century ruins of **Brougham Castle** are just outside

A steamer showing visitors the delights of Lake Windermere

the town, and remnants of a Roman fort built by Agricola are near by. Beautiful **Lowther Park and Adventure Park** is a few miles south and is set in 100 acres (40 hectares) of parkland. **The Gloucester Arms**, dating from 1477, is one of the oldest inns in England, and the Duke of Gloucester, later Richard III, is said to have lived here. The wild, open spaces round Penrith may be bleak, even in summer, and crossing the Pennines can prove difficult in winter.

[i] Robinson's School, Middlegate

Follow the A686 through Langwathby towards Alston. Turn left on to the A689 then right along an unclassified road to Haltwhistle.

Haltwhistle, Northumbria

11 This small, grey market town is a good starting point for **Hadrian's Wall**, built in the 2nd century AD to ward off Scottish tribes. **Holy Cross Church**, founded in 1178, is a fine example of Early English architecture. There is no tower, and the sanctuary preserves three carved coffin lids which are thought to date from the 14th century. The **South Tynedale Railway**, England's highest narrow-gauge railway, runs from Alston for a few miles towards Haltwhistle. Further along the A69, at **Greenhead**, the Roman wall, turret, fort and museum recall life 2,000 years ago.

[i] Sycamore Street, Haltwhistle

From Greenhead take the B6318 and unclassified roads to rejoin the A69. Continue through Brampton to Carlisle.

2 days – 153 miles (246km)

ACROSS THE BACKBONE OF ENGLAND

Richmond, one of Britain's most glorious towns, dominated by its 11th-century castle

ⓘ Minster Road, Ripon

Take the A6108 for 10 miles (16km) to Masham.

Masham, North Yorkshire

1 Masham's importance as a market town is illustrated by the huge market square, dominated by its Market Cross, which survives even though the market no longer takes place. Masham is full of interesting features: a four-arched **bridge** over the Ure dates from 1754, and **St Mary's Church** is even older, with its 15th-century spire standing on top of a Norman tower. The town is the home of **Theakston's brewery**, famous for its dark and rich 'Old Peculier' ale. Five miles (8km) from town is **Jervaulx Abbey**, in an attractive riverside setting. This Cistercian abbey was founded in 1156 and later destroyed in the 15th century, though enough of it remains to show how impressive it once was.

Follow the A6108 for 8 miles (13km) to Middleham.

Middleham, North Yorkshire

2 Grandiose building traditions of the past can be seen in the ruins of 12th-century **Middleham Castle**, a former seat of the Neville family, where some of the walls are 12 feet (3.5m) thick. This was the childhood home of Richard III and its massive keep is one of the largest ever built. The view from the top is magnificent, looking out across Wensleydale over

Ripon • Masham • Middleham • Leyburn Richmond Barnard Castle • Brough • Sedbergh Hawes • Bainbridge • Buckden • Grassington Pateley Bridge • Fountains Abbey • Ripon

The green valleys and wild, often wind-swept moors of Yorkshire provide a rich variety of scenery, with ever-changing views. Curiously weathered rocks add an eerie atmosphere to the landscape of hills and vales, and castles and monastic ruins recall the prosperity of the Middle Ages on this tour which crosses the Pennines twice.

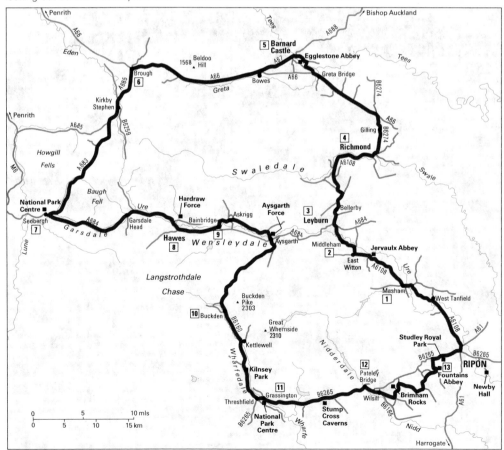

Imposing Barnard Castle, destroyed by Cromwell's army

FOR CHILDREN

Four miles (6km) southeast of Ripon is **Newby Hall and gardens**. This splendid Queen Anne house displays some of Robert Adam's finest work in its additions and interiors. The grounds cover about 25 acres (10 hectares) and include thrilling adventure gardens for children, a memorable ride on a miniature train and woodland discovery walks.

FOR HISTORY BUFFS

4 Lead mining helped the growth of Richmond and many of the surrounding villages in the 17th and 18th centuries. There are numerous footpaths leading to the old mine workings, where you can see the crushing floors and other remnants, and perhaps find tiny fragments of lead glistening in the sunlight. Primitive techniques such as 'hushing' were used, which created the narrow gullies visible on the hillsides.

wild but beautiful moorlands. Now an important horse breeding and training centre, Middleham is a good base for exploring Wensleydale.

Continue north on the A6108 to Leyburn.

Leyburn, North Yorkshire

3 Leyburn has developed into a major trading centre for the area. Its appearance is that of a prosperous late Georgian market town, and even though most shop fronts have become largely modern, some 18th-century houses survive, notably around Grove Square; the **Bolton Arms** and **Leyburn Hall** are probably the best examples. This is another good Wensleydale centre, and there are fine views from **The Shawl**, a 2-mile (3km) limestone scar not far from the town centre.

[i] Thornborough Hall

Keep on the A6108 to Richmond.

Richmond, North Yorkshire

4 There is a great deal to see in this capital and gateway to Swaledale, which is thought by many to be the finest of all Yorkshire Dales. From every angle **Richmond Castle** dominates the town. This fine Norman fortress, built on to solid rock, was started in 1071 overlooking the Swale, Britain's fastest river, but was never finished. The large, cobbled market place is surrounded by such architectural gems as the Georgian **Theatre Royal**, built in 1788, which was restored and reopened in 1962. You can see the home of the original

'sweet lass of Richmond Hill', of whom the famous song was written in 1785, and the award-winning **Green Howards Museum** covers the history of this famous regiment, including a unique collection dating from 1688 of war relics, weapons, medals and uniforms. Other interesting sights include **Greyfriars Tower**, the one surviving feature of an old abbey, and the **Holy Trinity Church**, whose main building is divided from the tower by shops and offices which are incorporated into the structure.

[i] Friary Gardens, Victoria Road

Take the B6274 to the junction with the A66 and continue to Greta Bridge. After crossing the River Greta turn right on to unclassified roads to Barnard Castle.

Barnard Castle, Durham

5 Medieval Barnard Castle, after which the town is named is now a ruin, but in its great days it stood guard over a crossing point of the River Tees. The town boasts one of the finest museums in Britain, **Bowes Museum**, housed in a splendid French château-style mansion which was built in 1869 by John Bowes, son of the Earl of Strathmore. It contains an outstanding collection of paintings, porcelain, silver, furniture and ceramics. A few miles south, off the B6277, are the ruins of **Egglestone Abbey**, in a delightful setting on the bank of the Tees, and southwest, along the A67, is the village of Bowes, where the local boarding schools gave author Charles Dickens the idea for Dotheboys Hall in his novel *Nicholas Nickleby*. William Shaw, the unfortunate model for sadistic schoolmaster Wackford Squeers, is buried in the churchyard. The **Church of St Giles** contains a Roman dedication stone, one of many relics of the Roman invasion in the area. **Bowes Castle**, like the church, used Roman stone for its building.

ⓘ 43 Galgate

Take the A67 to Bowes and follow the A66 west along the line of an old Roman route to Brough.

Brough, Cumbria

6 Standing on the site of Roman *Verterae*, **Brough Castle**, now in ruins, was built by William II and later restored by Lady Anne Clifford in the 17th century. This old settlement was a coaching town in the 19th century and used to hold an annual horse fair, now held at Appleby. Surrounded by isolated fells and woodland, this area has many miles of good walking.

Take the A685 to Kirkby Stephen, then the A683 to Sedbergh.

Sedbergh, Cumbria

7 Sedbergh is an old weaving town, and the Weavers' Yard still exists behind the King's Arms. The town is now more important as a tourist centre, and the rich natural history and beautiful scenery of the area have given rise to the creation of a **National Park Centre**. The **Public School** has gained a national reputation for its academic standards, and is noted for its sporting traditions. The **A684** east takes you through **Garsdale**, whose only community is a line of houses called The Street.

ⓘ 72 Main Street

Continue east along the A684 to Hawes.

Hawes, North Yorkshire

8 Hawes is a centre for sheep-marketing and a focal point of Upper Wensleydale life. Just off the main street are quaint alleyways and old cottages which have not changed much for 200 years. The **National Parks Information Centre** is located near the **Upper Dales Folk Museum**, which is housed in an engine shed of the old railway. **Hardraw Force**, the highest waterfall in England, is also considered to be the most spectacular, and is accessible only by foot through the grounds of the **Green Dragon Inn**. The water drops 90 feet (27m) over the limestone **Hardraw Scar**, into a narrow valley, once the venue for brass band competitions.

ⓘ National Park Centre, Station Yard

Take the A684 for a further 4 miles (6km) to Bainbridge.

Bainbridge, North Yorkshire

9 This little Dales village, with its lovely stone buildings set round the green, was the former centre of the once great Forest of Wensleydale. **Low Mill**, on the east side of the green, has been restored and is occasionally open to the public. Brough Hill, a natural grassy hillock to the east is the setting for a Roman fort, and gives fine views of Wensleydale and the village. A little further along is Askrigg, another charming village, built of local stone and set among hills, valleys and waterfalls. Most of the buildings are 18th- and 19th-century, built as a result of increasing prosperity in the clock-making, lead-mining and textile industries. Waterfalls are numerous, but especially dramatic is **Aysgarth Force**.

From Bainbridge cross the River Ure and turn right, continuing on unclassified roads, then at Aysgarth take the B6160 to Buckden.

All creatures bought and sold at Hawes' weekly market

Buckden, North Yorkshire

10 Buckden, in Wharfedale, is a very popular holiday and walking area. Kettlewell, further down the valley, was formerly part of the estate of the Percy family, ancestors of the Dukes of Northumberland. This stretch of road passes the imposing limestone outcrop of **Kilnsey Crag**, one of Yorkshire's most distinctive landmarks, alongside the all-weather attraction of **Kilnsey Park**, which has been established as a Visitor Centre.

Follow the B6160 south and turn left at Threshfield on to the B6265 into Grassington.

Grassington, North Yorkshire

11 This is Wharfedale's principal village and another National Park Centre, for the **North York Moors**. Its small passageways, cobbled market place, medieval bridge and interesting old buildings all add to the appeal. There are Bronze and

(1.6km) from town is **Foster Beck Hemp Mill**, now a restaurant, which features a huge 17th-century water wheel, the second largest in the country. East of town, along the B6165 (turn off at Wilsill) and unclassified roads are **Brimham Rocks**. These curious rock formations have been sculpted out of the millstone grit by wind and rain over thousands of years, and there are wide views from the surrounding moorlands.

i 14 High Street

Leave by the B6265 turning right after 1 mile (1.6km) on to the B6165. At Wilsill turn left and follow unclassified roads past Brimham Rocks to Fountains Abbey.

Fountains Abbey, North Yorkshire

13 Founded by Cistercian monks in 1132, Fountains is the largest and perhaps the finest abbey in England. Particularly notable are the tower, nave and lay brothers' quarters. The

The haunting profile of Brimham Rocks, high on the moors

Iron Age settlements at Lea Green, north of the village, and further east, along the B6265, are the underground caverns of **Stump Cross**. The main cave has been developed into an impressive floodlit show cave, with weird and wonderful stalagmite and stalactite formations.

i Grassington National Park Centre, Hebden Road

Continue along the B6265 to Pateley Bridge.

Pateley Bridge, North Yorkshire

12 This pleasant town has been the focus of everyday life in Nidderdale since ancient times. The picturesque ruins of **Old St Mary's Church** stand above the village on the hillside, and the **Nidderdale Museum**, in a former Victorian workhouse, has fascinating exhibits including the Victorian Room and a replica cobbler's shop. A mile

abbey was acquired by William Aislabie in 1768 and became the focal point of his magnificent landscaped gardens at nearby **Studley Royal Park**, which contains typical ornaments of the period, such as a lake, a temple and statues. The park's original house burned down in 1945, but there are still estate cottages, huddled round a 19th-century church designed by William Burges. Deer and other livestock can be seen grazing in the park.

Return to the B6265 for the journey back to Ripon.

Ripon – Masham 10 (16)
Masham – Middleham 8 (13)
Middleham – Leyburn 2 (3)
Leyburn – Richmond 11 (18)
Richmond – Barnard Castle 14 (23)
Barnard Castle – Brough 17 (27)
Brough – Sedbergh 19 (31)
Sedbergh – Hawes 15 (24)
Hawes – Bainbridge 4 (6)
Bainbridge – Buckden 17 (27)
Buckden – Grassington 11 (18)
Grassington – Pateley Bridge 11 (18)
Pateley Bridge – Fountains Abbey 10 (16)
Fountains Abbey – Ripon 4 (6)

1/2 days – 152 miles (245km)

The geological curiosity of Malham Cove lends an other-worldly air to this spectacular area

OVER HILLS & PLAINS

ⓘ Station Buildings, Morecambe

From Morecambe take the A5105, then the A6 for 7 miles (11km) to Carnforth.

Carnforth, Lancashire

1 Carnforth is a small Victorian market town on the west coast railway line to Scotland. The main attraction is **Steamtown**, the largest operating railway centre in the country, whose 30 engines include the legendary *Flying Scotsman*. In summer many of them are 'in steam'. Other railway memorabilia include coaches, a coaling plant and working models, and you can take a ride on the narrow-gauge miniature railway.

Turn left out of Steamtown and follow the unclassified road 2 miles (3km) to Warton.

Warton, Lancashire

2 The peaceful village of Warton has an unusual claim to fame. George Washington had ancestors living here, and legend has it that the famous 'Stars and Stripes' come from the family's coat of arms, which can be found in the 14th-century church. Not far from Warton is 18th-century **Leighton Hall**, built on the site of an earlier medieval house. In 1826 the estate was bought by Richard Gillow, a distinguished maker of fine furniture, and the house is a treasure chest of priceless pieces.

Continue on unclassified roads, across the A6 just south of Burton-in-Kendal then join the B6254 at Whittington and follow to Kirkby Lonsdale.

Kirkby Lonsdale, Cumbria

3 Kirkby Lonsdale is a fascinating town to explore. Look out for the three-arched **Devil's Bridge** spanning

Morecambe • Carnforth • Warton • Kirkby Lonsdale Ingleton• Clapham • Settle • Malham • Skipton Clitheroe • Slaidburn • Ribchester • Blackpool Lancaster • Morecambe

Lush green valleys, wild grouse moorland and one of the liveliest seaside resorts in the country are included in this tour which starts at Morecambe, on the edge of the Irish Sea, and climbs to the Pennines, before returning to the coast.

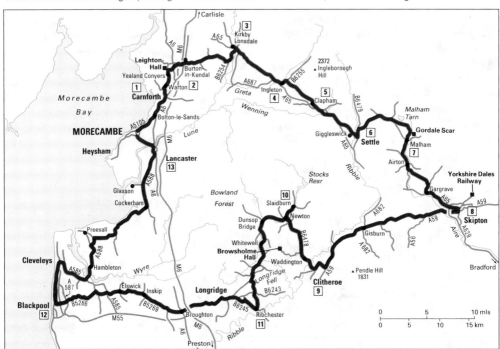

Settle, North Yorkshire

6 Settle is one of the most attractive towns in Ribblesdale, with its picturesque narrow streets, secluded courtyards and Georgian houses. By far the most outstanding building is **The Folly**, built in 1675, an extravaganza of windows and fine masonry, Tudor in appearance and quite out of place in the Dales. The 71-mile (114km) railway line from Settle to Carlisle runs through the Ribblesdale valley and is one of the most scenic routes in the country. Just outside the town is **Giggleswick Scar**, a rock wall caused by massive earth movements millions of years ago. In 1838 the chance discovery of **Victoria Cave** led to the retrieval of many bones of prehistoric animals long extinct in the British Isles.

i Town Hall, Cheapside

Take the B6479 north from Settle turning off right at Langcliffe on to unclassified roads to Malham Tarn and Malham.

Malham, North Yorkshire

7 Malham is a focal point for geographers and geologists, and the **Yorkshire Dales National Park Interpretation Centre** is based here. If you have time, stroll up the Pennine Way to **Malham Cove**, a 250-foot (76m) limestone amphitheatre. It used to be a spectacular waterfall, but the river now crawls out at the foot of the cliff. To the east is **Gordale Scar**, an almost vertical gorge thought to be a collapsed cavern and boasting a dramatic waterfall.

Follow the road from Malham to Gargrave, then take the A65 to Skipton.

Skipton, North Yorkshire

8 This pleasant market town is dominated by **Skipton Castle**, one of the most complete medieval castles in England. It was originally built in Norman times and was partly rebuilt in the 1650s after being damaged in the Civil War. Opposite the castle entrance is the **Craven Museum**, with exhibits on geology and local folk history. Near by, at Embsay, is the **Embsay Steam Railway** which runs 20 locomotives on its short track.

i 8 Victoria Square

Take the A59 west for 19 miles (31km) to Clitheroe.

Clitheroe, Lancashire

9 After the Civil War the small keep of **Clitheroe Castle** was presented to General Monk, and today it still stands boldly on its limestone knoll overlooking the town. The town itself was once filled with the harsh sound of looms – first wool, then cotton brought prosperity in the last century. Sinister **Pendle Hill**, associated with the notorious trial of several Lancashire women who were accused of being witches, rises to 1,828 feet (557km) on the east side of Clitheroe.

BACK TO NATURE

1 The RSPB reserve at Leighton Moss, 3 miles (5km) northwest of Carnforth, is famous for its reed-beds and wetland wildlife. Otters are regularly seen, and bitterns and bearded tits can be spotted by persistent observers. **Arnside Knott**, further north, is a limestone outcrop which shows fine examples of limestone pavements. Interesting flowers grow in the cracks and crevices, including several species of ferns and dark red helleborines.

SCENIC ROUTES

The whole area offers a variety of exciting scenery. Spectacular views can be found as you pass through the mountainous spine of England, the Pennines, on the road from Malham to Skipton before it joins the **A65**. The dramatic form of Ingleborough dominates the landscape, especially from Kirkby Lonsdale and along the **A65**.

RECOMMENDED WALKS

7 Malham village is close to the highly dramatic Malham Cove and Gordale Scar. Walk up the steep path to the top of the cove, and continue along the route of the old river, now dried up. You will soon reach the point at which the stream disappears underground through a series of holes. Retrace your steps or turn right and follow the signs to Gordale, where you can scramble down a waterfall and walk through a gorge on the way back to the village.

---

the River Lune. Possibly as old as the 13th century, it is one of the finest ancient bridges in the country. John Ruskin, the 19th-century writer and painter, loved this area of the Lune valley. The 'Ruskin Walks', which start near the churchyard, are well signposted. Cowan Bridge, just down the road, has further literary links, for it was here that novelists Charlotte and Emily Brontë endured a harsh boarding school education from 1823 to 1825. Now only a few cottages mark the site of the **Clergy Daughters' School**, immortalised by Charlotte as Lowood in her novel *Jane Eyre*.

i 24 Main Street

Continue on the A65 for 6 miles (10km), then turn left on to the B6255 into Ingleton.

Ingleton, North Yorkshire

4 Ingleton thrives as a centre for visitors to the Yorkshire Dales. The limestone hills to the north are honeycombed with caves, many of which are accessible only to experienced potholers, but **White Scar Cave** is open to everyone. It is tucked below the heights of Ingleborough, 2,373 feet (723m) which, with Whernside at 2,419 feet (737m) and Pen-y-ghent at 2,273 feet (693m), forms the most formidable trio of peaks in the Dales.

i Community Centre Car Park, High Street

Take the unclassified road along the foot of Ingleborough for 4 miles (6km) to Clapham.

Clapham, North Yorkshire

5 Tiny Clapham is the unlikely Fleet Street of the Dales, for it is here that *The Dalesman* magazine is published. The village has a **Yorkshire Dales National Park Information Centre**, and like Ingleton is a noted potholing centre. To the north of the village is **Ingleborough Cave**, and the famous **Gaping Gill** pothole, 378 feet (123m) deep, with a central chamber large enough to hold a small cathedral.

From Clapham take the B6480 to the A65 and follow before branching off left to Settle.

⊡ 14 Market Place

Follow the B6578 north for 8 miles (13km) to Slaidburn.

Slaidburn, Lancashire

10 The little village of Slaidburn, on the River Hodder, was for centuries the administrative 'capital' of the **Forest of Bowland**. This wild region of grouse moor and high fells was one of the ancient royal forests of Saxon England. At the centre of the village is an inn called **Hark to Bounty**. Legend says Bounty was a foxhound belonging to a local vicar, and that its barking was easily distinguishable from the rest of the pack. **Gisburn Forest**, northeast of the village, is an extensive coniferous plantation sloping down to **Stocks Reservoir**, which takes its name from the village drowned to create it during the early 1930s.

Take the B6478 back to Newton, then branch off on to unclassified roads through Dunsop Bridge, Whitewell and over Longridge Fell to Ribchester.

Ribchester, Lancashire

11 In Roman times the wild country round Ribchester was guarded by a fort known as *Bremetennacum*, built around ad80. In the 18th century a schoolboy found a Roman ceremonial helmet, and since then its extensive remains have been excavated and you can see many of the finds in the **Museum of Roman Antiquities**. Two Roman columns support the oak gallery in 13th-century **St Wilfred's Church**, and the pillars at the entrance of the **White Bull Inn** are said to come from a Roman temple. The **Museum of Childhood**, along Church Street, has dolls, toys and models on display.

Take the B6245 to Longridge and then the B5269 west via Broughton and Elswick to join the B5266 to Blackpool.

Blackpool, Lancashire

12 Brash and cheerful Blackpool stretches in a long, multicoloured ribbon by the sea, punctuated with three piers and dominated by its splendid 519-foot (158m) tower. Built between 1891 and 1894, **Blackpool Tower** was for many years the highest building in Britain, and it gives a breathtaking view of the surrounding coast. The heart of Blackpool, the **Golden Mile**, is in fact more like a quarter of a mile. It is possible to walk the whole length of the sea front between Fleetwood in the north and Squires Gate in the south, but it is much more fun to go on one of the trams which still run along the promenade. During autumn evenings, the whole front is ablaze with more than 375,000 bulbs, laser beams, animated displays and tableaux.

⊡ 1 Clifton Street and 87a Coronation Street

Follow the trams along the promenade to Cleveleys, before

For all its air of repose, Clapham is a busy centre of information

turning inland on the B5412 then right on to the A586. Turn left on to the A588 to Lancaster via Pilling and Cockerham marshes.

Lancaster, Lancashire

13 This county town was England's chief port for the American trade throughout the 18th century. The elegant **Customs House**, designed by Robert Gillow of Leighton Hall, is a reminder of its former prosperity. The massive Norman keep of **Lancaster Castle** now serves to keep people in rather than out: it is the county gaol. It contains a well tower where prisoners languished while awaiting trail – including 10 Lancaster witches convicted and hanged in 1612. On show are grim relics such as the clamp and iron used to fasten a criminal's arm while the initial 'M' (for malefactor) was burned on to his hand. The **City Museum** in Market Square is also the **Museum of the King's Own Royal Lancashire Regiment**, and the **Judges' Lodgings** on Castle Hill contain a **Museum of Childhood**.

⊡ 29 Castle Hill

Cross the River Lune on the A589, and a short drive of 3 miles (5km) takes you back to Morecambe.

Morecambe – Carnforth	7 (11)
Carnforth – Warton	2 (3)
Warton – Kirkby Lonsdale	10 (16)
Kirkby Lonsdale – Ingleton	7 (11)
Ingleton – Clapham	4 (6)
Clapham – Settle	6 (10)
Settle – Malham	9 (14)
Malham – Skipton	11 (18)
Skipton – Clitheroe	19 (31)
Clitheroe – Slaidburn	8 (13)
Slaidburn – Ribchester	16 (26)
Ribchester – Blackpool	24 (39)
Blackpool – Lancaster	26 (42)
Lancaster – Morecambe	3 (5)

FOR HISTORY BUFFS

9 A few miles northwest of Clitheroe, just beyond Bashall Eaves, is **Browsholme Hall**. Pronounced 'Broozum', it is a modified Tudor mansion set in beautiful gardens laid out in honour of the Prince Regent and Mrs Fitzherbert. It contains fascinating collections of tapestry work, armour, furniture and pictures.

SPECIAL TO...

9 **Clitheroe Castle** contains a fine collection of carboniferous fossils from the local rocks. Similar fossils can be found in the limestone areas around Malham or Ingleton. Brachiopods look like some of the modern shells you can find on beaches today and there are pieces of coral from a warm ocean floor of 300 million years ago, and crinoids, which look like screws made out of stone.

FOR CHILDREN

12 Blackpool is a paradise for children, with so much to do at every turn, including the **Pleasure Beach amusement park**, with the first 360-degree 'loop the loop' roller-coaster in Britain, and **Sandcastle**, the world's greatest 'inside seaside' with tropical fun pools and a 300-foot (91m) water slide.

1/2 days – 85 miles (138km)

DERBYSHIRE'S WHITE PEAK

Macclesfield • Castleton • Eyam • Chatsworth
Matlock and Matlock Bath • Bakewell • Tideswell
Buxton • Macclesfield

This tour of the Peak District explores the gentler southern side, the White Peak, with its high close-cropped sheep pasture, limestone dry walling and pretty wooded valleys, but our route also offers a small glimpse of the Dark Peak – bleaker moorland and angular outcrops of blackened millstone grit.

Those with a head and stomach for heights can take the cable car ride up the Heights of Abraham at Matlock Bath. With a tower above and caves below, it's a good day out

ℹ️ Town Hall, Macclesfield

Leave Macclesfield by the A5002 to Rainow, then in 4 miles (6km) cross the A5004, taking the B5470 to Chapel-en-le-Frith. Take the A625 signed Rushup and Edale, then turn right and shortly left signed Castleton Caverns for Castleton.

Castleton, Derbyshire

1 Dominating this pretty Peak village is **Peveril Castle**, built by William Peveril, illegitimate son of the Conqueror, and immortalised in Sir Walter Scott's 1825 novel *Peveril of the Peak*. Although roofless, Henry II's huge keep still stands. Castleton has a 200-year history of visitors, who come mainly to see the spectacular caverns in the limestone hills. Follow the stream to **Peak Cavern**, which has Britain's largest natural cave entrance. You can still see evidence here of the rope makers who lived and worked in the cavern: their speciality was hangman's nooses. There are other local caverns, carved out by miners looking for lead and the lovely Blue John Fluorspar. **Treak Cliff**, **Speedwell** (explore it by boat) and **Blue John Caverns** are all open to visitors. A trip behind Mam Tor, 'the shivering mountain', leads to nearby Edale, which lies snugly in the Noe Valley and is the starting point of the **Pennine Way** footpath. The gritstone **Kinder Scout** at 2,088 feet (636m), broods above.

Go east on the A625, then turn right in 3 miles (5km) on to the B6049. Soon turn left on unclassified roads to Great Hucklow, through Foolow to Eyam.

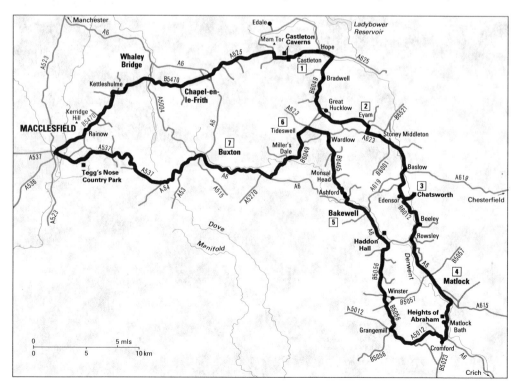

The subterranean light of the Peak Cavern at Castleton

Eyam, Derbyshire

2 In 1665, the year of the Great Plague in London, a chest of clothes was sent from the capital to the little stone village of Eyam, high up among the moors. Soon four out of every five villagers were dead. But what made Eyam special was the extraordinary sacrifice that these villagers made. Led by the rector, William Mompesson, they resolved to isolate themselves and prevent the disease from wiping out neighbouring communities. The churchyard's graves reflect this sad story and every August a service is held in a nearby dell, known as **Cucklet Church**, where Mompesson held his open-air services. Near his wife's grave is a unique sundial, telling the time throughout the world.

> *Turn right on to the B6521 then left on to the A623. At Baslow turn right on to the A619 then shortly left on to the B6012. In 5 miles (8km) turn left again at Edensor For Chatsworth.*

Chatsworth, Derbyshire

3 Set in the lush Derwent valley, Chatsworth is one of the grandest country houses in England, popularly known as the 'Palace of the Peak'. The Elizabethan house, built in 1555 by Bess of Hardwick, was virtually replaced with the 1st Duke of Devonshire's baroque mansion of the late 17th century, finished by the 6th Duke in the 1820s. Although Capability Brown landscaped the grounds, their crowning feature is Joseph Paxton's stunning Emperor Fountain, at 260 feet (80m) the tallest in Britain. When you rejoin the main

road, take a look at the golden stone village of Edensor. Before 1839 the village lay in full view of the big house, so the 6th Duke had Paxton demolish it and rebuild it out of sight!

> *Leave Chatsworth and turn left on to the B6012. At Rowsley turn left on to the A6 for Matlock.*

Matlock and Matlock Bath, Derbyshire

4 These two towns are of similar name but very different character. Matlock is the administrative centre of Derbyshire, a busy town built around an ancient stone bridge across the river. Next door is Matlock Bath, a 19th-century spa town, where the water still bubbles up at a constant 20°C, although the **Pavilion** where Victorians used to take it is now an entertainment centre. Commanding the heights above Matlock Bath are the **Victoria Prospect Tower** and the strange folly of **Riber Castle**. Behind this imposing front is not the mansion one would expect, but a **wildlife park** for rare breeds and endangered species. A mile (1.6km) on from Matlock is Cromford, an important benchmark in the development of England as an industrial nation. Here, in 1771, Richard Arkwright built the world's first mechanised textile factory. It survives today, with the new village Arkwright built for his workers.

ⓘ The Pavilion, Matlock Bath

> *Leave Matlock Bath on the A6 to the south and at Cromford turn right on to the A5012 signed Buxton. Turn right on to the B5056 then the A6 to Bakewell.*

Bakewell, Derbyshire

5 The fine five-arch stone bridge built in 1300 to span the River Wye, is

FOR HISTORY BUFFS

5 Haddon Hall, near Bakewell, is reputed to be England's most complete and authentic medieval manor house, and is certainly one of Derbyshire's finest buildings. Unlike many large country houses, it remains very much as it was 300 years ago..

SPECIAL TO...

The **National Tramway Museum** at Crich, just south of Cromford, is unique. Over 40 trams from all over the world, built between 1873 and 1953, are kept here in pristine condition by a band of volunteers, and on any one day several trams are guaranteed to be running. For the price of admission you can hop on and off as much as you like anywhere along the 1 mile (1.6km) route. Open from April to October.

RECOMMENDED WALKS

The **Monsal Trail** was created from the former Manchester-St Pancras railway line, and it runs through some of the most scenic parts of the Peak National Park. The path stretches, with occasional breaks, a total of 8 miles (10km) from Wyedale to Bakewell, often over viaducts and bridges. A good place to sample it is at Monsal Head on the **B6465** north of Ashford.

the principal feature of this fine market town. The Romans came here first for the warm springs; the Saxons named it Bad Quell or 'bath well'. Most of the buildings are 17th- and 18th-century, but the **Old House Museum** (off Church Lane), with its wattle and daub walls, is at least a hundred years older. The town boasts more than 50 shops, including the **Old Original Bakewell Pudding Shop**, a very popular eating place. Bakewell Pudding – don't dare call it 'tart' here – is supposed to have originated in the kitchens of the **Rutland Arms Hotel**, when a cook poured egg on to the jam instead of the pastry.

ℹ️ Old Market Hall, Bridge Street

> Go north on the **A6** from Bakewell. At Ashford turn right on to the **B6465** and, in 4 miles (6km), left on to the **A623**, then soon turn left into Tideswell.

Tideswell, Derbyshire

6 Tideswell grew with the medieval wool trade – being granted market status as early as the 13th century. Over the intervening years it has become a sleepy backwater away from the main roads, and little remains to indicate the town's heyday, with one glorious exception. The 14th-century **Church of St John the Baptist**, with its soaring tower, is known as the 'Cathedral of the Peak'. Tideswell is a venue for well-dressing, the tradition of decorating wells with flowers, which takes place at the end of June or very early in July.

Buxton is a sophisticated and elegant Georgian spa set high amidst wild and beautiful Derbyshire countryside

> From Tideswell go south on the **B6049** then join the **A6** heading west to Buxton.

Buxton, Derbyshire

7 At 1,007 feet (307m), Buxton is one of the highest towns in England, sheltered by hills all around. People have sought the town out since Roman times for its springs of mineral water. Not only is it good for rheumatics, but it tastes nice too. Bring a bottle and help yourself, free, from **St Anne's Well**; you can even swim in warm spa water in the **Pavilion**'s indoor pool. It was in the 18th century that the town took off as a spa resort, thanks to the 5th Duke of Devonshire, who built the beautiful Doric-style **Crescent** and the huge domed riding school and stables, now the **Royal Devonshire Hospital**. The town has two golf courses, an elegantly restored **Opera House** and the lovely **Pavilion Gardens**. Walks are plentiful; one that offers a panoramic view of the town is the round trip up to **Solomon's Temple**, a folly on Grinlow.

ℹ️ The Crescent

> Leave Buxton on the **A53**, going right on to the **A54**. Turn right again on to the **A537** signed Macclesfield and in 5 miles (8km) left on to unclassified roads past Tegg's Nose Country Park into Macclesfield.

Macclesfield – Castleton 19 (31)
Castleton – Eyam 10 (16)
Eyam – Chatsworth 6 (10)
Chatsworth – Matlock 8 (13)
Matlock – Bakewell 14 (23)
Bakewell – Tideswell 8 (13)
Tideswell – Buxton 8 (13)
Buxton – Macclesfield 12 (19)

The White Horse of Kilburn. White horses are thought to have been devotional objects of ancient tribes, but no one knows for sure

FROM VALE TO MOOR

York • Malton • Pickering • Goathland
Grosmont • Danby • Rosedale Abbey • Hutton-le-Hole
Kirkbymoorside • Helmsley • Kilburn • Coxwold
Wass • Sutton-on-the-Forest • York

ⓘ De Grey Rooms, Exhibition Square, York

Take the A64 and turn left on to an unclassified road before Whitewell-on-the-Hill, passing Castle Howard, through Coneysthorpe to Malton.

Malton, North Yorkshire

1 Malton is divided in two by the site of a Roman station. New Malton is the busy market town, and Old Malton, a mile (1.6km) northeast, is a small village. **Malton Museum**, in the town, contains extensive Romano-British remains from the fort of Derventio and other settlements. Northwards is **Eden Camp Military Museum**, a former prisoner-of-war camp, where displays include women at war and the rise and fall of the Nazi Party. Six miles (10km) southwest of Malton, on a signed road, is **Castle Howard**, a magnificent 18th-century house designed by Vanbrugh. It has been the home of the Howard family for nearly 300 years and its notable features include the central dome, the Temple of the Four Winds and Hawksmoor's mausoleum.

ⓘ Old Town Hall, Market Place

Follow the road to Old Malton, cross the A64 on to the A169, turning almost immediately left on to an unclassified road through Kirby Misperton, rejoining the A169 north to Pickering.

Pickering, North Yorkshire

2 This ancient market town is the starting point for the **North Yorkshire Moors Railway**, which runs on 18 miles (29km) of track between Pickering and Grosmont. Parts of the **Church of St Peter and St Paul** date from the 11th century and it contains some splendid medieval wall paintings, notably *St George and the Dragon* and *John the Baptist's Head*. The ruins of **Pickering Castle** include a motte which was probably constructed in the days of William the Conqueror, and the **Beck Isle Museum of Rural Life** is housed in a fine Georgian building and is packed with bygones of the Victorian era.

ⓘ 7 Eastgate Car Park

Continue along the A169 for about 12 miles (19km) then turn left on to an unclassified road to Goathland.

Goathland, North Yorkshire

3 Goathland is one of the most picturesque villages in the North York Moors, with its grey stone buildings set round the large village green. This is a marvellous centre for walking and the area is renowned for spectacular waterfalls, including **Nelly Ayre Foss**, **Mallyan Spout** and **Thomason Foss**.

Return to the A169 for a short distance, then turn left on to unclassified roads to Grosmont.

This area of the North Riding extends from the gentle farm lands of the Vale of York to the wild beauty of the North York Moors, taking in delightful villages and evocative ruins.

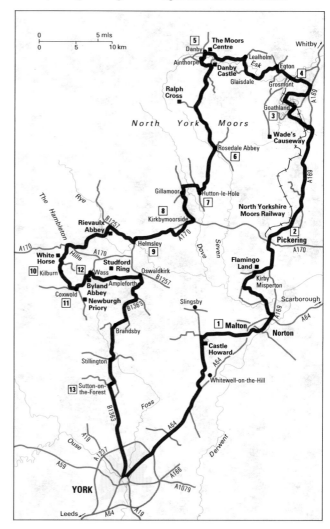

Grosmont, North Yorkshire

4 Grosmont is the northern terminus of the **North Yorkshire Moors Railway**, and its popularity owes much to the railway. A trip on the **Moorsrail** will take you back to a gentler and slower age, and the locomotive sheds are worth a visit to see engines being prepared and restored.

Continue west along unclassified roads for 11 miles (18km) through Glaisdale to Danby.

Danby, North Yorkshire

5 The **Moors Centre** is located in Danby in a former shooting lodge, with exhibitions and impressive gardens. Southeast of the village are the ruins of 14th-century **Danby Castle**, where Catherine Parr, Henry VIII's sixth wife, once lived. The route now goes on to the moors past two old crosses **Fat Betty**, and the **Ralph Cross**, which is used as the symbol for the North York Moors National Park.

> ⓘ The Moors Centre, Danby Lodge, Lodge Lane

Follow unclassified roads south for 10 miles (16km) to Rosedale Abbey.

Rosedale Abbey, North Yorkshire

6 Rosedale's 12th-century Cistercian abbey no longer exists: only a few stones remain in the village. Ruins of railways and kilns at **Chimney** Bank Top are reminders of the old 19th-century ironstone industry. The famous chimney, once visible for miles, was demolished in 1972 when it was declared unsafe.

Continue south for 5 miles (8km) to Hutton-le-Hole.

Hutton-le-Hole, North Yorkshire

7 Hutton-le-Hole's **Ryedale Museum**, in an ancient cruck-type building, features a marvellous collection of farm equipment, and reconstructed buildings. There are two 3½-mile (6km) walks signposted from the centre of the village into the surrounding countryside.

> ⓘ Road Ryedale Folk Museum

Continue on unclassified roads, crossing the River Dove and through Gillamoor to Kirkbymoorside.

Kirkbymoorside, North Yorkshire

8 Situated at the edge of the moor, this small, peaceful town is just off the main road, with quiet streets and squares. The **church** dates from the 12th century and retains some fine Norman masonry and fragments of a Saxon cross.

*Take the **A170** for 6 miles (10km) to Helmsley.*

Wild, beautiful and free: the North York Moors National Park

Helmsley, North Yorkshire

9 Roads from Cleveland, Thirsk and York converge upon the town square, making Helmsley a busy trade centre. **Helmsley Castle,** sometimes called Furstan Castle, dates from 1186 and was once inhabited by the Duke of Buckingham, court favourite of James I and Charles I. Two miles (3km) west of Helmsley is **Rievaulx,** one of the largest Cistercian abbeys in England. The 12th-century ruins are surrounded by wooded hills, and above the abbey wall is **Rievaulx Terrace,** a beautiful landscaped garden with mock-Greek temples completed in 1758.

[i] Town Hall, Market Place

Follow unclassified roads from Rievaulx through Scawton to rejoin the A170, then turn left to White Horse Bank and Kilburn.

Kilburn, North Yorkshire

10 Kilburn White Horse is the only turf-cut figure in the north of England. Almost 314feet (96m) long by 228feet (70m) high, it can be seen from the central tower of York Minster, 19 miles (30km) away. The village is well known for its woodcarvings, the work of Robert Thompson, who died in 1955. His trademark, a mouse, is still carved into the items produced by craftsmen at his works.

Continue on unclassified roads for 2 miles (3km) to Coxwold.

Coxwold, North Yorkshire

11 Coxwold's most outstanding building is the 15th-century octagonal-towered **church.** In the churchyard is the gravestone of the 18th-century author Laurence Sterne, who named his house **Shandy Hall,** after the hero of his novel *The Life and Opinions of Tristram Shandy;* today it is a museum devoted to his life and works. Just beyond the village is **Newburgh Priory,** a 17th- and 18th-century house with a lake and gardens.

Castle Howard, one of the architect Vanbrugh's finest works

Return to Coxwold, then take an unclassified road to Wass.

Wass, North Yorkshire

12 Wass was partly built from the ruins of nearby **Byland Abbey** ,the largest Cistercian church in the country, with a 26-foot (8m) diameter window dating from the 13th century. Two miles (3km) west of Wass is **Ampleforth,** which was chosen as the site of a school by English monks escaping from the French Revolution. **Ampleforth College** is now England's premier Roman Catholic public school. Nearby **Studford Ring** is thought to date from the Bronze Age and is probably the finest earthwork enclosure in the area.

Turn right along the B1363 and continue east on unclassified roads to Oswaldkirk, where you continue south to Sutton-on-the-Forest.

Sutton-on-the-Forest, North Yorkshire

13 Set in the undulating Howardian Hills, this is an unusual brick-built village with a stone **church. Sutton Park,** an early Georgian house, contains antique furniture by Chippendale and Sheraton and a collection of porcelain.

Return to York via the B1363.

York – Malton 18 (29)
Malton – Pickering 8 (13)
Pickering – Goathland 15 (24)
Goathland – Grosmont 7 (11)
Grosmont – Danby 11 (18)
Danby – Rosedale Abbey 10 (16)
Rosedale Abbey – Hutton-le-Hole 5 (8)
Hutton-le-Hole – Kirkbymoorside 6 (10)
Kirkbymoorside – Helmsley 6 (10)
Helmsley – Kilburn 10 (16)
Kilburn – Coxwold 2 (3)
Coxwold – Wass 2 (3)
Wass – Sutton-on-the-Forest 16 (27)
Sutton-on-the-Forest – York 8 (13)

RECOMMENDED WALKS

The 100-mile (160km) **Cleveland Way** curves round the edge of the Moors, and certain stretches along it make ideal short walks.

9 Highly recommended is the 3½ miles (6km) from Helmsley to Rievaulx, which runs along the richly wooded valley of the River Rye.

SCENIC ROUTES

Between Kilburn and Ampleforth the route along unclassified roads is a succession of scenic views, and the **A169** from Pickering to Goathland reveals splendid open moorland before descending into the village. Between Danby and Rosedale are the heather-covered moorlands of the North York Moors, the largest expanse of heather in England.

SCOTLAND

Inverness

Inverness is the capital of the Highlands. Industry is confined to one fringe area, and the town can boast some fine old buildings among clumsy modern developments. Inverness makes a feature of its riverside walks, overlooked by a 19th-century castle, and footbridges cross to the Ness Islands. There are cruises on the Caledonian Canal, a good local museum, and the curious claim – which you can judge on wooded Tomnahurich Hill – that the town has the most beautiful burial ground in the country!

Aberdeen

Aberdeen is the grey Granite City, the capital of North Sea oil, but the granite of its buildings comes to life and sparkles in the sun. There are excellent museums and galleries, such as Provost Ross's House and Provost Skene's House, golf courses and a long beach, while parks its parks rival any in Britain. Aberdeen is a regular top prizewinner in the Britain in bloom competition: look for the 100,000 roses planted along one city dual-carriageway.

Edinburgh

Even if no longer a seat of government, Edinburgh is obviously a capital city. The New Town is one of the most graceful examples of Georgian planning, and few shopping streets have such an imposing backdrop as Princes Street, dominated by the castle rock. Edinburgh houses Scotland's national galleries and some splendid museums as well as being, every August and September, a world-famous festival city. Within the city limits, look for Dean Village, a remarkable survival of lovely buildings by the Water of Leith, and for Cramond, once an oyster-fishermen's village, where the Almond Water flows into the Forth.

Dumfries

Dumfries is the Queen of the South, the principal town in the region which stretches from the English border to the Mull of Galloway, Scotland's southwestern tip. Its museums are varied and impressive,

Looking west across Loch Garry on Tayside

Cross the border from England to Scotland, and you will find that the landscape, architecture and historical emphasis all change. This is part of the United Kingdom which retains its own educational and legal systems, banknotes and established church. Scotland joined the Union in 1707, but many of its castles and historic houses, heroes and battlefields are from the time when England was 'the auld enemy'. Football and rugby internationals retain something of that ancestral rivalry.

The ruined Border abbeys are evidence of the old raiding days. Along the Galloway coast, revenue duties on brandy, wine, silks and other goods were so resented that generations of Solway men made their living by smuggling contraband from the tax-free harbours of the Isle of Man. This was no casual trade. Several smuggling companies were proper businesses, with shareholders and accurate, if secret, books of accounts.

Further north, in the Highland and Grampian glens, it was whisky taxes that were bitterly disliked. Pure mountain water, often flavoured by the peaty ground through which it flowed, was the basis of hundreds of illicit whisky stills. Some respectable modern distilleries happily admit to a raffish past.

Scotland is a nation with its own character and its own history. At the turn of the 13th and 14th centuries the story was one of avoiding an English conquest, and Scotland's independence was re-asserted during the reign of Robert I – Robert the Bruce. His descendants founded the dynasty of the Stuart kings and queens, and the story of the Highlands in the first half of the 18th century is largely bound up with the efforts of the Stuarts – notably in the charismatic figure of Bonnie Prince Charlie – to regain the British throne. All their attempts were failures, but the history of the Jacobites, the followers of the prince's father James Stuart, is still well remembered.

The tours which follow will take you to Jacobite country, to the land of the Solway smugglers, to ground fought over in the Border wars, and to lonely northwestern districts, where the people were forced off their holdings by 19th-century landlords wanting the larger rents offered first by incoming sheep-farmers and then by wealthy deer-stalkers. In places you will wonder why the land seems so empty: it was not always so.

one featuring an old windmill adapted to house a camera obscura. Robert Burns is remembered affectionately in Dumfries, his home in later years. His house is one of the town museums and his favourite pub, the Globe Inn, retains many Burns mementoes.

Dumbarton

Once upon a time Dumbarton was the capital of the Celtic kingdom of Strathclyde. Later, it became an innovative shipbuilding centre and, almost in passing, a pioneer of the

The dramatic cascade of the Falls of Measach tumbling 150 feet (46m) in Corrieshalloch Gorge

helicopter and the hovercraft. It is still an exhilarating experience to climb to the viewpoint summit of Dumbarton Rock, the old Celtic stronghold and later a fortress of the Crown. Although the shipyards have been abandoned, the Denny Experiment Tank, where scale-models of hulls were tested to see how they performed in miniature storms still survives.

3/4 days – 281 miles (451km)

HISTORY & MYSTERY

Inverness • Culloden • Drumnadrochit
Eilean Donan Castle • Applecross • Torridon
Beinn Eighe • Gairloch • Inverewe Garden
Strathpeffer • Inverness

History and magnificent scenery are ever present on this tour from Inverness. Just outside town lies Culloden, where Bonnie Prince Charlie's defeat in 1746 ruined the last hope of a Stuart restoration to the British throne. To the west, much of the landscape is in the hands of conservation bodies. There are glorious sea, loch, island and mountain views, and who knows what may be lurking in the dark waters of Loch Ness?

The palm tree on Plockton's shorefront imparts a holiday air

i Castle Wynd, Inverness

Leave Inverness on the B9006 to the battlefield of Culloden.

Culloden, Highland

1 Cared for by the National Trust for Scotland, **Culloden Moor** is a place of sombre memories. It was here, on 16 April 1746, that the Duke of Cumberland's army crushed the Jacobite rising led by Prince Charles. The battlefield is laid out with plaques showing the disposition of the opposing forces, and in the visitor centre you can follow the story of this last major battle on British soil. Displays illustrate the confusing political climate of the times, when there were Scots – and even different Highland clans – fighting on both sides. The bitter aftermath of the battle, when government troops were sent on a murderous rampage through the glens, is also described.

Return to Inverness and leave on the A82 as for Fort William.

Drumnadrochit, Highland

2 This is the site of the **Loch Ness Centre**, with its exhibition about the search for the world's most famous monster, said to lurk in the chill waters. You may arrive feeling sceptical, but you will almost certainly leave with the feeling that there is *something* here to be explained. Follow the 'Divach' sign off the A82 to the graceful **Falls of Divach**, and visit the striking lochside ruins of 13th-century **Urquhart Castle**, and the roadside monument to John Cobb, the landspeed record holder who was killed on Loch Ness in 1952 trying for the water-speed record.

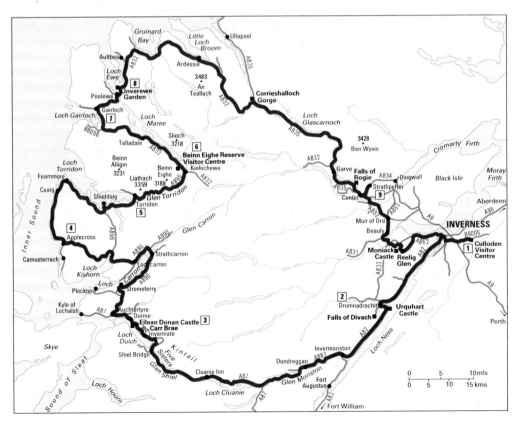

☐ Loch Ness Centre

Continue on the A82 to Invermoriston, then take the A887 and go straight on along the A87. Continue through Inverinate and turn right up Carr Brae. Go into Dornie and turn left for Eilean Donan Castle.

Eilean Donan Castle, Highland

3 Probably the most photographed castle in Scotland, Eilean Donan was rebuilt on its splendid islet site between 1912 and 1932, after lying in ruins since the Jacobite Rising of 1719. The MacRaes have been its Constables since 1509. Principal apartments open to visitors are the barrel-vaulted billeting room and the small but impressive banqueting hall. In the hall, look for the letter from Bonnie Prince Charlie – 'Being fully persuaded of yr loyalty and zeal for the King's service…' – sent to clan chiefs on behalf of his father, seeking their support in the 1745 Rising.

Leave Dornie on the A87 as for Kyle of Lochalsh, then turn right on to the A890, left on to the A896 through Lochcarron and Kishorn, and left for Applecross.

Applecross, Highland

4 If you do not like narrow mountain roads, skip Applecross; if you are prepared to brave them you will find a beautifully located crofting village, facing the splendid skyline of the Cuillin Hills on Skye. St Maelrhuba is the local saint, and after his death in ad722, villagers carried soil from his grave on long or perilous journeys. Potter southwards to the lovely rocky bay beyond Camusterrach and take a picnic behind the rippled sandbanks of Applecross Bay. On the lonely road north, look for the pathway which, until a generation ago, was the only land link between the scattered settlements of North Applecross.

Across the upper reaches of Loch Torridon, there is a splendid view of Beinn Alligin

---

☐ Main Street, Lochcarron, or Applecross campsite

Leave Applecross following the 'Shieldaig' sign. Turn left at a T-junction to rejoin the A896.

Torridon, Highland

5 The Torridon landscape has no peers in mainland Scotland, with shapely **Beinn Alligin** and its outliers soaring from the sea-loch and, further east, **Liathach's** seven-peaked pinnacled ridge towering over Torridon village and glen. Both ranges are owned by the National Trust for Scotland, and a classic 9-mile (14km) walk on Trust ground explores the wild country behind Liathach. In summer, the Trust Visitor Centre explains the history, geology and wildlife of this glorious district, and there is an exhibition and audio-visual presentation on red deer near by.

☐ NTS Visitor Centre

Continue on the A896. Turn left on to the A832.

Beinn Eighe, Highland

6 This magnificent mountain range, with quartzite summit rocks which give the impression of a permanent dusting of snow, was Britain's first National Nature Reserve. The Visitor Centre on the A832 illustrates the fascinating layered wildlife of the mountain – warblers and redstarts in the birchwoods, crossbills among the pines, otters and black-throated divers on the margins of **Loch Maree**. Two fairly rough waymarked trails – one to 1,700 feet (518m) – offer tremendous views over the loch.

☐ Aultroy Visitor Centre

Continue on the A832 to Gairloch.

FOR HISTORY BUFFS

3 Beside the **A87** in wild Glenshiel a plaque describes the battle fought there during the short-lived Jacobite Rising of 1719. The defeated Jacobite army included a company of Spanish troops – the last foreign soldiers to fight on Scottish soil.

8 Turn off the **A832** into Aultbea and look behind Pier Road for the board describing how, during World War II, the sheltered anchorage of Loch Ewe was the gathering-point for Arctic convoys to the Soviet port of Murmansk.

SCENIC ROUTES

Down Glenshiel, the **A87** slices through a landscape of steep green mountainsides. After Inverinate, Carr Brae leads to a wonderful high-level viewpoint and, later, the **A890** opens up dramatic views around Loch Carron.

RECOMMENDED WALKS

4 Lochcarron Environmental Group publishes a guide to 15 hill, coast and forest walks. One, climbs the Allt nan Carnan gorge above three waterfalls, with glorious views over Loch Carron and the Attadale hills.

9 Turn off the **A835** after Tarvie for the Falls of Rogie. Footpaths cross a bridge over the rock pools and rapids, and pass a salmon ladder built to allow fish to swim upstream in the spawning season.

Gairloch, Highland

7 Gairloch is really a cluster of crofting settlements on the shores of a very attractive sea-loch, which has become a resort with fine sands, a fishing harbour and one of the most beautifully located golf courses in Scotland. **Gairloch Heritage Museum** has fishing boats in its courtyard, an old lighthouse tower installed at ground level, and indoor displays on the fishing, crofting and archaeological history of the heartland of the MacKenzies.

ⓘ Gairloch Community Centre

Beinn Eighe from Glen Torridon

sturdy Victorian villas in wooded grounds. Strathpeffer's redundant **station** has been restored to house craft shops, and in a **pavilion** in the square, you can sample some of the mineral-rich waters from local springs. Be prepared for a strong taste of sulphur! In the old days, spa visitors were expected to take vigorous exercise; so there is an excellent golf course, as well as a network of paths in a pleasant pinewood and, on the southern hills patrolled by kestrels and sparrowhawks, to the commanding viewpoint summit of **Knock Farril**.

ⓘ The Square

Continue on the A832 through Poolewe.

Inverewe Garden, Highland

8 Maintained by the National Trust for Scotland, this is perhaps the most famous garden in the whole of Scotland. Its Victorian creator transformed a bare, windswept promontory into a pine-sheltered woodland where, helped by the benign effect of the Gulf Stream, a spectacular collection of rhododendrons, primulas, deep blue meconopsis and hundreds of other plants and flowering shrubs now flourishes.

Continue on the A832, turn right on to the A835 then left at Contin on the A834.

Strathpeffer, Highland

9 What was once Europe's most northerly spa remains a fine-looking resort centred on a gathering of

Return to Contin and turn left on the A835. Turn right on the A832 then right on the A862 through Beauly. Turn right to Moniack and pass Moniack Castle. Turn right at a T-junction following the Rebeg sign, pass the start of the Reelig Glen forest walk, then continue over a bridge and uphill. Take the first tarred road left, past a house called Kilninver, turn left at a T-junction and immediately first right, then right at a Give Way sign to Inverness.

THE CASTLES OF MAR

One of the marvellous wealth of gardens open for the public's enjoyment at Crathes Castle

ℹ️ St Nicholas House, Broad Street, Aberdeen

Leave Aberdeen on the B9077. Turn right on the A957, then left on the A93 to Crathes Castle.

Crathes Castle, Grampian

1 One of the finest properties of the National Trust for Scotland, 16th-century Crathes Castle was the home of generations of the Burnett family. It is a typical design by the Bells, master masons of Aberdeen and its hinterland, with a tower-like structure and an intriguing ornamented roof-line. Look for the lovely painted ceiling of the Nine Nobles Room, and in the Green Lady's Room ponder the story of the Crathes ghost. There are eight splendid individual gardens, and one of their major attractions is the array of massive yew hedges, planted in 1702. Topiarists trim them into sweeping shapes, a task which takes three weeks every year.

Continue on the A93 to Aboyne.

Aboyne, Grampian

2 Set among pinewoods and built in Victorian times round a spacious green, Aboyne was previously a base for the 'floaters', the intrepid characters who made rafts of timber, cut up-river, and then steered them down the Dee to Aberdeen. There is a well-kept **golf course** not far from the water-skiing centre at Aboyne Loch. Anglers fish the Dee, and there are pleasant riverside walks backed by banks of broom. Aboyne Highland Games, held every August on the green, are among the most famous in Scotland.

ℹ️ Ballater Road Car Park

Leave Aboyne to the south. Turn right on the B976, left on the A97 as far as Ordie. Turn left on to the B9119 and left on the A93 to Ballater.

Ballater, Grampian

3 Close to the Royal Family's Balmoral estate, this sturdy granite-built town has many shops showing

Aberdeen • Crathes Castle • Aboyne • Ballater Balmoral Castle • Kildrummy Castle • Alford Craigievar Castle • Drum Castle • Aberdeen

Aberdeen is the gateway to Royal Deeside and to the great spread of historic houses known as the Castles of Mar. The Royal Family's Scottish home is here, where pine and birch-woods line the riversides and heathery grouse moors rise to the skyline hills. Salmon and trout anglers fish the Dee and its companion river, the Don. Gliders soar above Aboyne and Dinnet, while older transport is the fascination at Alford. Much of this area is, strictly speaking, in the northeast of Scotland rather than in the highlands, but there is a strong tradition of Highland Games.

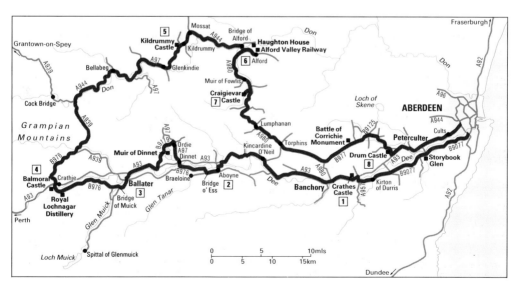

what must have been the grandest ever building fund bazaar.

Turn left on the A93, right on the B976, left on the A939, right on the A944 then straight on along the A97 to Kildrummy Castle.

Kildrummy Castle, Grampian

5 Built in the 13th century, this was the first great stone fortress in the north of Scotland. Even in decay it remains an impressive place. Modern Kildrummy Castle, once a mansion house, is now a hotel. The quarry from which it was built was transformed in Victorian times into a Japanese-style rock and water-garden with woodlands, pools, waterfalls, shrubs and flower beds linked by paths and stairways in a narrow ravine.

Continue on the A97, then right on the A944 to Alford.

Alford, Grampian

6 If it runs on wheels, Alford welcomes it. The **Grampian Transport Museum** houses a fine collection of cars, commercial and farm vehicles, models and transport *memorabilia*. Look for the *Craigievar Express*, a steam wagon built in the 1890s by a local postman; and a Sentinel steam lorry from a distillery, whose wares it

A loving home for veterans at the Grampian Transport Museum

SCENIC ROUTES

For much of the way to Balmoral, the **A93** and **B976** run past birch and pine woods through which the sparkling River Dee is often seen.

There is a beautiful outlook over the Muir of Dinnet from the **A97**; and beyond Balmoral the **B976** climbs from Deeside to give wide-ranging views of narrow cultivated valleys and sweeping heather hills.

the royal warrant. Golf, angling and walks by the Dee are once again favourite recreations here, but there are also enjoyable footpaths on Craigendarroch and Craig Coillich, the two wooded viewpoint hills which squeeze the town towards the river.

In the now redundant railway station there is a display on the Deeside Line and its most celebrated passengers: the Royal Family used to arrive by train at Ballater and continue by road to Balmoral.

ⓘ Station Square

Leave Ballater to the south and turn right on the B976 to the car park for Balmoral Castle.

Balmoral Castle, Grampian

4 The Royal Family's Scottish home is their private property, and not one of the great state houses. Prince Albert collaborated closely with the architect commissioned to build the present castle in Scottish Baronial style. From May till the end of July, the beautiful grounds are generally open to visitors. The ballroom houses an exhibition on the history of the estate. Across the river from the car park, Crathie parish church is where the Royal Family worship when in residence at Balmoral. They also helped to finance it; Queen Victoria opened the grounds of Balmoral to

BACK TO NATURE

Follow the **A92** north of Aberdeen, turning right on to the **A975** to reach the **Sands of Forvie** and **Ythan estuary**. Terns, shelduck and eiders breed in the dunes here and, where the vegetation is firmly established, ling, crowberry and creeping lady's tresses can be found. The estuary is the winter haunt for thousands of waders and wildfowl, most notably for bar-tailed godwits, redshanks, shelduck and sanderling.

The grounds of Balmoral are open to the public at certain times

advertises as most suitable for medicinal purposes.

Outside, the museum operates a little motor-racing circuit where sprints for modern and vintage cars are held. Close by, the old station has been restored as a **railway museum**.

ⓘ Alford Station

Return from Alford along the A944 straight on along the A980, then right to Craigievar Castle.

Craigievar Castle, Grampian

7 Although they were not building for fairytales, the Bell family of master masons combined a firm grasp of technique with a glorious lightness of touch. With its profusion of towers and turrets, Craigievar demonstrates this very clearly. Built for 'Danzig Willie' Forbes, who made his fortune in the Baltic trade, it was completed in 1626. Craigievar's five floors of rooms include such features as a grand heraldic fireplace carved from granite, pine and oak panelling, intricate plaster ceilings and the first of the Craigievar gaming tables which had a vogue among 18th-century card players.

Continue on the A980 and go straight on along the B977 and the B9125, then immediately

after Flora's Shop, turn right, following the 'Hopeton' sign. Turn right at a crossroads, avoiding a farm road straight ahead, then follow signs to Drum Castle.

Drum Castle, Grampian

8 The Irvine family have been lairds at Drum Castle for 24 generations before giving the property to the National Trust for Scotland. They lived in a complex of linked buildings: a 13th-century keep, a Jacobean mansion and Victorian additions. Drum is well furnished with valuable pieces from different centuries. Among the portraits is one of Washington Irving, author of the classic *Rip van Winkle*, whose family left Scotland to live in America.

Rejoin the public road, then turn left on to the A93 to return to Aberdeen.

Aberdeen – Crathes Castle 17 (27)
Crathes Castle – Aboyne 16 (26)
Aboyne – Ballater 17 (27)
Ballater – Balmoral Castle 8 (13)
Balmoral Castle – Kildrummy Castle 27 (43)
Kildrummy Castle – Alford 10 (16)
Alford – Craigievar Castle 7 (11)
Craigievar Castle – Drum Castle 22 (36)
Drum Castle – Aberdeen 10 (16)

FOR CHILDREN

1 Turn left off the **B9077** for **Storybook Glen**, with its tableaux of children's stories, ranging from *Jack and the Beanstalk* and *Little Jack Horner* to the *Incredible Hulk* and *ET*.

6 From Alford station the narrow-gauge **Alford Valley Railway** runs into Haughton House country park, where there is an adventure playground in the birchwoods.

RECOMMENDED WALKS

2 After Aboyne, turn left off the **B976** at the grand gateway by the Bridge o' Ess into beautiful **Glen Tanar**. Call in at the interpretive centre at Braeloine for information on the footpath routes beside the Water of Tanar, to forest viewpoints and along part of the Firmounth road, one of the historic rights of way across the Grampians.

SPECIAL TO...

2 Aboyne is just one place which hosts annual **Highland Games**. Tossing the caber, shot-putting and hill races as well as normal track events are featured at Ballater and further up Royal Deeside. The Lonach Gathering at Bellabeg, on the A944 in Strathdon, is preceded by a march of the green-clad Lonach Highlanders.

4 Single malt whisky is a classic Highland product. Turn left off the B976 before Balmoral for a tour of **Royal Lochnagar Distillery**, which received its royal warrant after a friendly visit from its neighbours Queen Victoria and Prince Albert.

FOR HISTORY BUFFS

5 **Kildrummy Castle** never witnessed a more gruesome deed than in 1306, when its English besiegers promised to reward the blacksmith who betrayed it to them with gold. They kept their promise by melting the gold pieces and pouring them down his throat to kill him.

8 On the B977, look to the left for the granite monument to the Battle of Corrichie in 1562. Mary Queen of Scots' army crushed the Gordons, the most powerful family in the northeast, in this battle. The Earl of Huntly, the head of the family, died in the battle, and his corpse was taken to Edinburgh to 'hear' the sentence that forfeited his lands and titles.

2/3 days – 134 miles (216km)

EXPLORING A RIVER VALLEY

Edinburgh • Hillend Country Park • Peebles
Traquair House • Innerleithen • Melrose
Kelso • Coldstream • Haddington
Aberlady • Edinburgh

Hills are an important part of this tour from Edinburgh, which visits the Pentlands, the Eildons and the Lammermuirs, and looks south to the Cheviots. But the valley of the River Tweed, one of Scotland's great trout and salmon waters, is the most significant element as the journey reaches the Border country, taking on many guises from Peebles and Innerleithen, Abbotsford, Melrose and the farmlands of the Merse of Berwickshire. Two of the graceful Border abbeys are on the tour; so are a veteran printing works, historic houses and a year-round ski centre right on the edge of Edinburgh.

A study in unspoiled tranquillity: the River Tweed near Innerleithen in Border country

i Waverley Station, Princes Street, Edinburgh

Leave Edinburgh on the A702 and turn right into Hillend Country Park.

Hillend Country Park, Lothian

1 This is one of two similar parks in the exhilarating Pentland Hills, which rise directly from Edinburgh's southern suburbs. Footpaths climb steeply to the grassy viewpoint summits of Caerketton and Allermuir, the boyhood hills of Robert Louis Stevenson.

These paths link up with others across the rounded passes in the Pentlands, and alongside the many reservoirs which supply the city. **Hillend Ski Centre** is a year-round mountain resort in miniature.

i Pentland Hills Ranger Service Office

Continue on the A702, then straight on along the A703 and follow the A701 and B7026 through Auchendinny. Take the A6094 and the A703 again to Peebles.

Peebles, Borders

2 No development is allowed to encroach upon Peebles' tree-lined riverside walks by the Tweed, and the town itself has a traditional charm. The **Tontine Hotel** in the High Street, retains the old front yard where stagecoaches used to sweep to a halt. There is a well-stocked

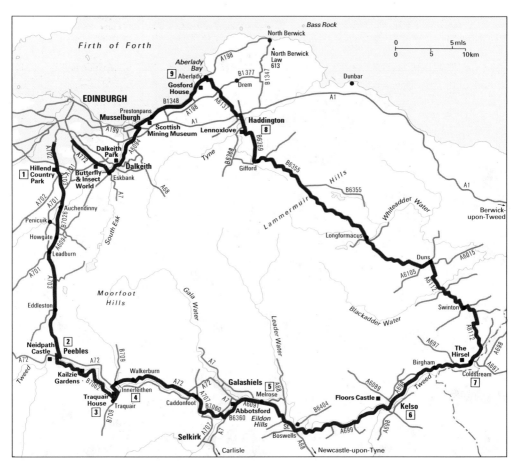

Tweeddale Museum, and the **Scottish Museum of Ornamental Plasterwork** is close by, where you will be encouraged to don wellies and an apron, and try your hand at the craft. Peebles has extensive public parks and an interesting town walk. Medieval **Neidpath Castle** stands dramatically above an up-river wooded curve of the Tweed. Its walls still show signs of the bombardment in 1650 by Cromwell's artillery.

ⓘ Chambers Institute, High Street

Leave Peebles on the B7062 and turn left for Traquair House.

Traquair House, Borders

3 Twenty generations of Stuart lairds made Traquair House their home, but it dates from well before their time – from 1107 at least – and is the oldest inhabited house in Scotland. Traquair retains mementoes of such famous Stuarts as Mary Queen of Scots and Bonnie Prince Charlie. As well as having valuable collections of glass, porcelain and embroideries, it is famous for its one derelict 18th-century estate brew-house. The present laird restored the copper, the mash tun, the coolers and fermenters, and now brews the rare Traquair Ale in quantities of no more than 210 barrels every year.

Continue on the B7062 then turn left on the B709 to Innerleithen.

Innerleithen, Borders

4 The founder of this little textile town had the idea of using London names so addresses here include The Strand and Bond Street. Cashmere cloth is still woven in Innerleithen's mills, and the National Trust for Scotland has completely restored **Robert Smail's Printing Works**, closed as a family business

only in 1986. A tour of this fascinating place recalls the otherwise lost technology of planers, reglets, quoins and sidesticks, and you may be given the chance to hand-set some type yourself. At a glorious viewpoint high in the town, the little blue-and-white spa pavilion of **St Ronan's Wells** has also been restored.

Leave Innerleithen on the A72. Bear right on the A707, then left on the B7060. Turn right on the A7, left on the B6360, right on the A6091 as for Jedburgh, and left on the B6374 into Melrose.

Melrose, Borders

5 One of the pleasantest of the Border towns, Melrose is notable for the mellow ruin of its abbey, where the heart of Robert the Bruce is buried, and for **Priorwood Garden**, in which something like the old monks' orchard has been revived. The restored station houses an exhibition on the disappeared Waverley Line, and there is a small **motor museum**. Two walks explore the town, and the Southern Upland Way includes a lovely riverside stretch along the meadows by the Tweed.

ⓘ Priorwood Garden

Leave Melrose on the A6091 as for Jedburgh. Turn right on to the A68 then left on the A699 and left on the A698 into Kelso.

Kelso, Borders

6 Here is a Border market town with a ruined abbey, the oldest cricket club in Scotland, a racecourse and a reputation for providing some of the best angling beats on the Tweed.

Walter Scott declared Kelso the most beautiful village in Scotland

FOR CHILDREN

1 Hillend Ski Centre is the largest of its kind in Europe. Children's courses start for those aged six. On the return to Edinburgh, the **Butterfly and Insect World** on the A772 houses hundreds of exotic butterflies as well as scorpions, tarantulas and stick insects.

RECOMMENDED WALKS

2 The **Sware Walk** at Peebles heads west along the wooded riverbank below Neidpath Castle, crosses Manor Bridge and Old Manor Bridge, then climbs to the wide-ranging Tweeddale viewpoint at Manor Sware.

5 Starting from B6359 in Melrose, the waymarked **Eildon Walk** climbs to the 1,325-foot (404m) Eildon North Hill, a magnificent viewpoint where a Roman signal station overlooked the Dere Street route from the Cheviots to the Forth.

SPECIAL TO...

4 After Innerleithen, pause at Walkerburn to visit the **Museum of Scottish Woollen Textiles**, which illustrates all the processes from sheep-rearing to spinning, weaving and knitting.

8 In Newtown Street, Duns, the **Jim Clark Memorial Room** commemorates the great world race-driving champion who won 25 Grand Prix races and the Indianapolis 500.

FOR HISTORY BUFFS

5 Abbotsford was the home of Sir Walter Scott, author of the *Waverley* novels. The tour includes his impressive library and study.

8 Memorials at Gifford recall the Rev John Witherspoon, who signed the American Declaration of Independence and was president of the college which became Princeton university.

Off the **B6369**, Lennoxlove House is the home of the Dukes of Hamilton. It contains many mementoes of Mary Queen of Scots, including the ring which, on her way to the scaffold, she bequeathed to the Hamiltons.

BACK TO NATURE

4 The tidal inlet, saltmarsh and dunes at **Aberlady Bay Nature Reserve** attract great numbers of waders. Regular reports are posted of bird observations: hundreds of sandwich terns, for instance, and godwits, dunlin and plover.

On the return towards Edinburgh, **Dalkeith Park** nature trails link the River North Esk and the South Esk through extensive estate woodlands.

SCENIC ROUTES

The B7062, past Kalizie Gardens, and the A72 follow the Tweed as it winds among woodlands, farms and hillside forests. You can follow a tree-lined road on the B7060 over the shoulder of a hill between two stretches of the Tweed.

Kelso has an elegant Georgian centre, and its cobbled square retains a bull ring – a pattern of stones marking the place where bulls were tethered during livestock sales. Turret House is the local **museum**.

Outside the town, **Floors Castle**, home of the Duke of Roxburghe, is richly furnished with paintings, tapestries and porcelain, and has a window for every day of the year.

ⓘ Town House Square

Leave Kelso on the A698 for Coldstream.

Coldstream, Borders

7 This is the closest Scottish town to the English border. The Coldstream Guards, under an earlier name, were stationed in the town in 1660 when they marched south to assist in the restoration of King Charles II to the throne. There is a **museum** here dedicated to the regiment and its impressive heritage.

Just outside Coldstream, the **Hirsel** estate has a comprehensive museum and a craft centre, several walks and a colourful collection of rhododendrons in Dundock Wood.

ⓘ Henderson Park

Leave Coldstream on the A6112 for Duns, then take the A6105 as for Earlston. After leaving Duns, watch for the right turn to Gifford. Turn right to Haddington on the B6369 and B6368.

Haddington, Lothian

8 Haddington is famous for the dozens of listed buildings along its streets, lanes and riverside walks. St Mary's Church – the Lamp of Lothian – contains the Lauderdale Aisle, scene of an annual ecumenical pilgrimage. Near by, **St Mary's Pleasance** is a garden laid out in an old Scottish style. Features to look for on a stroll round

The Victoria Bridge spanning the River Tyne at immaculately preserved Haddington

Haddington include the town history display in **Lady Kitty's Doocot** (dovecote); **Jane Welsh Carlyle's House**, with its memories of the Victorian writer Thomas Carlyle; the **Nungate Bridge**; and the statue of two goats fighting. A goat eating grapes is Haddington's unusual coat of arms.

Leave Haddington on the A6137 for Aberlady.

Aberlady, Lothian

9 Once the seaport for Haddington, Aberlady is now a residential village with carefully preserved buildings, including a fine **parish church** and attractive 18th- and 19th-century houses in the High Street. Aberlady's golf course, **Kilspindie**, shared the ground with a rifle range when it was opened in 1898; hence the names of holes such as the Target and the Magazine. West of the village, **Gosford House** is the home of the Earl of Wemyss. The magnificent entrance hall houses Gosford's imposing portrait gallery.

Leave Aberlady on the A198 as for Edinburgh, then straight ahead on the B1348. Turn left on the A199 then right on the A6094 through Dalkeith. Turn right on the A772 and return to Edinburgh.

Today's visitor to Rockcliffe, popular for its quiet charm, will feel a lot safer than an 18th-century ancestor, who would have found its bays and inlets much-used by smugglers of wine and tobacco

---

i Whitesands, Dumfries

Leave Dumfries on the A710 to New Abbey.

New Abbey, Dumfries and Galloway

1 Here, 'new' is a relative term. It refers to the lovely ruined abbey of mellow red sandstone which stands on the south side of the village. This is **Sweetheart Abbey**, new in the 13th century when it was founded by the family which also endowed Balliol College at Oxford. New Abbey also has a splendidly restored 18th-century **corn mill**. Among the pinewoods at the entrance to the village, Shambellie House is the site of Scotland's **Museum of Costume**.

Continue on the A710 to Kirkbean.

Kirkbean, Dumfries and Galloway

3 American visitors often come to this attractive village in 'the garden of Galloway' to trace the roots of Paul Jones, organiser and first commander of the Navy, who was baptised John Paul in the parish church here. His birthplace cottage on the **Arbigland** estate is a museum of his life and exploits, which included raiding his home coast during the American War of Independence! Arbigland itself has attractive sheltered gardens stretching to the Solway shore, where Paul Jones' father was employed. Also near Kirkbean, Carsethorn is a Solwayside village with salmon stake-nets out on the treacherous tidal sands. Facing the Cumbrian shore, it was built to house the men of a 19th-century coastguard station, in the days when the coastguards' preoccupation was stopping the smugglers.

Continue on the A710. Turn left off it, first to Rockcliffe and then to Kippford.

ALONG THE SMUGGLERS' COAST

Dumfries • New Abbey • Kirkbean
Rockcliffe and Kippford • Castle Douglas
Kirkcudbright • Gatehouse of Fleet • Kirroughtree
Forest • The Queens Way • Dumfries

Mountains, forests and beautiful stretches of coastline are the accompaniment to this tour from Dumfries. The huge Galloway Forest Park offers walks and trails, exhibitions, nature reserves and fishing waters. Along the coast, the Solway smugglers once brought contraband from the Isle of Man. The whiff of that secret trade is still in the air. Robert Burns knew Galloway well, and so did Paul Jones, founding commander of the US Navy, whose boyhood home here preserves his memory.

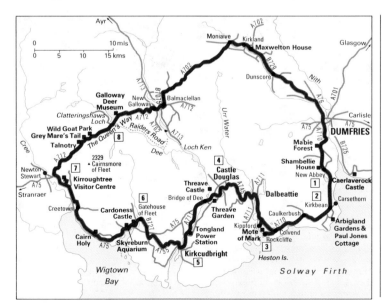

SCENIC ROUTES

Beyond Dumfries, the **A710** gradually comes within sight of the wide Solway sands and, across the water, the faraway Lakeland hills. After Gatehouse, the **A75** offers beautiful high-level views over the bird-watcher's paradise of Wigtown Bay.

The Queens Way is not crushed between spruce plantations; there is room to admire the craggy summits above the forest and, across Clatteringshaws Loch, the remote and atmospheric Rhinns of Kells. After Moniaive, the **A702** and **B729** follow the Cairn Valley through a fine landscape of farms, woods and stone-dyked fields.

Rockcliffe and Kippford, Dumfries and Galloway

3 These are the principal villages of the Colvend coast, the most beautiful stretch of the Solway Firth. Rockcliffe with its rock flakes in a curving bay, was a Victorian seabathing resort. Kippford, near the mouth of the River Urr, used to make its living from boat-building and quarrying. Now it is the main sailing centre on the Solway.

A still life at low tide. The estuary of the Dee at Kirkcudbright in evening light

gardens. **Threave House** is the Trust's School of Horticulture, and the whole 60 acres (24 hectares) are impeccably kept.

ⓘ Market Hill

> *Turn left at a roundabout, go along the A75, then turn left on to the A711 to Kirkcudbright.*

Kirkcudbright, Dumfries and Galloway

5 Built as the county town, this is a place of elegantly proportioned and colour-washed Georgian houses. It comes as no surprise that it attracted

Almost all the land between the villages is owned by the National Trust for Scotland. Both offer outstanding views over the wooded peninsulas around Rough Firth. Above Rockcliffe stands the **Mote of Mark**, site of a 6th-century fortress and now a glorious viewpoint.

ⓘ Colvend Post Office, **A710**

> *Continue on the A710, then follow signs for Castle Douglas on the A711 and A745. Turn left at a roundabout and go through the town centre.*

Castle Douglas, Dumfries and Galloway

4 A light and lively market town, Castle Douglas is lucky in having, as its principal public park, the land around **Carlingwark Loch**. Here you can hire a rowing boat to potter round the wooded islets and reedbeds where swans and great crested grebes nest and raise their young.

West of the loch, watch for the road on the left to **Threave Garden**. A property of the National Trust for Scotland, it features springtime daffodil displays as well as herbaceous borders, peat, woodland and rock

turn-of-the-century artists, and their successors still live and work here. **Broughton House**, an 18th-century mansion, was presented to the town by the painter E A Hornel. It hosts art exhibitions and is well furnished with a fine antiquarian library and features such as a 1920s-style laundry. Outside, you may be surprised to find a **Japanese garden**; Hornel was influenced by Oriental themes.

Maclellan's Castle, now an ancient monument, is the ruin of a grander and earlier town mansion. The **Stewartry Museum** holds a fascinating local collection, including a room devoted to Kirkcudbright shipping, in which Paul Jones features strongly.

ⓘ Harbour Square

> *Leave Kirkcudbright on the A755 then follow the B727 through Gatehouse of Fleet.*

Gatehouse of Fleet, Dumfries and Galloway

6 Gatehouse by the River Fleet is one of the most intriguing country towns in Scotland full of restored buildings from its brief heyday – from 1790 onwards – as a cotton town.

Robert Burns visited Gatehouse during the boom years, and it was in a room at the **Murray Arms Hotel** that he wrote what was to become Scotland's unofficial anthem, *Scots, wha hae*. The town is surrounded by delicious woodland country. Try the **Fleet Oakwoods** interpretive trail. A shorter open-ground stroll leads to the field-top viewpoint on Venniehill, which identifies the features of Gatehouse and its surroundings. Beyond Venniehill, **Cardoness Castle** is an imposingly situated 15th-century tower which was the home of the notoriously hot-tempered McCullochs.

ⓘ The Car Park, High Street

Turn right on to the A75 (heading west) and in Palnure watch for a right turn to Kirroughtree Visitor Centre.

Kirroughtree Forest, Dumfries and Galloway

7 The oldest South of Scotland plantations of the Forestry Commission cover a landscape of hills and a river valley overlooked by the great bulk of Cairnsmore of Fleet. An audio-visual presentation explains the workings of the forest, and outdoor attractions include a forest garden with plots of more than 60 tree species, from redwoods and monkey puzzles to cypress and rarities such as the Englemann spruce. Four trails explore the upper parts of the forest, visiting hill lochs and viewpoints, and you should certainly follow the separate Papy Ha'bird trail above the

Annie Laurie of Maxwelton was immortalised in song by a suitor

Palnure Burn, habitat of warblers, woodpeckers, dippers, goosanders, shelduck, jays and ravens.

ⓘ Visitor Centre

Rejoin the A75, then go right on to the A712.

The Queens Way, Dumfries and Galloway

8 Several visitor areas of the Galloway Forest Park are concentrated along the stretch of A712 known as the Queens Way. The start is signalled by the hilltop **obelisk** at Talnotry commemorating Alexander Murray, a local shepherd's son who became the greatest Oriental linguist in early 19th-century Britain.

Look for the **Grey Mare's Tail** waterfall, the wild goats and their kids in the roadside reserve at **Craigdews Hill**, the red deer range and the **Galloway Deer Museum** among a stand of pines above the shore of Clatteringshaws Loch.

ⓘ Talnotry campsite or Galloway Deer Museum

Continue on the A712 through New Galloway. Turn right on the A713, left on the A712, left on the B7075 and right on the A702 through Moniaive. In Kirkland, turn right on the B729 and return to Dumfries.

RECOMMENDED WALKS

3 For one of the most beautiful walks in Scotland, leave Rockcliffe by the **Jubilee Path** with its gorgeous views over the estuary. At Kippford, turn left by the post office along the shore road, then return to Rockcliffe by grassy pathways. Except in May and June when the terns and oystercatchers are nesting, you can extend the walk – with care – along the tidal causeway to Rough Island.

8 At Talnotry on the Queens Way, marked trails explore the steep forested hills. Do not be misled by the wide path at the start; much of this is roughish going. The trails go to viewpoints and an old lead mine, and follow the 'lost' 18th-century Edinburgh-Wigtown coach road.

FOR HISTORY BUFFS

4 At the roundabout after Castle Douglas, take the second exit for the walk and short ferry trip across the Dee to **Threave Castle**, the ruined island fortress of the Black Douglases, rebels against the crown, in the River Dee.

7 Turn right off the A75 for the standing stones of **Cairn Holy**, overlooking the Solway. On the return to Dumfries, **Maxwelton House**, on the B729, was the birthplace of the heroine of Scotland's famous love song, *Annie Laurie*.

4 days – 246 miles (396km)

THE BEAUTIFUL WESTERN HIGHLANDS

Dumbarton • Helensburgh • Inveraray • Crinan Canal
Kilmartin • Easdale • Oban • Sea Life Centre
Port Appin • Ballachulish • Glen Coe and the Black Mount
Loch Lomond • Dumbarton

Some of the most striking seascapes, mountains, forests and moorland scenery in the West Highlands form the landscape of this tour, based on the firmly Lowland town of Dumbarton. Woodland gardens tumble down lochside glens, and ancient monuments are scattered across a beautiful valley which was the first tiny kingdom of the Scots. You can explore islands where generations of slate-quarriers toiled, and sense the atmosphere in Glen Coe, where the mountains loom over the scene of a shameful massacre committed in the king's name.

Winter colours adorn the hills surrounding Kilchurn Castle

ⓘ Milton, by Dumbarton

Leave Dumbarton on the A814 through Cardross, Helensburgh, Rhu and Shandon.

Helensburgh, Strathclyde

1 Think of this residential town rising from the estuary of the River Clyde when you switch on your television. John Logie Baird, the television pioneer, was born here in 1888. Another inventive Helensburgh man was Henry Bell, whose *Comet*, launched in 1812, was the world's first seagoing steamboat. Both men are commemorated in the town.

Charles Rennie Mackintosh, the most famous of Scotland's 20th-century architects, completed **The Hill House** in 1902. You may share the feelings of many visitors that the elegant interiors, showing Mackintosh's amazing attention to detail, seem to become more rather than less modern as the decades pass.

In summer, ferries sail across the Clyde from Helensburgh. There are sailing races, and dozens of yachts lie moored off Rhu – where the woodland garden of **Glenarn** is an early-season attraction – and Shandon. After Shandon the main road passes the **Clyde Submarine Base**, home port of Britain's nuclear fleet.

ⓘ The Clock Tower

Take the third exit from the roundabout, follow the A814 to Arrochar and turn left on the A83. Ignore a left turn for the A815, bear left on an

SCENIC ROUTES

On the **A814**, after you go under the railway bridge at Whistlefield, there is a startling view of the forested and rocky hills of Ardgoil rising steeply from the fiords of Loch Goil and Loch Long. From the head of Loch Fyne via the Crinan Canal, almost to Oban, there is beautiful coast, hill and forest scenery, with many island views. Glen Coe is majestic in fine weather when clouds cap the ridges and buttresses, and seep down the gullies; and Loch Lomond is simply the most beautiful area easily accessible from the towns and cities of Lowland Scotland.

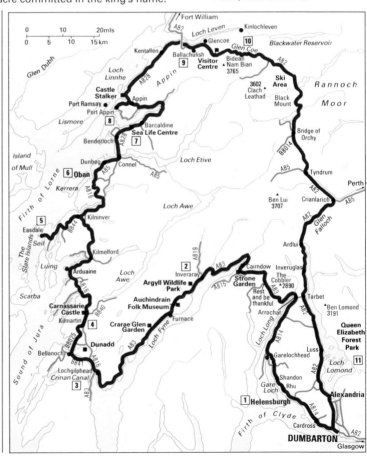

unclassified road through
Cairndow, and rejoin the **A83**
for Inveraray.

Inveraray, Strathclyde

2Once the county town of Argyll,
this gem of 18th-century architecture is reflected in the waters of Loch
Fyne near **Inveraray Castle**, home of
the 12th Duke of Argyll, who is also
chief of Clan Campbell. The castle's
public rooms include an imposing
armoury hall, a tapestry drawing
room and a state dining room with
elaborate plasterwork.

In the grounds, **Cherry Park** houses
a **Combined Operations Museum**
recalling how a quarter of a million
troops were trained at Inveraray for
seaborne landings of World War II.
There are also pleasant woodland
walks. If you are fit and sure-footed,
try the steep climb through roe deer
territory to the viewpoint summit of
Dun na Cuaiche.

The town's 20th-century bell tower
acts as the Clan Campbell war
memorial; and **Inveraray Gaol** is one
of the finest theme museums in
Scotland. In the courtroom, sitting
among lifelike figures of lawyers and
jurymen, you can hear the tape-
recorded transcript of an actual trial
held in 1850, all the characters' lines
being spoken by Inveraray folk of
today.

[i] Front Street

*Continue on the A83 to
Lochgilphead. Turn right on the
A816, bear left on the B841 to
cross the Crinan Canal, then go
right at Bellanoch on the B8025.*

Crinan Canal, Strathclyde

3Built to save fishing boats and trading ships the risky journey round
the Mull of Kintyre, this 9-mile (14m)
waterway is now used mostly by
yachts and motor cruisers. To the

*Some mementoes of Rob Roy are
amongst the interesting things to
see at Inveraray Castle*

south of the summit level, spruce
plantations clothe the hills where
reservoirs store the canal's essential
water supply. From the picnic site at
Dunardry a forest walk looks down
on the canal, its locks and towpath,
and an attractive tree-backed lagoon.

*Bear left on the A816 to
Kilmartin.*

Kilmartin, Strathclyde

4The lovely Kilmartin valley was the
heartland of the 6th-century kingdom of Dalriada, which expanded to
become the kingdom of Scotland.
The valley also contains Bronze Age
burial cairns and **standing stones**,
some set out in a straight linear align-
ment.

Kilmartin **church** and **churchyard**
house many medieval grave slabs,
and Carnassarie Castle, high above
the village, offers a magnificent view,
unobtainable from road level, into the
narrow canyon which swings down
from Loch Awe.

*Continue on the A816, then left
on the B844 and follow signs to
Easdale.*

Easdale, Strathclyde

5The steeply-arched 'bridge over the
Atlantic' to Seil joins one of Argyll's
Slate Islands to the mainland.
Easdale is the name both of the old
quarry village on the west side of
Seil, and of the smaller offshore
island facing it. A deep quarry at
Easdale village, breached by the sea
during a ferocious storm in
November 1881, survives as an open
bay.

The village retains its rows of
whitewashed quarriers' cottages. In

FOR CHILDREN

2South of Inveraray, **Argyll
Wildlife Park** covers 60
acres (18 hectares) of open
ground, forest and lochside.
There are wildfowl pools as
well as badgers, wildcats,
foxes, pine martens and deer,
and the residents of Owl
Avenue stare imperiously
down.

6A World in Miniature, on
the North Pier at Oban, displays amazingly intricate one-
twelfth scale model scenes.
Look for the country pub with
its tiny dartboard, the charming music room and the workshop where all the
miniaturised tools work like
their full-scale counterparts.

FOR HISTORY BUFFS

2Beside the A83,
Auchindrain is a farming
museum. In and around a
cluster of restored cottages
once lived in by families of
MacCallums, MacCoshams,
MacNicols and Munros you
can see furnishings and displays of agricultural
techniques of generations
long gone by.

4Few places are as atmospheric, for Scots or descendants of Scots, as **Dunadd**,
south of Kilmartin. With its
lovely panoramic views, this
hilltop fortress was the capital
of the kingdom of Dalriada
and the coronation site of the
first Scottish kings.

Elsewhere in the town you can watch glass-blowers and paper-weight-makers at work, and visit the **distillery** founded in the 18th century. Footpaths climb to outstanding viewpoints such as **Pulpit Hill** and **McCaig's Tower**, built in the style of the Colosseum at Rome. Gallanach Road leads south to the little ferry slip for Kerrera, where a family prepared for changeable West Highland weather could enjoy an exhilarating island walk round a 7-mile (11km) circuit of paths and farm roads.

⒤ Argyll Square

Leave Oban on the A85. At Connel, turn right on the A828 as it swings over Connel Bridge.

Sea Life Centre, Strathclyde

7 As you admire the agile seals here you may have the feeling that they are watching the parade of visitors just as much as the other way round. Similarly, the rays rise up from their low-level tank to look enquiringly at the tourists. It is intriguing to see the herring shoal swim clockwise round their specially-shaped tank, then suddenly, at a mysterious group signal, all change direction.

Continue on the A828 into Appin village then turn left for Port Appin.

Port Appin, Strathclyde

8 On one of the finest stretches of the coast of Argyll, this little village looks out to the long island of Lismore and, beyond it, to the lonely hills of Kingairloch. There is a peninsula walk past a natural archway in the cliffs, and another excursion could start with a ferry trip to the north end of Lismore. Walks there include one to the former limeworkers' village of Port Ramsay. North of Port Appin, look for **Castle Stalker**, romantically located on a tidal islet.

Return to the A828 and turn left. Pass Ballachulish Hotel and turn left on the A82.

Ballachulish, Strathclyde

9 The 'Village at the Narrows' used to be well-known for its ferry across Loch Leven, which has been replaced with a modern bridge. A flight of steps after the Ballachulish Hotel climbs to a memorial marking the site of the gibbet where, in 1755, James Stewart of the Glen was hanged for the murder – which he did not commit – of government agent Colin Campbell. After he was dead, Stewart's body was left hanging for three years. The mystery of who really did commit the Appin Murder is still discussed, and Robert Louis Stevenson made it the central theme of his novel *Kidnapped*.

Extensive landscaping has disguised the fact that between 1697 and 1955 Ballachulish was a major centre of the slate industry. A comprehensive display in the visitor centre describes its rise and decline.

⒤ A82 Car Park

Continue on the A82, diverting left into Glencoe village, then return to the main road for Glen Coe itself.

RECOMMENDED WALKS

8 The most spectacular of the Forestry Commission walks around Barcaldine on the A828 starts from **Sutherland's Grove**. Paths lead up Glen Dubh – the Dark Glen – to a footbridge over the ravine where the river rampages down.

10 After the river bridge at Glencoe village, turn left for the **Lochan Trail**, which circles an ornamental lake backed by Corsican pines. On a calm day it reflects like a mirror the striking outline of Ben Vair – the Peak of the Thunderbolt.

McCaig's Folly was begun as a ploy to relieve local unemployment but was never finished

contrast, high walls and a wooded cliff protect the garden of **An Cala** – with its gentle stream, ponds, herbaceous borders and flowering shrubs – from the salt-laden wind.

Across the narrow sound on Easdale Island, the workings of a now vanished trade and the way the quarry communities created their own lively social life are explained in a fascinating museum.

⒤ Easdale Island Museum

Return to the A816 and turn left for Oban.

Oban, Strathclyde

6 Clustered on a hillside round a curving bay, Oban is a major car-ferry port and hosts several important yacht races. **St Columba**'s, the 20th-century cathedral with carved oak panels showing scenes from the life of the famous Celtic saint, is the heart of the Roman Catholic diocese of Argyll and the Isles.

Glen Coe and the Black Mount, Strathclyde

10 Now the tour heads into its most dramatic phase. At the village of Glencoe the informative local museum recalls how, one night in February 1692, the MacDonalds of Glencoe were slaughtered in their homes by troops billeted on them – an atrocity which has never been forgotten. The story of the massacre is retold in a National Trust for Scotland Visitor Centre a little way up the glen. It also features the wildlife and geology of the district. The northern wall of Glen Coe is a forbidding mountain ridge, while a glorious succession of towers, buttresses, gullies and hanging valleys marches along its southern side.

Beyond the isolated Kings House Hotel, desolate **Rannoch Moor** stretches away to the left. Further on, notably from a chill roadside loch edged with boulders, there are tremendous views into the corries of the Black Mount.

ℹ️ National Trust for Scotland Visitor Centre, **A82**

Continue on the A82.

The tragedy that occurred at Glen Coe casts a shadow on even the finest day

Loch Lomond, Strathclyde

11 Having swooped down Glen Falloch, the route reaches Ardlui at the head of Loch Lomond. In the north, the loch fills a narrow glacial trough between crammed-in mountains. Luss, with its low sandstone cottages and fine Victorian **church**, lies where Loch Lomond broadens out to become part of a gentler Lowland scene with lovely wooded islands. Like Ardlui, Inveruglas, Tarbet, Inverbeg and Balloch, Luss is a port of call for ferries. You can cruise through the islands or cross the loch, walk on the West Highland Way through spruce, larch, birch and oakwoods under the shoulder of Ben Lomond, and sail back to the western shore.

ℹ️ Main Street, Tarbet

Continue on the A82 and return to Dumbarton.

Dumbarton – Helensburgh 8 (13)
Helensburgh – Inveraray 40 (64)
Inveraray – Crinan Canal 27 (43)
Crinan Canal – Kilmartin 7 (11)
Kilmartin – Easdale 29 (47)
Easdale – Oban 16 (26)
Oban – Sea Life Centre 11 (18)
Sea Life Centre – Port Appin 14 (23)
Port Appin – Ballachulish 18 (29)
Ballachulish – Glen Coe 5 (8)
Glen Coe – Loch Lomond 50 (80)
Loch Lomond – Dumbarton 21 (34)

SPECIAL TO...

9 Railway enthusiasts often trace the old line from Oban via Connel Bridge to Ballachulish. It features handsome turn-of-the-century stations, one of which is the Holly Tree Hotel at Kentallen.

11 The most famous but most elusive fish for Loch Lomond anglers is the powan, unique to Scotland. This freshwater herring had to adapt to life away from the sea after glacial debris blocked out the tidal waters.

BACK TO NATURE

11 Loch Lomond is the largest freshwater lake in Britain. Goldeneye, red-breasted mergansers and other ducks can be seen on the water during the summer months, and in winter, parties of whooper swans visit from time to time. Nearby **Queen Elizabeth Forest Park** harbours woodland birds, including woodcock and wood warbler, while on the higher ground of Ben Lomond there are golden eagles, ptarmigan and mountain flowers.

INDEX

Reference to captions are in *italic*.

ACKNOWLEDGEMENTS

The Automobile Association would like to thank the following library and photographers for their help in the preparation of this book.

INTERNATIONAL PHOTOBANK Cover Cottage Emery Down, New Forest.

All remaining pictures are held in the Association's own library:

AA PHOTO LIBRARY 1 How Hill (A Souter), 2 Godrevy Lighthouse (A W Besley), 3 Canterbury Cathedral (D Noble), 4 Cwm Idwal & Tryfan (E Roberts), 5 Bibury (A Souter), 6 Ben Lawers (H Williams), 8 & 9 Mevagissey, St Michael's Mt (A W Besley), 10 Newlyn (A Lawson), 11 Land's End (A W Besley), 12 Zennor (H Williams), 13 Cadgwith, 14 Boscastle (A Lawson), 15 Camelford (R Newton), 16 Tintagel (T Teegan), 17 Exmoor, 18 Thatcher (A Lawson), 19 Oare Church (H Williams), 20 Dorchester (J Baker), 21 Cerne Abbas (P Baker), 22 Sherborne Castle (R Czaja), 23 Glastonbury Tor (H Williams), 24 Stonehenge (E Meacher), 25 Stourhead (W Voysey), 26 Tunbridge Wells (D Noble), 27 Seven Sisters C P (A Baker), 28 Tenterden Railway, 29 Hever Castle, 30 Chartwell, 31 Tenterden, 32 Bodiam Castle, 33 Chilham, 34 Rye, 35 St Margaret's Bay (D Noble), 36 Hillier Arboretum, 37 Winchester Cathedral, 38 R Test (P Enticknapp), 39 Queen Elizabeth C P (H Williams), 40 New Forest (R Fletcher), 41 Christchurch (P Enticknapp), 42 Fordingbridge (W Voysey), 43 Wimborne Minster (P Enticknapp), 44/5 Elan Valley (H Williams), 45 Pen-y-fan (C Molyneux), 46 Chepstow Castle (H Williams), 47 Brecon & Monmouth Canal (C & A Molyneux), 48 Symonds Yat (A Hopkins), 49 Tenby, 50 St David's (M Allwood Coppin), 51 Boathouse (J Gravell), 52 Abergwesyn (C Molyneux), 53 Builth Wells (E Meacher), 54 Nr Devil's Bridge (M Allwood Coppin), 55 Cader Idris (R Eames), 56 Trawsfynydd, 57 Talyllyn Railway (M Allwood Coppin), 58 Betws y Coed (R Newton), 58/9 Caernarfon Castle (M Allwood Coppin), 60 Portmeirion (T Timms), 61 Llanberis Pass (A Greerley), 62/3 Cley-next-the-Sea (S & O Mathews), 62 Hemingford Grey (P Baker), 64 Sherwood Forest Visitors' Centre, 65 Heckington Windmill (M Birkitt), 66 Newark Castle (R Surman), 67 Hunstanton (S & O Mathews), 68 Ten Mile Bank (A Souter), 69 Hunstanton (S & O Mathews), 71 Finchingfield (S & O Mathews), 72 Clare (T Woodcock), 73 Banbury Cross (M Birkitt), 74 Grt Rollright Stone Circle (A Souter), 75 Broughton Castle (V Greaves), 76 Mary Arden's House (H Williams), 77 Royal Shakespeare Theatre (V Greaves), 78 Chipping Campden (A Souter), 79 Much Wenlock (R Surman), 80 Bridgnorth Castle (M Allwood Coppin), 81 Ironbridge (A Baker), 84 Ashness Bridge (M Birkitt), 86 Windermere (E A Bowness), 87 Richmond, 89 Hawes (S & O Mathews), 90 Brimham Rocks, 91 Malham Cove (H Williams), 92 Devil's Bridge (J Beazley), 93 Clapton (A Baker), 94 Heights of Abraham, 95 Peak Cavern (M Birkitt), 96 Buxton (A Baker), 97 White Horse, Kilburn (C Molyneux), 98 Danby Dale (R Newton), 99 Castle Howard (J Beazley), 100 L Garry (A Greerley), 101 Falls of Measach (H Williams), 102 Plockton, 103 Upper L Torridon (J Beazley), 104 Beinn Eighe (D Hardley), 105 Crathes Castle Gardens, Grampian Transport Mus (J Beazley), 107 Balmoral Castle (R Weir), 108 R Tweed, 109 Kelso Abbey, 110 Haddington, 111 Rockcliffe (J Beazley), 112 Kirkcudbright (S & O Mathews), 113 Maxwelton House (J Beazley), 114 Kilchurn Castle (D Hardley), 115 Inverary Castle, 116 Oban (J Beazley), 117 Glencoe (D Hardley).

Copy editors: Nia Williams, Dilys Jones